THE
LINEBACKER RAIDS

THE
LINEBACKER RAIDS
The Bombing of North Vietnam, 1972

John T. Smith

ARMS AND
ARMOUR

ARMS & ARMOUR PRESS
An imprint of the Cassell Group
Wellington House, 125 Strand, London WC2R 0BB

Distributed in the USA by Sterling Publishing Co. Inc.,
387 Park Avenue South, New York, NY 10016-8810

British Library Cataloguing-in-Publication data:
A catalogue record for this book is available from the British Library.

ISBN 1 85409 450 5

Edited and designed by Roger Chesneau/DAG Publications Ltd

Printed and bound in Great Britain by
Creative Print and Design (Wales), Ebbw Vale

By the same author
ROLLING THUNDER

CONTENTS

THE THEORY OF STRATEGIC BOMBING AND AMERICAN AIR POWER DOCTRINE

T HE 'Linebacker I' bombing campaign took place between May and October 1972. The American President Richard Nixon ordered the bombing of North Vietnam in retaliation for the North Vietnamese invasion of South Vietnam. For a 5½-month period North Vietnam was subjected to extremely heavy bombing in an attempt to change the North's policy towards South Vietnam. 'Linebacker II' took place over an eleven-day period at the end of December 1972 and was the most concentrated bombing campaign inflicted on any country up until that time. In this chapter it is hoped to give some idea of what the American military, rather than their political masters, thought could be achieved by the bombing.

The senior officers were working within a tradition of air power that stretched back to the early years of the century and an American bombing doctrine that went back to the 1920s. Before we can reach any decision on the bombing we must consider within exactly what parameters the people who planned the bombing were working.

The theories of the strategic use of bombing aircraft and the associated deterrence theories are the only new strategic views of warfare developed during the twentieth century. Throughout the century airmen have constantly claimed that the development of aircraft has given them a special place in the conduct of warfare. Aircraft were seen as having the ability to pass unhindered over the ground and above naval forces and to be able to strike an enemy directly in his homeland. It was thought possible to win a war by the use of air power alone, by forcing an enemy to surrender while the army and navy were incapable of intervening. These ideas were always highly contentious and under dispute, before the development of nuclear weapons confirmed the destructive potential of air power. Now the deterrent use of air power, in the form of nuclear missiles, is the major strategic stance of all the nuclear powers.

Along with their counterparts in many other countries, American Air Force officers during the 1920s and 1930s viewed air power as the decisive factor in any future wars. These theories remained central to Air Force thinking until the start of the Vietnam War and had been used by the Air Force to campaign for separation from the US Army in 1947. By the start of the Vietnam War the young officers who had developed the strategic bombing theories during the 1930s were the senior staff of the US Air Force. The idea that bombing alone can win wars has persisted in the American military and played a large part in what was thought could be achieved by the bombing of North Vietnam.

There has always been a general fear of bombardment from the air, and as early as 1899 a conference at The Hague on arms reductions ratified an article prohibiting the dropping of projectiles and explosives from flying machines. At a second conference in 1907 this general ban on aerial bombing was changed to encompass only the bombing of open or undefended towns and cities, in conformity with existing land and naval limitations. The bombing of 'legitimate' military targets was now permitted. The years between 1899 and 1907 saw the line of development of military aviation change from that of unpowered balloons to the use of powered, heavier-than-air machines, and, although the practical use of aircraft was still some way off, the majority of the nations at The Hague did not appear to want to lose the potential use of aircraft for military purposes.

At this early stage of aeronautical development the use of dirigible balloons seemed to offer the best chance of practical use and both France and Germany put types of airship into military service, the French with Lebaudy machines and the Germans with Zeppelins. Both countries experimented with the dropping of bombs from airships.

The public at large seems to have learned of these developments with dismay. H. G. Wells captured these feelings in his book *War in the Air*, published in 1908, in which he envisaged a fleet of airships crossing the Atlantic and bombing New York. These developments were taking place against the background of the naval race between Germany and Britain. In Britain massive amounts of money were being spent on the construction of a battleship fleet, but H. G. Wells and other writers (R. P. Hearn, Harry Harper, Claude Grahame-White) foresaw that the nature of warfare had been changed by the development of aircraft. All the early advocates of air power realised that existing aircraft were totally incapable of carrying out even a small part of the tasks that were predicted for them, but thought that, over time, and with technical development, things would change. In July 1909 the French airman Louis Blériot crossed the English Channel, and, although this journey was undertaken in a lightweight, single-seat machine, it showed what was possible for the future. It also demonstrated the fact that the Royal Navy, which had held supremacy for 150 years, could no longer guarantee Britain's safety from outside attack.

The major European nations all created air arms attached to their armies or navies in the period leading up to the First World War. The first use of aircraft in combat was by Italy in 1911, in North Africa against the Turks. This involved the use of aircraft in reconnaissance and bombing attacks, and the first pilot to die on active service—the first of many thousands over the rest of this century—was killed in October 1912. The value of these operations can only have been marginal at best, bearing in mind the aircraft available. Very small numbers of aircraft were also used in the Balkan and Moroccan wars in 1912.

The Royal Flying Corps was created as a branch of the Army in 1912 under the command of David Henderson, who was a cavalry reconnaissance specialist. Churchill had already established the Royal Naval Air Service in 1911. The American Army founded its air section as part of the Signal Corps in 1907, but it took another two years before an aircraft was purchased from the Wright brothers and its first pilot learned to fly from a correspondence course. The military establishments of most countries were very slow to appreciate the possibilities presented by aircraft. In Britain General Haig stated, in 1911, that 'Flying can never be of any use to the army.'

By the start of the First World War there had been steady development in military aviation, Russia, Germany and France leading the way with around 600 aircraft between them. The RFC only managed to send 40-odd aircraft to France to support the Army. With the aircraft then available the only practical mission was reconnaissance in support of ground forces, but the Germans did carry out a series of ineffectual bombing raids on Paris in 1914 and the RNAS attempted to bomb the airship sheds in Düsseldorf. However, in general aircraft were still incapable of carrying out the schemes of their more extreme advocates.

General Henderson was replaced as the head of the Royal Flying Corps in late 1915 by Hugh Trenchard, who had transferred to the service in 1912 after learning to fly at his own expense. Trenchard was a staunch supporter of the offensive use of aircraft, and during the rest of the war the RFC was used aggressively against the German Army and Air Service. In many ways this offensive stance placed the RFC at a disadvantage as most of its activities took place over the German lines. This led during the course of the war to a much higher loss rate for the RFC than for the Germans. Trenchard believed in the essential offensive nature of aircraft, and the RFC was ordered to attack enemy aircraft and airfields whenever possible, to restrict the enemy's action while allowing friendly aircraft to operate at will. However, he saw this only in terms of support for the Army. Later in his life Trenchard came to support the strategic use of aircraft, but during most of the First World War the Royal Flying Corps was subordinated directly to the needs of the Army.

The Germans used their Zeppelin airships to carry out a sporadic bombing campaign against Britain and France, starting in daylight but later changing to night after several airships were lost to the defences. These raids were only of limited success, little damage being done. However, after the Germans introduced the Gotha twin-engine heavy bomber in early 1917, they began to carry out bombing raids over Britain with more effect. The Gothas raided Folkestone in May 1917, and on 13 June 1917 London was bombed by seventeen Gothas each carrying a bomb load of 1,000lb.

The Gotha raids continued on London until 10 May 1918; starting as daylight raids, they later continued as a series of night raids, after the defences against daytime air attack had been strengthened. The raids forced the recall of considerable numbers of fighter aircraft from the front in France, much to Trenchard's chagrin. The damage caused by the raids compared to Britain's war effort was negligible, but the shock affected both the government and the people. It was shown that production slumped in the days following the raids because of absenteeism, and hundreds of thousands of people were leaving London every night. The main effect of these raids was on British morale. Speaking of the earlier Zeppelin raids, R. P. Hearne said,

> It is particularly humiliating to allow an enemy to come over your capital city and hurl bombs upon it. His aim may be very bad, the casualties may be few, but the morale effect is wholly undesirable.[1]

The Gotha raids also caused considerable trouble for the government in parliament, and the reaction to the raids was the Smuts Report. As a member of the War Cabinet, General Smuts, who later became the prime minister of South Africa, was asked to produce a report on British air policy. The historian A. J. P. Taylor's view of the Smuts report was that

---

[1] Hearn, R. P., *Zeppelins and Super Zeppelins*, John Lane (London, 1916).

His report, completed in October 1917, was an epoch-making document. There stem from it all the great achievements of our contemporary civilization: the indiscriminate destruction of cities in the Second World War; the nuclear bombs dropped on Hiroshima and Nagasaki; and the present preparations for destroying mankind.[1]

Smuts suggested that the British should indeed retaliate for the German raids, but he went considerably further than this. He recommended that the RAF should be created as a separate force by combining the Royal Flying Corps and the Royal Naval Air Service. A separate Air Ministry was formed in December 1917 and the RAF was formed on 1 April 1918. The Smuts Report observed that

> As far as can at present be foreseen there is absolutely no limit to the scale of its [air power's] future independent war use. And the day may not be far off when aerial operations with their devastation of enemy lands and destruction of industrial and populous centres on a vast scale may become the principal operations of war, to which the older forms of military and naval operations may become secondary and subordinate.[2]

The creation of the RAF made little difference to the way in which aircraft were used in practice. In very general terms bombing can be divided into three categories—what are now called close support, interdiction and strategic bombing. Close air support is direct action in support of the army; interdiction is the bombing of enemy supply lines; and strategic bombing is the bombing of an enemy's homeland, factories and centres of power. The Army still wanted the tactical use of all available aircraft directed towards the winning of the ground battle, and in reality the Smuts view of strategic bombing was technically still very marginal.

Under the command of Trenchard the Independent Bombing Force was created in France in June 1918. Trenchard, who had always been a supporter of the tactical use of aircraft, had resigned as Chief of Staff of the RAF and he was the most experienced air officer available to command the Independent Force. He became a convert to strategic bombing and, during the 1920s, one of its leading proponents. In 1928 he wrote,

> It is not, however, necessary for an air force, in order to defeat the enemy nation, to defeat its armed forces first. Air power can dispense with that intermediate step, can

---

[1] Taylor, A. J. P., *English History 1914–1945*, Penguin Books (London, 1975), p. 136.
[2] Questor, George H., *Deterrence before Hiroshima*, John Willey & Sons (New York, 1966), p. 38.

pass over the enemy navies and armies, and penetrate the air defences and attack direct the centres of production, transportation and communications from which the enemy war effort is maintained.[1]

The Independent Force was stationed in France but outside the control of the Allies' command structure. The idea of the force had been based on the promise of large numbers of aircraft being available in 1918, but, since these had never appeared because of production difficulties, the numbers of aircraft actually used was quite small. The force was never very popular in France, and when the Germans began to retaliate for the attacks on Germany it was against French targets. Although the force was intended for strategic use, for political reasons (that is, to placate the Allied High Command) part of its effort was taken up in tactical attacks. A large proportion of its attacks were also directed against German air force targets, and so the number of raids against German industrial facilities was strictly limited. Gradually, however, the force built up its expertise, and by the end of the war the Handley Page V/1500, which had the range to bomb Berlin, was just coming into service.

The German bombing of Britain over a period of four years had caused £2m worth of damage. This was the equivalent of just one day's expenditure of munitions on the Western Front, and the public, although shocked by the bombing, had come nowhere near breaking. The French and British bombing of Germany had caused more damage, especially in the Rhineland, but it followed the same pattern, with marginal damage and the public at first shocked by the attacks and then coming to terms with them. The supporters of the theories were left with the argument that the technical developments necessary for the success of strategic bombing were just around the corner. During the 1920s and 1930s the theories continued to be developed in all the major countries, sometimes in isolation and sometimes as part of an international school of thought. The RAF and the Italian Air Force were the only independent air forces, and it seemed for a time that, for financial reasons, the RAF would return to being part of the Army.

During the war and in the years afterwards the leading British theorists were F. W. Lanchester, P. R. C. Groves and Frederick Sykes. A clear statement of the theories developed during the 1920s and 1930s was that

The fundamental doctrine is that the airplane possesses such ubiquity and such advantages of speed and elevation as to possess the power of destroying all surface

---

[1] Quoted in Hastings, Max, *Bomber Command*, Pan Books (London, 1981), p. 46.

installations and instruments, ashore or afloat, while itself remaining comparatively safe from the ground.[1]

Aircraft, it was argued, had added a completely new dimension to warfare: naval and ground forces did not now have to be defeated, or even faced up to, but could be safely ignored while the enemy's heartland was destroyed from above. In some ways the death toll on the Western Front had focused attention on a way of breaking the stalemate that had developed, and the strategic bombing theories were an attempt to see how wars could be won without the slaughter of trench warfare.

Giulio Douhet became the foremost exponent of the power of bombing, developing a set of ideas that gained international acceptance amongst military professionals. He commanded the Italian Army Air Service for a short period before the First World War, but during the war he was sentenced to one year's imprisonment, by court martial, for criticising his superiors. He was released from jail and exonerated after the Italian defeat at Caporetto had shown up the kind of deficiencies about which he had complained. He retired from the Army after the war but served as Mussolini's Secretary for Aeronautics for a period in 1922.

In the first book he wrote on air power, written as early as 1909, Douhet stated, 'For if there are nations that exist untouched by sea there are none that exist without the breath of air.' For Douhet the essence of air power was offensive. His main work, *Command of the Air*, was published in 1921, expanded editions appearing in 1927 and 1931. At the start of any future war both sides would begin with bombing attacks on the enemy's air force in an attempt to destroy it on the ground. Once one side had obtained command of the air the war would be won by bombing the enemy's homeland, factories and population. Any diversion of aircraft away from this strategic campaign would be a waste of effort.

Douhet defined 'command of the air' as follows:

Command of the air means being in a position to prevent the enemy from flying and at the same time guaranteeing this faculty for oneself . . . Command of the air means victory and to be beaten in the air means defeat and the necessity of accepting whatever conditions it may please the enemy to impose . . . In order to guarantee national

---

[1] Warner, Edward, 'Douhet, Mitchell, Siversky: Theories of Air Warfare', in *Makers of Modern Strategy* (ed. Earl, Edward Mead), Princeton University Press (Princeton, 1971), p. 485.

defence, it is necessary and sufficient to be in a position to obtain command of the air, in the event of a conflict.[1]

The phrase 'command of the air' was used in the same way that the naval strategist Mahan had used the phrase 'command of the sea': it was not possible to stop the enemy from flying his aircraft, but he would be unable to put to any major use a particular section of air space. Douhet downgraded the use of fighter aircraft, believing that, because bombing aircraft had the initiative and could mass to attack any one point, the numbers of fighters needed would be prohibitive. He also thought that the bomber would stand a good chance against the fighter. His ideal type of aircraft was the general-purpose, twin-engine, multi-seat bomber with a good self-defence capability.

It was generally thought unlikely that modern bombing aircraft could be stopped by any kind of defence. In a statement on defence in the House of Commons in 1932, the British Prime Minister remarked,

> I think it is well also for the man in the street to realise that there is no power on earth that can protect him from being bombed. Whatever people may tell him, the bomber will always get through.[2]

It was only through counter-strike forces that it was possible to deter an enemy from launching his bombers first. This echoed Douhet's thoughts exactly.

The two major wars that have taken place this century have been total wars, involving entire societies fighting for their very survival. If an entire nation is at war then every member of that nation is a combatant. The person who produces the rifle is as important as the one who fires it. The strategic bombing theorists needed this view of war to allow them to strike at the enemy's homeland—at least, this was the argument used as a justification for civilian deaths. If we accept Clausewitz's dictum 'War is an act of violence whose object is to constrain the enemy to accomplish our will', then the enemy's will and morale become a legitimate target.

With this view, the mind of the government and that of the people become legitimate objects for attack. Any war only ends when the leaders of one side mentally admit defeat. Trenchard had stated that the RAF's bombing in the Rhineland during the First World War had been twenty times as effective on the psychological level as the material level. The idea that bombing can be

---

[1] Douhet, Giulio, *The Command of the Air*, Rivista Aeronautica (Roma, 1958), pp. 20, 23.
[2] Quoted in Questor, George H., op. cit., p. 67.

used to force an enemy government to change its policy or to behave in a certain way—essentially what was intended by the United States at the start of the 'Linebacker' campaigns—has been part of the strategic bombing theories from the very beginning.

William Mitchell became the leading American exponent of strategic bombing. He had served in France during the First World War as the commander of the US Army Air Section combat squadrons. After the war he became a fervent believer in the use of air power. Early in the 1920s tests were carried out by Mitchell on the effects of bombs on naval vessels in order to justify his claim that aircraft had rendered the battleship obsolete because of the latter's vulnerability to air attack. Old American ships and surrendered German ships, including the battleship *Ostfriesland*, were indeed sunk, and the lesson of the tests was, according to Mitchell, that the Navy was no longer capable of protecting the country. However, the Navy's view was that the sinking of a few old ships at anchor in fact proved very little.

Mitchell made many enemies and he was finally foolish enough to describe his superiors as incompetent. He was court-martialled in 1925 and lost his position as Assistant Chief of the Air Service. The court sentenced him to five years' suspension from the Army, but he chose to resign instead. He continued to campaign for air power with a messianic fervour until his death in 1935.

Mitchell was in agreement with most of Douhet's theories, as were that international group of airmen who were campaigning for the strategic use of air power. Mitchell wrote in 1930,

> The advent of airpower which can go straight to the vital centers and entirely neutralize or destroy them has put a completely new complexion on the whole system of making war. It is now realized that the hostile army in the field is a false objective and the real objectives are the vital centers.[1]

Mitchell was almost religious in his belief in aircraft and even envisaged the creation of a new class of warrior:

> It is probable that future wars will be conducted by a special class, the air force, as it was by the armoured knights in the Middle Ages. Again, the whole population will not have to be called in the event of national emergency, but only enough of it to man the machines that are the most potent in national defence.[2]

---

[1] Mitchell, William M., *Skyways* (Philadelphia, 1930), p. 255.
[2] Mitchell, William M., *Winged Defence*, Putnam & Sons (London, 1925), p. 19.

The Air Corps Tactical School, at Langley, and later Maxwell, Air Base, from 1920 onwards acted as a centre for the development and spreading of the strategic bombing theories. Although Mitchell's work was well known, there is some disagreement about the influence of Douhet at the school. But, consciously or not, the school spent most of the inter-war years teaching a version of Douhet's ideas to a whole generation of air force officers. The school developed the concept of a modern industrial state as having a web of production. This involved the idea of industries interlocking together, with each of the parts dependent on all of the others, and led to the notion that it was not necessary to destroy all of a nation's industrial capacity, but only certain industrial bottlenecks, in order to bring a nation's war production to a halt.

Thus it was only necessary to destroy certain 'vital targets' to bring an enemy to its knees: what was needed was not the capacity to obliterate large areas but 'surgical precision' to destroy certain factories. These ideas influenced thinking for many years. (Jerry Green wrote an article in the May 1965 issue of *Air Force Magazine* entitled 'Air Power in Vietnam—Scalpel rather than Broadsword', and the bombing of Libya in 1986 is still termed a 'surgical strike'.) High precision required daytime bombing, and this led to the development of the highly accurate Norden Mk XV bomb sight and the B-17, B-24 and the B-29 day bombers with a heavy defensive armament. The bombing theories needed the hardware to carry them out, and with the introduction of the B-17 it seemed as if technology were finally catching up with doctrine. Many of the criticisms of the air power theorists had been based on the fact that their ideas had been predicated on 'paper' aircraft.

If critical precision targets did exist, then this meant that the selection of these targets became the central point of the theories. Douhet had foreseen this as early as 1922 when he wrote,

> . . . in actual fact the choice of targets, their grouping into areas and the order in which these areas are to be destroyed constitute the most delicate and difficult part of air warfare and might be defined as Air Strategy.[1]

Just before the entry of the United States into the Second World War President Roosevelt asked for a statement from the air service of the amounts of equipment needed for victory if America were to become involved in the war. This statement became known as AWPD/1 (Air War Plans Division 1), was a

---

[1] Douhet, Giulio, op. cit., p. 42.

clear exposition of the strategic bombing position and called for the creation of large numbers of long-range bombing aircraft and the logistic back-up to mount a strategic bombing campaign. The report was drawn up by four Air Force officers, all of whom had been stalwarts of the Air Corps Tactical School, and can be seen as the final development of nearly 20 years' work by the school. The numbers of men and aircraft asked for seemed enormous, but they were achieved by 1944 and to a large extent the plan was implemented.

The view of AWPD/1 was that Germany could be defeated by the use of air power, and a list of targets was drawn up, the destruction of which, it was thought, would be enough to eliminate Germany's war-making capability. One of the four people who drew up the report, Colonel Hansel, stated,

> Many factors formed vital links in Germany's industrial and military might. The over-riding question was: which were the most vital links? And among these, which were the most vulnerable to air attack? And from among that category, which would be most difficult to replace or to 'harden' by dispersal or by going underground?[1]

Here again, the emphasis is on crucial links and the unstated presumption of precision accuracy.

The experience of bombing during the Second World War proved to be at odds with the pre-war theories. Early in the war the RAF found it almost impossible to operate during daylight because of heavy losses and so turned to night bombing. Until 1942 only one in ten of the RAF's aircraft dropped its bombs within five miles of the target. The difficulties involved in precision bombing, other than with specially selected and trained crews, forced the RAF to turn to 'area' bombing in order to 'de-house' (as it was euphemistically termed) the German population.

The US Army Air Forces were heavily committed to daylight bombing, but their experience of operating from British bases against Germany was to show the difficulties involved in strategic bombing. The German fighter force disproved Douhet's and Mitchell's view that fighter aircraft were ineffectual: the bomber could not 'always get through'. Until the availability of the very long range P-51 fighter aircraft in 1944, the existing P-38s and P-48s could not escort the bombing aircraft all the way to the target on deep-penetration raids. The American raids in October 1943, especially those on the Schweinfurt factories, suffered such heavy losses that the daylight raids were scaled down

---

[1] Hansel, Haywood S., *The Air Plan That Defeated Hitler*, Higgins-McArther Longino & Porter (Atlanta, 1972), p. 79.

until fighter escort was available all the way to the target. But, once such escort was available, the USAAF continued with daylight precision raids and the German fighter force was practically destroyed in the air and on the ground.

The pre-war faith in the effects of strategic bombing was never quite justified in practice. Germany continued to increase industrial production until very late in the war, when for practical purposes the ground war was nearly over. No one can doubt the immense damage caused by the American and British bombing of Germany, but industrial society had proved much more resilient than expected. 'Vital points' or 'bottlenecks' that could close down production had been hard to find, and the Germans, an industrious and resourceful people, had reacted to and absorbed the bombing. Probably the most famous precision raid of the war was that undertaken by the 'dam busters'on the Ruhr dams. This was a brilliantly planned and executed attack by specially trained and selected crews, but, although it caused considerable devastation and disruption, no long-term damage was caused to the German economy, which rolled with the punches and adapted.

The idea that a nation's morale would break under heavy bombing has proved equally illusory. In China, Spain, Britain, Germany and Japan the populations stoically endured heavy bombing. Morale might have been severely shaken but nowhere did it break; almost unbelievably, one American survey even found that many of the survivors of Hiroshima had been prepare to continue fighting the war. In fact, the early stages of a bombing campaign seem to have strengthened the population's commitment to the war.

In essence, before the war the strategic bombing theories had been just that— theories: nobody could point to a bombing campaign that had been fully carried through either to prove or to disprove these ideas. The supporters of the theories could say that the examples of the First World War had not been carried through to a conclusion and that technological development had rendered them irrelevant. But the experience of the Second World War had shown that, if not completely mistaken, strategic bombing campaigns were extremely difficult to organise and very expensive in men and machines—exactly the lessons of the first war. It has been claimed that the industrial capacity taken up by the British bombing campaign in particular was more destructive to the British economy than to the German economy until very late in the war. The Germans only surrendered when the Allied ground forces met in the centre of Germany. The central points of the doctrine taught at the Tactical School were difficult to justify. Fighter aircraft were effective; vital points in an economy either did not exist or were very difficult to find; and precision bombing was nearly impossible to achieve.

Giulio Douhet's theories contain a quasi-mathematical slant and he talks about a 20-ton bombing unit, but his estimation of what could be achieved with this unit proved to be wildly optimistic. In fact Douhet never learned to fly, and there is a lack of practical feeling in his writing. For Douhet, aircraft would always fly (they would never be shot down by enemy fighters); they would always find their target irrespective of the weather; and their bombs would always hit the target and destroy it. Douhet's enemy always had a weak government, a fragile or brittle industrial economy and a morale that would break under pressure (to be fair, he did envisage the use of gas). All the objectives *could* be achieved by air power—but only at truly enormous effort and cost.

After the destruction caused at Hiroshima and Nagasaki by atomic weapons, it began to seem that the ideas of the original strategic theorists would finally come true—that air power really was the crucial factor in modern warfare. Bringing a nation to its knees, irrespective of its military capabilities on land or on the seas, was much more feasible with atomic weapons. The air power theorists had always presumed that technological development would bring about the supremacy of air power. The amount of time and effort needed to crush an adversary from the air now seemed to be within acceptable limits, and American strategy until the early 1960s was based completely on nuclear weapons, even on the tactical level. The independent role of strategic bombing carried out by the US Army Air Forces during the war, together with the nuclear deterrent theories prevalent, played a large part in the separation of the Air Force from the Army in 1947.

Thus the accepted doctrine of the US Air Force—that air power was the decisive factor in war-survived the Second World War intact and was enhanced by the introduction of nuclear weapons. The doctrine also managed to survived the experiences of the Korean War. After the first months of the conflict all the major targets in North Korea had been destroyed and all the effort, including that of the long-range heavy bombers, was concentrated on the interdiction campaign to stop the passage of supplies from the Chinese border to the front line. Operation 'Strangle' which lasted from 1951 to 1952, was one attempt to destroy the Korean road and rail network. However, although thousands of sorties were flown and over 300 aircraft lost, the North Koreans maintained their ground position at the front line. By using manual labour to repair the railways and roads, and if necessary to carry supplies, with enormous effort they kept the routes open.

The front line at this period of the war was static, which gave the Koreans the tactical initiative: they could increase or decrease their operations to suit the quantities of supplies available, and a North Korean division used less than 10 per cent of the daily supplies of an American division. While the United Nations forces did not hold the initiative on the ground and so force up the use of materials by the Chinese and North Koreans, no amount of bombing could be completely effective because it could not by itself compel the enemy to surrender. This is not to denigrate the part played by air power—it did indeed play a very important role—but it cannot be seen as decisive.

After the Korean War the emphasis in the US Air Force on strategic bombing again reasserted itself. Air Force Manual 1-8, *Strategic Air Operations*, was produced in May 1954 and was not revised until December 1965. The manual states:

> Somewhere within the structure of the hostile nation exist sensitive elements, the destruction or neutralisation of which will best create the breakdown and loss of will of that nation to further resist.[1]

The experience in Korea was seen as a special case with no relevance to general American air policy. General Momyer, who commanded the Seventh Air Force in Vietnam, could still write in 1978, 'Airpower can be strategically decisive if its application is intense, continuous, and focused on the enemy's vital systems.'[2] The emphasis on independent use, precision and 'vital systems' from the early days of the Air Corps Tactical School in the 1920s and 1930s was still evident.

The leading civilian American strategist in the 1950s and 1960s was Bernard Brodie, who published his influential book *Strategy in the Nuclear Age* in 1959. This book sets out the basics of the nuclear deterrent strategy, which has in practice been followed by the United States over the last forty years. In this book Brodie analyses Douhet's conclusions and seems to say that they are still relevant with respect to nuclear weapons:

> ... one would seem justified in drawing the following conclusion: barring revolutionary and presently unforeseen advances in air defence, including extensive hardening

---

[1] Clodfelter, Mark, *The Limits of Air Power*, The Free Press (New York, 1989), pp. 27–8.
[2] Momyer, William W., *Air Power in Three Wars*, US Government Printing Office (Washington, 1979), p. 339.

of targets, an unrestricted strategic air campaign in a war in which the United States is engaged is bound to be decisive.[1]

He also stated that, before thermonuclear weapons,

Even with fission weapons numbering in the hundreds, there was still a real—and difficult—analytical problem in choosing targets that would make the campaign decisive rather than merely hurtful.[2]

The doctrine is still that air power is decisive and that targeting is the essence of strategy.

It was thought, after the end of the Korean War, that this type of conflict would be unlikely to occur again. The view was that the principal role of the Air Force was to undertake a nuclear attack upon the Soviet Union. The emphasis was on the development of Strategic Air Command and there was a decline in the tactical use of aircraft. American strategy during this period was one of 'massive retaliation': there would be no more small wars, and if the Soviet Union were seen to be behind any aggression, anywhere in the world, the response would be a massive attack on Russia. It is doubtful whether this doctrine was ever really valid, especially after the Soviets had developed as many nuclear weapons as the Americans. The doctrine for the use of tactical aircraft also foresaw the use of small 'tactical' nuclear weapons to support the Army; the use of conventional munitions dropped from aircraft was seen as passé. It was also thought that the day of air-to-air combat had gone, and little effort was put into the development of 'air superiority' aircraft and tactics.

The view of the senior military within the US armed forces on air power doctrine remained constant for many years before the start of the Vietnam War. In essence, this was that air power was decisive, that precision bombing could be carried out and that countries had 'vital centres'. However, in the ten years prior to the Vietnam War little effort was directed towards either the aircraft or the tactics that were in fact used to fight the war. The bombing of North Vietnam during 1965–68 failed to achieve its purpose, but the military believed that special factors were at work that had stopped air power from succeeding. When the 'Linebacker' bombing started in 1972 opinions within the American military saw the campaign as a final chance for air power to show what it was capable of at a strategic level.

---

[1] Brodie, Bernard, *Strategy in the Missile Age*, Princeton University Press (Princeton, 1959), p. 165.
[2] Ibid, p. 153.

CHAPTER 1

THE AIR WAR IN SOUTH-EAST ASIA

THE bombing of North Vietnam up to 1972 was only part of the air war in South-East Asia, which in reality was not one air war but four, overlapping in time and space. The air war in South Vietnam was for the Americans essentially a ground support conflict, with aircraft assisting the US troops committed to the fighting Viet Cong and North Vietnamese forces. In Laos the air war was mainly an interdiction campaign to stop the flow of men and materials from North to South Vietnam down the Ho Chi Minh Trail. The American bombing in Cambodia was both a ground support campaign and an interdiction campaign against the North's supply lines. The US bombing of North Vietnam was a strategic bombing campaign designed to force the North Vietnamese leadership to change its policy towards the South.

For the United States the Vietnam air wars were a time of great change, and they lasted long enough for new tactics and technology to be developed to combat the difficulties that were encountered. The Vietnam War was the first of the modern air wars. Although such weapons had all been used before, the conflict saw the first large-scale general use of air-to-ground missiles, ground-to-air missiles, air-to-air missiles (the original F-4 Phantoms did not have a gun armament), air-to-air refuelling and AWACS (Airborne Warning & Control System) aircraft.

All of Indo-China had been part of the French colonial empire before the Second World War, but when the French attempted to regain control from the Japanese after the end of the war they found a well-organised, well-equipped army under Ho Chi Minh waiting for them. After a savage, bloody conflict the French were finally defeated at Dien Bien Phu in 1954. Although the Viet Minh had been equipped by China and the Soviet Union they were a genuine Vietnamese nationalist group. The settlement of the war with France included the temporary division of the country into North and South of the 17th Parallel, with the Viet Minh controlling the North. The United States came increasingly to support the South and stopped the elections to unite the country from taking place, because it was thought that Ho Chi Minh had enough support in the South to have won the elections.

The Viet Cong, or National Front for the Liberation of South Vietnam, was created in 1960. At this stage of the war it was a genuine Southern movement, with considerable help from the North. By the end of 1961 the Viet Cong were estimated to number 17,000. During 1961 Nikita Khrushchev, the Soviet leader, announced that the communist revolution would be spread by means of 'wars of liberation', and in response the United States used the South-East Asia Treaty Organisation (SEATO) to supply arms to South Vietnam, Thailand, Laos and Cambodia.

During the late 1950s and early 1960s the US Air Force had been equipped and trained for a major international war, using both tactical and strategic nuclear weapons, and, under the command of General Curtis LeMay, Strategic Air Command (SAC) had received most of the investment and attention during this time. Most of the higher echelon of officers in the Air Force at this time had been bomber pilots during the Second World War, and the result was that the Air Force was ill-equipped and ill-trained for what were seen as the forthcoming 'wars of liberation'.

When John Kennedy became US President in 1961 he instructed the American military to prepare for what he termed counter-insurgency (COIN) warfare. The US Air Force's answer to this was to create the 4400th Combat Crew Training Squadron at Eglin AFB in April 1961. The squadron was equipped with Second World War-vintage C-47s, B-26s and T-28 armed trainers. The 4400th was transferred to South Vietnam in October, with, ostensibly, a training role for the South Vietnamese Air Force. By the end of 1961 large parts of South Vietnam were under the control of the Viet Cong, and under the code-name 'Farm Gate' the 4400th began to fly combat missions, although these were only permitted when crews were accompanied by a Vietnamese observer.

The US Air Force in South-East Asia in November 1961 set up the 2nd Air Division, at Tan Son Nhut air base near Saigon, to control USAF forces in the area, which were commanded by General R. H. Anthis; the 2nd Air Division was under the command of the Thirteenth Air Force, which in turn was under the control of the Pacific Air Force (PACAF). Although under the command of the Thirteenth Air Force, the 2nd Air Division was under the operational control of the Military Assistance Advisory Group (MAAG) in Saigon. Euphemistically referred to as 'advisers', American ground troops began to build up

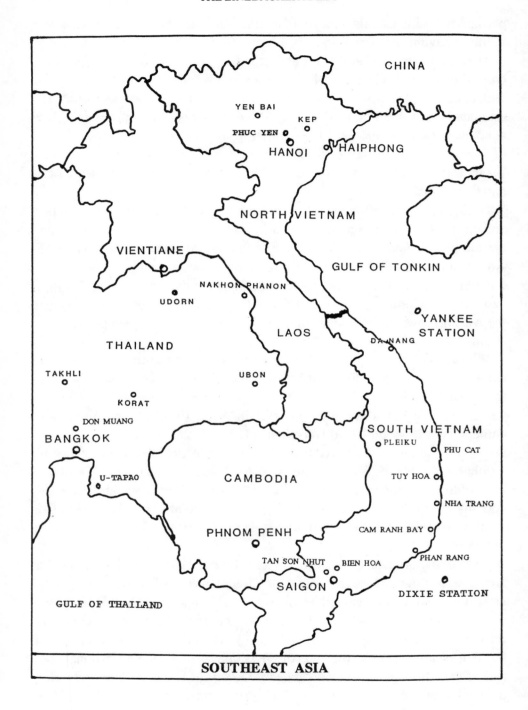

SOUTHEAST ASIA

in South Vietnam, and during October and November 1961 four RF-101 Voodoo reconnaissance aircraft were stationed at Tan Son Nhut to photograph areas of South Vietnam and Laos.

In 1961 the majority of the American public had never even heard of Vietnam, and Laos was seen as the possible future trouble spot. The CIA had been funding and controlling a war in Laos against the communist Pathet Lao, and Air America, the CIA airline, had been providing transport and support. The Soviets were also flying in supplies to the Pathet Lao. US Air Force pilots carried out reconnaissance flights over Laos, flying RT-33s of the Philippines Air Force, with Laotian markings, and operating from Thailand.

In early 1962 US Army General Paul Arkins became overall American commander in Vietnam. During January 1962 C-123 transports equipped with spraying equipment were moved into South Vietnam. This was the now infamous 'Ranch Hand' operation. The idea was to use the defoliant Agent Orange to deny the Viet Cong the use of jungle hideouts. The dioxin in the chemical is still causing medical problems with many Air Force personnel and even more Vietnamese. By the time the operation ended in 1971 6.5 million acres had been sprayed, with little effect on the Viet Cong.

After a radar system had been set up in South Vietnam large numbers of unaccountable aircraft were detected and four F-102A interceptors from the 509th FIS were stationed at Tan Son Nhut in March 1962, but no enemy aircraft were intercepted. As the US Air Force's commitment to the area increased a large-scale effort was put into the building or enlarging of air bases. These bases included Pleiku, Cam Ranh Bay, Bien Hoa and Da Nang in South Vietnam, plus Takhli, Ubon, Korat, Udorn and U-Tapao in Thailand.

The government in South Vietnam had been controlled by President Diem after the French had left. There was little popular support for the Diem regime in South Vietnam, although he seems to have obtained 99 per cent of the votes cast in presidential elections. Diem was killed during a *coup* on 1 November 1963. The new president was General 'Big' Minh. Over the next few years there was a succession of corrupt military regimes in South Vietnam, none of which had strong popular support.

President Kennedy was murdered in November 1963, and decisions concerning Vietnam now had to be taken by President Johnson, whose stated wish was that he would not be the first President to lose a war and who drew America ever further into the conflict. The Vietnam War was essentially Johnson's war. By 1964 the aircraft used by the 'Farm Gate' detachment were beginning to suffer structural failure after much hard use. One of the B-26s lost a wing on 11 February that year and several T-28s suffered structural collapse during combat missions. There was a major conference in Honolulu during June 1964 involving the US Secretary of Defense Robert McNamara and the chiefs of staff. The decision was taken that the United States would continue to back South Vietnam and provide military support, but only on a limited basis. The Air Force Chief, Curtis LeMay, had wanted an all-out air attack on North Vietnam but this was rejected.

A Navy reconnaissance jet, an RF-8, was shot down over the Plain of Jars in Laos on 6 June 1964. The next day an F-8 escorting another RF-8 was also shot down by ground fire. In retaliation, anti-aircraft sites were attacked on 9 June by US Air Force F-100s on temporary detachment to Takhli Air Base. These were the first of many USAF strikes on Laos.

One of the major turning points in the war was the Gulf of Tonkin Incident that occurred on 2 August 1964. The American destroyer USS *Maddox*, sailing close to the coast of North Vietnam, was attacked by North Vietnamese torpedo boats. This event was followed two days later by an incident in which the USS *Maddox* and the USS *Turner Joy* claimed to have been attacked again by North Vietnam; it now seems that the second attack never took place, but the claims were believed at the time. On 5 August Navy aircraft attacked the torpedo boats' bases in North Vietnam in reply, in Operation 'Peace Arrow'. Two aircraft were shot down and Lieutenant E. Alvarez became the Navy's first POW; he remained a prisoner for nine years. Two days later, on the 7th, the US Congress passed the Gulf of Tonkin Resolution which became the legal basis for Presidential control of the undeclared war in Vietnam. Also on 7 August, the North Vietnamese reacted to the air attack by moving 36 MiG-15s and -17s on to the airfield at Phuc Yen from China. North Vietnamese pilots were receiving training in the Soviet Union, and the Soviets had also begun to build up the North's air defence system. The North also began to send large regular army formations into South Vietnam for the first time.

In response to the Tonkin Gulf Incident the US Air Force began to send more squadrons into Vietnam and Thailand. In South Vietnam 36 B-57s of the 8th and 13th TBS and eight F-100s of the 615th TFS were stationed at Bien Hoa and Da Nang, while in Thailand the 36th TFS, with 15 F-105Ds, was moved on to the air base at Korat. By the end of 1964 the USAF had two light bomber squadrons and nine tactical fighter squadrons in the South-East Asia theatre of operations.

On 14 December 1964, under Operation 'Barrel Roll', bombing operations were started against targets in eastern Laos. These missions were the first continuous US Air Force missions in the area, and were intended to support Laotian government forces by interdicting the flow of North Vietnamese men and equipment moving down the Ho Chi Minh Trail into South Vietnam. The Annamite mountain range runs along the western border of North Vietnam, and the routes into South Vietnam from the North crossed via three main passes through these mountains into Laos. The trail then ran through a mass of roads and tracks down into Cambodia and then into South Vietnam. Over the next nine years parts of the Ho Chi Minh Trail became the most bombed places on earth as US Air Force and Navy aircraft tried in vain to stop the movement of supplies.

The ground war in South Vietnam continued unabated and the Viet Cong continued to grow in numbers. The idea developed amongst the American military that, instead of trying to defeat the communist ground forces in South Vietnam, they should subject the North to a bombing campaign intended to force its leadership to terminate their involvement in the South. President Johnson hesitated to implement this suggestion, but when on 7 February 1965 the American air base at Pleiku was attacked by mortars and eight Americans were killed and seven aircraft destroyed he ordered a strike on North Vietnam by Navy aircraft under the code-name 'Flaming Dart'. The following day 30 USAF A-1s and F-100s attacked a North Vietnamese army barracks just north of the Demilitarised Zone, along the border between North and South Vietnam. The Viet Cong attacked an American barracks at Qui Nhon on 10 February and killed 23 Americans. Johnson again ordered air raids on the North, and the following day the US Air Force and Navy bombed military installations at Chanh Hoa and Vit in the southern part of North Vietnam. On 18 February the South Vietnamese ended the restriction that US Air Force aircraft had to carry a Vietnamese observer when carrying out combat missions, and on the 19th B-57s and F-100s began to carry out attacks on Viet Cong positions in support of American and South Vietnamese ground forces.

The continuing decline in the situation in the South forced Johnson to consider a sustained bombing campaign against North Vietnam. Under the code-name 'Rolling Thunder', this was intended to be a measured campaign starting with targets in the southern part of the North. At this stage 'Rolling Thunder' was meant to be a demonstration to the leadership in the North of what American air power could do, in order to force it to back down. It was never considered that North Vietnam could possibly withstand a major bombing campaign.

The first US Air Force 'Rolling Thunder' raid took place on 2 March 1965. Included in the raid were 44 F-105s from Thailand and 20 B-57s and 40 F-100s from South Vietnam. The targets were an ammunition dump at Xom Bong and a small port at Quang Khe. It came as a shock to the Americans that three F-105s and two F-100s were shot down. Captain Hayden J. Lockhart became the first US Air Force prisoner to be held by the North.

The number of raids flown over North Vietnam was progressively stepped up as the Northern leadership refused to change its policy towards the South. The Air Force commanders wanted to mount an all-out attack on the North, but the targets were only released by the political leaders intermittently for fear that China could be drawn into the war, as had happened in Korea.

The first US combat Marines were committed to the war on 8 March 1965 when they landed on the beach at Da Nang. The Air Force was not allowed to attack the North Vietnamese airfields or radar sites, and this permitted the North to build up its air defence system without interference. The first MiG attack on US Air Force aircraft occurred on 3 April 1965 when a flight of F-105s on the way to bomb the bridge at Than Hoa was attacked by MiG-17s. Two of the F-105s were shot down before the escorting F-100s could intervene. While they were carrying a full bomb load the heavily laden 'Thuds' could not 'mix it' with the much smaller and lighter MiGs. Many of the MiG attacks were merely intended to force the bomb-carrying aircraft to jettison their bombs prematurely.

The US Air Force introduced the F-4C Phantom into South-East Asia in April 1965 when the 45th Tactical Fighter Squadron was moved to Ubon Air Base in Thailand. The Phantom was the Air Force's air superiority aircraft and replaced the F-100 as escort for the 'Rolling Thunder' raids. On 10 July two Phantoms from the 45th TFS shot down two MiG-17s with Sidewinder missiles while escorting an F-105 raid on the Bac Giang bridge south of Hanoi. Reconnaissance photographs taken over the North showed that the Soviet-built SA-2 ground-to-air missile had been installed at several locations. However, these sites were still 'off limits' to the bombing aircraft. On 24 July a missile exploded close to a flight of four Phantoms operating near Hanoi, destroying one and damaging the other three. Even after American aircraft had been shot down the missile sites could not be attacked unless they were targeting aircraft with their radars.

The Navy aircraft carriers in South-East Asia were under the command of Task Force 77 and the Seventh Fleet. There were between one and five aircraft carriers stationed in the Gulf of Tonkin during the war, along with large numbers of support ships. In order to coordinate the Navy and Air Force attacks on North Vietnam the country was divided into six areas called 'route packages', with No 6 subdivided into two regions, A and B. The Air Force was given control in RP 1, 5 and 6A—this represented about 60 per cent of the area of North Vietnam—and the Navy controlled the rest. There were prohibited areas established around Hanoi, around Haiphong and along the Chinese border, where special permission was needed for bombing to take place. For attacks on the North the Navy's aircraft carriers were placed at Yankee Station, a notional point north-east of Da Nang in the Gulf of Tonkin. During 1965 and 1966 a carrier was also placed at Dixie Station, off South Vietnam, for air support in the South.

President Johnson kept strict political control of 'Rolling Thunder'. Many of the targets, and even the bomb loads and the direction of attack, were decided by Johnson and his close advisers. The US Air Force commanders in Vietnam had to apply for targets to the PACAF in Hawaii, and their requests were then passed on to Washington. This system caused frustration among the pilots and leaders carrying out the bombing raids.

Most of the targets released during the early stages of 'Rolling Thunder' were part of North Vietnam's transport system, in an attempt to stop the movement of supplies to the South. North Vietnam received military support from the Soviet Union, China and Eastern Europe. These supplies entered the country mainly through the port of Haiphong and along rail lines from China. The main targets were bridges on the rail lines from Haiphong to Hanoi, from China and from Hanoi to the south of the country. Major bridges on this system were the Canal des Rapides and the Paul Doumer bridges north of Hanoi and the Than Hoa bridge to the south. The bridges close to Hanoi were safe from the bombing but the Than Hoa bridge was continually bombed, with little effect, until it was destroyed in 1972.

As the bombing increased so did the number of US aircraft shot down. Most of the losses were brought about by anti-aircraft guns, thousands of which were supplied by the Soviet Union and China. In an attempt to reduce the losses the US Air Force developed specialised aircraft to identify and attack the air defence radars and missile sites. Known by the code-name 'Wild Weasel', four F-100Fs were equipped with radar warning and homing sets that

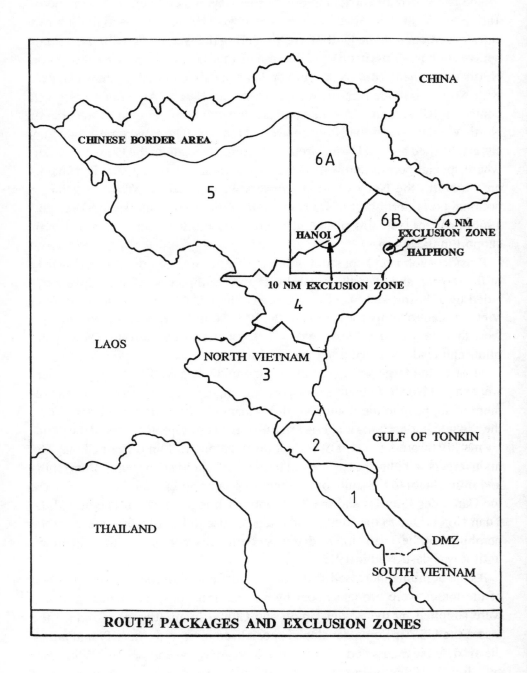

ROUTE PACKAGES AND EXCLUSION ZONES

could detect radar, and then show the direction of the radar. The F-100s were usually accompanied by F-105Ds in 'hunter-killer' teams, the F-100s identifying the sites and the F-105s then attacking them. After 26 November 1965 the F-100s operated from Korat Air Base. The first SA-2 site was claimed as destroyed on 22 November. To jam the missile radars the Air Force used EB-66s loaded with electronic equipment. Later the F-100s were replaced by F-105Fs equipped to fire the Shrike anti-radar missile.

To monitor the bombing raids over the North and to detect the North's MiGs the Air Force used a control system that included ground-based radars and Airborne Command & Control Centers (ABCCC). These were Lockheed EC-121 aircraft, based on the Constellation airliner, with a large radar placed on the back of the aircraft and operated under the code-name 'Big Eye'. Flying out of Tan Son Nhut Air Base, the EC-121s circled over Laos or the northern part of the Gulf of Tonkin with their radar covering North Vietnam. The Navy equivalent of this system was code-named 'Red Crown' and involved a ship stationed off Haiphong with its radar covering the Red River valley. Even with these systems in place some parts of North Vietnam were not covered and only general warnings could be given when the MiGs were airborne.

The distance from the air bases in Thailand to Hanoi was around 400 miles and the aircraft used could not have flown this far, carrying full bomb loads, without air refuelling. Originally KB-50J tankers were used, but later KC-135A tankers were stationed in Thailand at Don Muang and Takhli Air Bases. The tankers remained under the control of Strategic Air Command even though stationed in South-East Asia. Eventually as many as 80 tankers were involved. To operate, the KC-135s circled in oval 'race track' patterns over Laos and over the Gulf. Phantoms and F-105s were refuelled on the way into North Vietnam and on the way out.

There was an great need for reconnaissance over Vietnam and Laos to carry out both pre- and post-strike photographic coverage. RF-101s from the 15th and 20th TRS flew unarmed missions over the North, while strategic missions were flown by U-2s and SR-71As from Kadena Air Base on Okinawa. The Navy reconnaissance aircraft were the RF-8 Crusader and the RA-5 Vigilante (later in the war the Navy was forced to put the RA-5 Vigilante back into production, for use over the North). A large number of unmanned photographic drones were also flown over the North.

Under the code-name 'Arc Light', Strategic Air Command B-52s began to drop bombs on South Vietnam and Laos in June 1965. Bombing from a high level, the B-52s were used in vics of three aircraft and dropped their bombs on particular map references and in some cases never even saw the ground. After all the money spent on SAC, fighter-bombers were attacking the North while strategic bombers were dropping bombs on paddy fields. The B-52s were based originally outside the theatre on Guam but some were later based in Thailand.

As the situation on the ground continued to deteriorate in Vietnam, more and more US Air Force aircraft were drawn into the area. By the end of 1965 there were eleven squadrons of fighter-bombers stationed in South Vietnam and the entire 2nd Air Division had 500 combat aircraft. The bombing of Laos had now reached 200 sorties a day. Most of the movement along the Ho Chi Minh Trail took place at night and thus most of the bombing also took place at night, some aircraft dropping flares while others dropped the bombs.

The US Air Force's tactical and strategic transport fleets were also committed to the war in Vietnam. Military Airlift Command (MAC) was averaging 134 tons a day flown into Vietnam, and during critical periods as much as 1,875 tons a day were airlifted. When necessary, artillery, helicopters, trucks and even tanks could be carried on MAC C-141s and, later, C-5s. Inside South Vietnam C-130s, C-123s and elderly C-47s were used to carry supplies into even the smallest landing strips on a daily basis.

Some of the older transport C-47s were converted into gunships carrying four 7.62mm miniguns firing out of the side of the aircraft to provide concentrated ground support. The guns each fired 4,000 rounds a minute and only a cargo aircraft could carry enough ammunition to be effective. The gunships circled the target, firing down into it. Later, C-130s were converted to AC-130 gunships carrying a heavy armament, up to 105mm guns in some cases. These conversions were used in South Vietnam and Laos.

As the use of tactical fighter-bombers expanded the Air Force developed the use of Forward Air Controllers (FAC) to direct the tactical bombing. When ground troops asked for air support the FAC, flying in light Cessna O-1s or later in Cessna O-2As, assessed the situation and marked the target for the fighters to attack. Later in the war the F-100 was used to provide fast FAC. The FAC pilots became familiar with a particular area and working with the same troops.

The 2nd Air Division was upgraded to the Seventh Air Force on 1 April 1966. The Commander of the Seventh was Lieutenant-General William W. Momyer USAF, who was also deputy to the overall commander in Vietnam, Army General Westmoreland. With many temporary halts, the bombing of the

North continued to expand. In June 1966 the North Vietnamese oil and petro-leum storage facilities were bombed for the first time, and most of the large tanks and pipelines were destroyed. The first MiG-21 was shot down by an F-4C on 26 April 1966 and the first F-4 was shot down by MiG-17s on 21 September. During 1966 the US Air Force lost 379 aircraft in South-East Asia. This figure included 126 F-105s. Most of these were lost to ground fire over the North. Also included were 56 F-4Cs, 41 A-1s, 26 F-100s and 17 RF-101s. North Vietnam lost 13 MiG-17s and four MiG-21s to USAF aircraft.

Early in 1967 F-4s from the 8th TFW shot down seven MiG-21s in one day. The 8th TFW was commanded by Colonel Robin Olds, who later became the leading MiG scorer of the early years of the war, with four 'kills'. During 1967 many of the restrictions on the bombing of the North were removed and the attacks intensified. For the first time North Vietnamese airfields were bombed. The bombing in South Vietnam and Laos also increased, and during the course of the year the US Air Force flew 878,771 combat sorties and dropped 681,700 tons of bombs. In the entire theatre 421 USAF aircraft were lost, including 113 F-105s, 95 F-4s and 23 RF-4s. North Vietnam lost 42 MiG-17s and 17 MiG-21s to USAF aircraft.

On 30 January 1968 the Viet Cong and North Vietnamese launched the Tet offensive in South Vietnam. This was an enormous effort and there was fierce fighting throughout the country. When the offensive was finally defeated the Viet Cong were a broken force. North Vietnamese regulars attacked the US Marine base at Khe Sanh and the US Air Force flew 350 fighter-bomber and 48 B-52 sorties a day to support the Marines; large numbers of North Viet-namese were killed. The Americans had always wanted the guerrilla forces to come out into the open to fight conventionally and they made the most of the opportunity. The Tet offensive was a tactical defeat for the communist forces but a strategic success. The sight on American television of the fighting in-volved in the Tet offensive, after three years of American involvement, de-stroyed the hope that the war could ever be won.

President Johnson was forced to reduce the bombing of North Vietnam on 1 April 1968. Talks started with the North Vietnamese in Paris during May, and in November Johnson stopped the bombing of the North completely. But, even after the limitation of the bombing to below the 20th Parallel and the later ending of the bombing, no serious negotiations took place. The stumbling block was the position of the Viet Cong and the government in the South; even the seating arrangements required months of discussion. Following the US Presidential Elections in 1968 Richard Nixon became President and he pledged to end the war. The end of the bombing of North Vietnam enabled aircraft to be transferred to bombing duties in Laos and South Vietnam. Special sensors had been dropped along the Ho Chi Minh Trail and the information from these sensors allowed the trail to be attacked at night, and with greater accuracy. During 1968 the US Air Force flew 1,034,839 sorties in South-East Asia, the highest yearly total of the war.

In 1969 President Nixon announced the policy of 'Vietnamisation'. This involved a run-down in the numbers of American forces and an increase in South Vietnamese forces. It was hoped that air power would hold the communists at bay in the region until the South Vietnamese were strong enough to accomplish this on their own. At this stage of the war the American public had become deeply dissatisfied with the conflict in Vietnam and demonstrations against the war involving hundreds of thousands of people had became commonplace. In a democracy public opinion cannot permanently be ignored by any politician. Nixon stated that he wanted 'peace with honour', but this option was never really available to him. As part of the policy of ending the bombing the Americans thought they had an agreement with the North Vietnamese to allow reconnaissance flights to continue over the North unmolested. These flights continued under the code-name 'Blue Tree', but many of the aircraft involved in these raids were fired on by the North Vietnamese defences. An F-105 was shot down in January 1969 while accompanying a reconnaissance aircraft, and an HH-53 rescue helicopter was shot down by a MiG over Laos while attempting to rescue the crew. In early 1970, after unarmed reconnaissance aircraft had been shot down, President Nixon authorised what became known as 'protective reaction strikes' against any anti-aircraft sites that fired on the reconnaissance aircraft. Starting from single unarmed photographic aircraft the 'Blue Tree' flights developed into complex operations over the North. Fighter aircraft were included to cover the MiG airfields, 'Wild Weasel' aircraft blocked the defensive radar and strike aircraft were employed to attack the anti-aircraft sites. Large numbers of aircraft continued to operate over North Vietnam.

Until 1969 Cambodia had been nominally neutral in the war. However, the North Vietnamese had been using Cambodia as part of the Ho Chi Minh Trail, and as a safe storage area. On 18 March 1969 B-52s were used to bomb parts of Cambodia with the secret agreement of the Cambodian government, in the 'Menu' series of raids. Even the aircrews were not supposed to know the position of the targets when bombing by radar guidance from the ground. When these raids finally became public in March 1970 the US had carried out 3,630 sorties over Cambodia and dropped more than 100,000 tons of bombs.

An RF-4C was shot down over North Vietnam on 5 June 1969 and came down in the Gulf of Tonkin. President Nixon ordered a series of reprisal raids by the Air Force and Navy on the associated anti-aircraft batteries, radar sites and covering missile sites. By the end of 1969 779 attack and reconnaissance sorties had been carried out over North Vietnam by the US Air Force. Ho Chi Minh died in September 1969. His 'long war' strategy had meant that he would not live to see the conclusion of his life's work. During 1969 in South-East Asia 966,949 sorties were flown and 294 aircraft lost.

The first MiG shot down since the end of 'Rolling Thunder' was destroyed on 28 March 1970 by an F-4J from the USS *Constellation*. The Phantom had been taking part in protective reaction strikes against the defences in the North. The ending of the continuous bombing had given the North Vietnamese the opportunity to move their anti-aircraft defences south, to cover the US aircraft attacking Laos. The mobile SA-2s were also moved south in an attempt to destroy the B-52s. In February 1971 a reconnaissance aircraft was tracked by North Vietnamese radar from a SAM site. In retaliation for this a raid involving 67 sorties was mounted in the area around the Ben Kari pass, inside North Vietnam.

During 1970–71 the numbers of US Air Force aircraft in the region continued to decline as 'Vietnamisation' began to take effect. In 1970 711,440 missions were flown and 171 aircraft shot down; the 1971 totals were 450,031 sorties and 87 aircraft lost. Although air power was meant to hold the line, as the number of ground troops declined the number of aircraft in South-East Asia also declined. By the end of 1971 the total number of land-based aircraft available had shrunk to less than 500, stationed in Thailand and South Vietnam. Reconnaissance over the North had revealed a build-up of forces in the southern region of North Vietnam, indicating a major ground campaign planned for 1972. Operation 'Proud Deep Alpha' was a five-day bombing campaign, starting on 26 December 1971, intended to disrupt this build-up. The raids were all conducted south of the 20th Parallel and comprised 1,025 sorties, including over 400 from the carriers *Constellation* and *Coral Sea*. The targets were the SAM sites that had been moved south and selected anti-aircraft sites. Logistic targets, truck parks, POL (petrol, oil and lubricants) storage facilities and supply dumps were also hit.

The American strategic bombing of North Vietnam during the 'Rolling Thunder' campaign lasted from 2 March 1965 until 31 October 1968. The North had been bombed before, but only in isolated attacks. The campaign followed the same course as the war in general, that is, it was a long, slow process of escalation. 'Rolling Thunder' started as a series of individual specific raids directed at named targets in the southern region of North Vietnam and developed into a continuous strategic bombing campaign covering almost the entire country. The original raids had been intended as a threat to the North, to show the leadership there what would happen if it did not change its approach to the war in the South: the plan was gradually to increase the scope and intensity of the bombing until the government in the North stopped supporting the Viet Cong in the South. It had been thought that the level of bombing that would be required would soon be reached. But over the 3½ years of the bombing, the number of sorties and the tonnage of bombs dropped continued to increase substantially every year, except for short-term declines during bad flying weather. Even after this enormous effort the North Vietnamese still refused to change their policy towards the war.

The higher levels of the American military were still in thrall to the strategic bombing doctrine and nobody involved in the initial decision-making had really envisaged the campaign that was in fact waged. The idea that the bombing would last for 3½ years had never been considered. The way the campaign developed was in reality the outcome of a series of decisions taken in reaction to the North's refusal to change its basic policy. The campaign did not follow a carefully designed course but simply developed out of the impotent rage that the American leadership felt at the refusal of the North Vietnamese to give way under the pressure. The bombing of North Vietnam was carried out from bases in Thailand and South Vietnam by the US Air Force and from carriers in the Gulf of Tonkin by the US Navy. The weight of the bombing developed steadily—25,000 sorties dropping 63,000 tons in 1965, 79,000 sorties dropping 136,000 tons in 1966, 108,000 sorties dropping 226,000 tons in 1967 and 82,000 sorties dropping 180,000 tons in 1968. These figures only encompass the bombs dropped on North Vietnam: higher totals were dropped on Laos, Cambodia and South Vietnam. North Vietnam managed to shoot down 928 of the attacking aircraft during 'Rolling Thunder'.

Even after these large tonnages of bombs had been dropped, the North Vietnamese did not alter their stance. The Tet offensive in early 1968 proved that even after three years of bombing the North had both the will and the capability to mount major operations in the South. How was it possible for North Vietnam to continue to operate? Was the strategic bombing doctrine faulty or did the fault lie in the application of the theories? The bombing of the North developed slowly from a series of individual raids to the massive campaign it later became. The military leadership had advised against the gradual application of force against North Vietnam. The essence of air power is mobility, concentration and surprise, and the gradualist approach loses at least two of these advantages. Since the ending of the war in Vietnam the military have put forward this misuse of air power, in the gradualist manner, as one of the main causes of the failure of 'Rolling Thunder'.

The US political leadership chose to apply a steadily increasing amount of bombing to the North because it never really considered the possibility that the Vietnamese would be capable of resisting the Americans. The gradualist approach degenerated into a war of attrition between the attacking aircraft and the North Vietnamese air defence system. The gradualists did not consider the dichotomy between the American view of the conflict as essentially a limited war and the Vietnamese view of the war as total. For the Americans, the risks of forcing the Soviets or the Chinese to enter the war were to be kept to a minimum.

The level of bombing that would have forced the North Vietnamese out of the war in the South would have been reached when it became physically impossible for them to continue. This level of bombing was never achieved, and the self-imposed limitations were never to allow this level to be possible. The US leaders were operating in a democracy, which meant that, ultimately, they had to carry public support for their policy. As the war dragged on this support declined, making more commitment impossible.

A sudden, massive, all-out attack at the start of 'Rolling Thunder', before the North had built up its air defences and dispersed what industry it did have, would undoubtedly have had a greater impact. The shock effect of such a concentrated campaign on the Vietnamese leadership might have been salutary. But it is doubtful if these attacks would have been enough to change the views of the Northern Vietnamese leadership, many of whom had dedicated their lives to their cause.

The American military developed a version of the 'stab in the back' theory to excuse the failure of air power in Vietnam. The political leadership was blamed for many of the mistakes made. Admiral Sharp, the commander of American forces in the Pacific during 'Rolling Thunder', has written,

I believe that the air war was the most misunderstood part of the whole engagement. It was especially misunderstood by the civilians in the Pentagon who were making the broad decisions and many of the smaller decisions of the air war. The severe restrictions under which our Air Force operated resulted in markedly decreased effectiveness of the tremendous power we had available and resulted in wide misunderstanding of the effectiveness of airpower when properly used.[1]

The military sincerely believed that the way air power had been used was incorrect, and that they had been held back from winning the war, in the North, by civilian interference. The fact that the targets for most of the bombing were chosen by President Johnson and his advisers and only released in dribs and drabs, often ignoring the recommendations of the military on the spot, is given as one of the reasons for the failure. Experience is the hardest-won thing in war, and the targeting system devised by the political leadership ignored the experience of the people who were daily risking their lives over the North. The image of the President of the USA choosing individual targets in Vietnam 12,000 miles away, and even aircraft types, bomb loads and directions of attack, over the heads or the military leaders directly involved, is absurd.

The political leadership also imposed artificial restrictions on the areas that could be bombed in the North. The early raids were restricted to areas just north of the Demiltarised Zone. The raids spread over time to cover most of the country, but there remained areas along the Chinese border, around Hanoi and around Haiphong that could not be bombed without special permission. The pilots, not unreasonably, thought they were being exposed to all the dangers of carrying out the bombing but were being held back from really applying the full weight of air power. These arguments carry a great deal of authority and few could now deny that air power was not used to its best advantage in Vietnam. But, as the Pentagon Papers state,

> ... virtually all of the economic and military targets in NVN that could be considered even remotely significant had been hit. Except for simply keeping it up, almost everything bombing could do to pressurise NVN had been done.[2]

North Vietnam had a small industrial base before the bombing but was basically a subsistence agricultural economy. America had chosen a poor example to test out the strategic bombing doctrine.

---

[1] Sharp, U. S. Grant, 'Airpower Could Have Won in Vietnam', *Air Force Magazine*, Vol. 54 (September 1971), pp. 82–3.
[2] *The Pentagon Papers*, The Senator Gravel Edition, Vol. 4, Beacon Press (Boston), p. 216

The US Navy also operated a strategic bombing policy, and had been in conflict with the Air Force since before the Second World War over control of the strategic bombing mission. The Navy was heavily committed to the construction and use of aircraft carriers for the tactical and strategic use of air power. In a war with the Soviet Union aircraft launched from carriers would have used nuclear weapons in the strategic role. One of the essentials of command is the unity of that command, but there was never any one single commander for 'Rolling Thunder'. It would seem that the lessons of Korea were ignored, since both Navy and Air Force operations remained under individual control. The advantages of air power are its flexibility and its ability to concentrate in mass on individual targets. The division of North Vietnam into separate areas where the targeting was under the control of either the Air Force or Navy and the division of command had the effect of limiting this flexibility. Both the Air Force and the Navy would have welcomed a single commander, but only if it was someone from their own service.

Robert McNamara, the Defense Secretary, had before the Vietnam War introduced the systems analysis approach to the control of the American military, especially financial control. The essence of this approach is 'how much is enough?', or an attempt to quantify the input and the expected output of the military services. This was not found to be the most effective way of fighting a war. Each type of aircraft was given an expected daily sortie rate by systems analysis and this came to be taken as a quantifiable measure of success, as was the 'body count' in the South. The sortie rate dominated the Air Force's and Navy's approach to the war. The overwhelming majority of sorties were armed reconnaissance missions flying over areas that had already been picked clean with only limited chances of success, but once criteria had been established then officers attempted to achieve results measured by these criteria, even when this meant losing sight of the overall results. The real objective was to defeat North Vietnam, not simply to provide more sorties. McNamara's Planning Programming and Budgeting System became something of a liability in the actual fighting of the Vietnam War.

The Americans' attempt to stop the supply of men and equipment to the war in the South involved the dropping of thousands of tons of bombs, but the gradualist approach had given the initiative in the war to the North Vietnamese, the Americans only reacting to the actions taken against them. The amount of munitions being used in South Vietnam by the communist forces never reached the level of that in Korea (at least, not before 1972) and the air attacks in Korea never stopped supplies reaching the front line. The communist forces in the South held the initiative for much of the war, in that they only fought at the time and place of their choosing. They could scale their actions up or down to suit the level of supplies available. While the American ground forces could not pin down the Viet Cong and force up the amount of supplies used to a higher level than could be brought down the Ho Chi Minh Trail, the attempt to stop the North interfering in the South was bound to fail.

The overwhelming majority of military supplies used by North Vietnam were produced in the Soviet Union, China or Eastern Europe. The material that the North needed to continue the war was imported into the country and not manufactured there. As America had no intention of bombing the Soviets or the Chinese, the factories producing the equipment needed by the North were completely safe from 'Rolling Thunder': the 'vital targets' were elsewhere. While they could continue to import into the North the necessary supplies, the North Vietnamese leadership did not need to worry about the destruction of their own limited industrial production. There were no industrial facilities in the North that the leadership were not prepared to do without, if necessary, provided the aid from outside the country continued. It was estimated that 'Rolling Thunder' cost North Vietnam $600m, but during the same period they had received over $2,000m in aid from their allies. In other words, for every dollar's worth of damage caused by 'Rolling Thunder' the North had received over three dollars in aid from outside the country. During 1965, including aid from abroad, North Vietnam's gross national product had actually gone up by 6 per cent, in spite of the bombing. Most of this aid was imported through the port of Haiphong, and one of the major weaknesses of 'Rolling Thunder' was its failure to close the port down. The fear that this would have brought the Soviet Union or China into the war created a safe haven around the port for supply ships.

The war in the South was in reality a political conflict. The original American commitment had been to give breathing space to the government in South Vietnam to enable it to create a stable society that was capable of sustaining its own defence. But the population in the South never showed any real faith or belief in the various governments that held power there, and none of these had the loyalty or support of a large section of the people. All the American actions in Vietnam were doomed to failure while the majority of the people were not prepared to back what they saw as corrupt governments which had no relevance to their everyday lives. As the failure of the governments in the South became more and more obvious the Americans were forced to pour more and more resources into Vietnam to hold in place these unrepresentative governments. All the other failures in Vietnam stem from this failure to create a popular government in South Vietnam. By ignoring the political dimension of the war the Americans ensured that whatever strategy they adopted for the military side of the conflict, including 'Rolling Thunder', had little chance of success.

The strategic bombing doctrine had failed to deliver the goods in the 'Rolling Thunder' campaign in Vietnam, but the American military produced a whole series of reasons for the failure, some justified and some not. Even in the face of the events in Vietnam the Air Force still had full confidence in the strategic theories. During 'Rolling Thunder' 605,000 tons of bombs were dropped in 297,000 sorties, or some 460 tons of bombs and 230 sorties a day over a period of three years and eight months. These are only average figures as there were several long bombing pauses. The US lost 928 aircraft, averaging one for every 650 sorties. The heaviest year of the bombing was 1967, and the figures for that year alone were 299 sorties delivering on average 616 tons a day and one aircraft lost for every 330 sorties.

CHAPTER 2

THE SITUATION IN VIETNAM, 1969–72

W HEN Richard Nixon became Commander-in-Chief of the American armed forces in 1969 he had given the impression during the election that he would end the Vietnam War by introducing a new approach to the conflict. However, he was to find that he faced exactly the same problems as President Johnson, and that he had much the same resources to work with. One of Nixon's first actions was to appoint Henry A. Kissinger as his National Security Adviser, and the two men were to play the central part in America's decision-making process in relation to the Vietnam War over the next five years. President Johnson's primary aim in the conflict had been the preservation of a non-communist South Vietnam. Nixon also wanted to stop the North Vietnamese taking over in the South, but over a period of time his primary aim became the goal of what he called an 'honourable peace', which was a much smaller strategic aim and might even have been an achievable one.

One of the first tasks given to Kissinger by Nixon was the drawing up of a survey of America's present position in Vietnam. The finished document was known as National Security Study Memorandum 1, or NSSM1. This showed that there was very little agreement over the state of the war or over the future course of action that should be taken to end it. Far from having any ready-made new approach to the war, Nixon soon found the problems as intractable as his predecessor. The option of increasing the commitment to the ground war was not available as the public would no longer have accepted this and there was now little belief that the United States could win on the ground.

One of the few points that found general agreement in NSSM1 was that South Vietnam still could not survive on its own. This was the essence of Nixon's dilemma: there was no agreement over how the war could be won or if it could be won, and he could not see a way of leaving Vietnam with 'honour' unless the South could be massively reinforced with equipment and aid to the point were it could stand alone against the North. Nixon's personal preference seems to have been to use more force and even to have expanded the war.

But in the long run he knew that the American public would not allow the stalemate to continue while large numbers of Americans were dying.

When Nixon found that his options were so limited he fell back on the process of 'Vietnamisation' that Johnson had started. The truth was that the more fully the Americans had entered the war, the weaker the South Vietnamese had become. Concerning his 'Vietnamisation' programme, Nixon stated that

> The first [part] is the strengthening of the armed forces of the South Vietnamese in numbers, equipment, leadership and combat skills, and overall capability. The second component is the extension of the pacification programme in South Vietnam.[1]

The Americans would rely on a strengthened South Vietnamese army to allow them to withdraw with honour. In order to show his commitment to the new policy, on 20 April 1969 Nixon ordered the withdrawal of 150,000 US troops from Vietnam over the next year. Running alongside the 'Vietnamisation' policy was Nixon's belief that something could be gained through negotiations with the North. Johnson had started the talks in Paris in May 1968 but they had immediately got bogged down. Both Johnson and Nixon were products of the American political system where deal-making plays a large part in the operation of Congress. American congressmen expect concessions for their constituents in return for their votes. The art of succeeding in American politics is in putting together a deal that, at least partially, rewards everybody. Johnson and Nixon both clung to the idea that they could reach a deal with the North if they could only apply enough pressure and offer enough concessions. The North Vietnamese were working within a completely different paradigm.

When it became obvious that the public talks in Paris were getting nowhere Nixon entered into an exchange of letters with Ho Chi Minh that started the secret talks between Kissinger and the Northern politician Le Duc Tho, who had been a founding member of the Northern Party 40 years earlier. There were twelve secret meetings of the two sides between August 1969 and October 1971, but in reality these meetings became as deadlocked as the official talks.

Nixon had long had a reputation as a hard-line anti-communist, and he sought to use this reputation in his dealings with the North Vietnamese. He told Kissinger to intimate to the North Vietnamese that the US President was obsessed with winning the war and that he would stop at nothing to achieve his aim. He called this his 'madman strategy'. Kissinger told the Vietnamese that

---

[1] Palmer, David, *Summons of the Trumpet*, Presidio Press (San Rafael, 1977), p. 219.

if they did not reach agreement Nixon could be out of anyone's control even on a nuclear level. Nixon told his aide H. R. Haldemann,

> I want the North Vietnamese to believe I've reached the point where I might do anything to stop the war. We'll just slip the word to them that, for God's sake, you know, Nixon is obsessed about communism. We can't restrain him when he's angry and he has his hand on the nuclear button.[1]

Both the invasion of Cambodia and the Lam Son 719 operation in Laos were attempts by Nixon to give substance to his pressure on North Vietnam, in addition to the military aims.

The North Vietnamese view remained constant throughout and they were no more impressed by Nixon than they had been by Johnson. At the talks the North demanded the removal of all American forces and the establishment of a provisional government in the South. The Northern leadership had dedicated their lives to the unification of the country and saw no reason to change their views. After the enormous losses of the Tet offensive they knew that they would have to rebuild the North's forces and return to the 'long war' strategy they had temporarily abandoned during Tet. Whenever the North had attempted to defeat the Americans in a stand-up fight they had been beaten. But Nixon had already announced the American withdrawal. The support by the American public for the war was seen by the Northern leadership as continuing to decline. Time, it was felt, was on their side. Even after the death of Ho Chi Minh on 3 September 1969 the leadership did not change the North's commitment to the war.

Each side had a totally different view of what the talks were for. The classic communist-Marxist view of negotiations is not that they are intended to lead to an amicable agreement but that they should be used (a) to accept the surrender of an enemy, (b) to avoid a defeat or (c) to open another avenue for bringing pressure to bear on an enemy. North Vietnam's view of the Paris peace talks was that they were intended to embarrass America and give the North access to the world's press.

Nixon's foreign policy in general can be viewed as highly successful. He did manage to isolate North Vietnam partly from both China and the Soviet Union, which countries had been the North's main source of outside aid. Johnson had always been constrained in his use of air power against the North by his fear that either China or the Soviet Union would become directly involved, as

---

[1] Quoted in Maclear, Michael, *Vietnam: The Ten Thousand Day War*, Thames Methuen (London, 1981), pp. 387–9.

China had in the Korean War. But from 1969 onwards the relations between the Soviets and the Chinese continued to decline and a series of border clashes took place between them. As a result, both sought to improve their relations with the United States so as to strengthen their position against the other. Although they both continued to provide aid to North Vietnam, they each came to view it as a side-show that should not interfere with their relations with America. Nixon's policy of *détente* with the Soviet Union and *rapprochement* with China strengthened his hand against the North Vietnamese.

The Chinese needed to end the international isolation that had been imposed by the Americans since 1949. The Cultural Revolution had only increased this isolation. The Soviet Union had built up a major army of 44 divisions along the Chinese border and the Chinese came to feel that they needed American support to counterbalance this threat. The North Vietnamese had always taken everything that China had offered, but they viewed China as their long-term traditional enemy and indeed had done so for the last thousand years. Relations between China and North Vietnam were never close, and later, in 1979, they fought a major war. The Soviets had come to the conclusion that they could not win the arms race and wanted a strategic arms treaty to slow down the costs of the Cold War. Moreover, the Americans were practically the only source of the large amounts of grain that their failing agricultural policy could not provide for their population.

Having accepted the 'Vietnamisation' strategy, Nixon continued to increase the aid and weapons provided to the South Vietnamese, at the same time continuing to reduce the numbers of American forces. The situation during 1969–70 was relatively calm as the North Vietnamese tried to rebuild their forces after the defeat of the Tet offensive. In March 1970 Nixon announced a further reduction of 150,000 American troops in Vietnam. However, in an attempt to strengthen the position of the South while 'Vietnamisation' took place, he ordered what he called the 'incursion' into Cambodia, and on 1 May he announced that American and South Vietnamese troops had entered the country.

On 18 March General Lon Nol had become head of state in Cambodia and had ordered the North Vietnamese out of the country, but the Cambodian Army had proved incapable of enforcing this order. Lon Nol asked the Americans to intervene in support of the Cambodian forces. The North Vietnamese had stored large amounts of supplies in Cambodia close to the border with South Vietnam and the Americans and South Vietnamese captured considerable quantities of these stores. However, the North Vietnamese Army chose to retreat in front of the attack rather than fight. The 'incursion' did achieve its short-term aims of weakening the North's position in South Vietnam, but the political reaction in America showed Nixon the limits of what the Americam public would accept in South-East Asia. He had hoped that he would demonstrate his resolve to the Northern leadership by the move into Cambodia, but the message that was sent showed up the restrictions in American policy.

In reaction to the operation in Cambodia the US Senate voted in June 1970 to end the Tonkin Gulf Resolution of 1964, which had been the basis of Presidential control of the war in Vietnam. The Cooper-Church Amendment cut off all funds for American operations in Cambodia after 30 June, although the Seventh Air Force was allowed to continue bombing the country. The operation in Cambodia did buy some time for 'Vietnamisation' to take place, but it also showed the limits of Presidential power.

By 1971 Nixon had been President for two years, but he had little to show for either the talks with the North or the 'Vietnamisation' policy. The Lam Son 719 operation started on 8 February 1971 and was intended to show the strength of the South Vietnamese. With American air support the South Vietnamese army attacked North Vietnamese positions in Laos to destroy lines of communications and stocks of supplies. Although some units fought well, other units of the South Vietnamese Army collapsed and the operation came very close to disaster. The pictures of South Vietnamese troops clinging to helicopters in order to escape sent a message to everyone who saw them. Even though it had been strengthened, the South Vietnamese Army did not look as if it could stand up to North Vietnamese regulars.

Kissinger made the most extensive peace offer so far at the secret negotiations in May 1971. In return for the release of American prisoners held by the North, the United States would withdraw all its troops within six months of signing an agreement. The North demanded that President Thieu should be removed from office but the Americans refused. Thieu was returned to office in September after an election in which his opponents were removed by force. The United States now seemed to be committed to maintaining Thieu's undemocratic Presidency.

For 3½ years between 1965 and 1968 North Vietnam had suffered heavy and continuous bombing during the 'Rolling Thunder' campaign. Roads, rail lines and bridges had been destroyed and much heavy industry, including the cement works at Haiphong and the iron works at Thai Nguyen, put out of action. Lighter industry had been broken into small units and dispersed into the countryside. By 1971 most of the damage had been repaired and industry was working again with the help of aid from the Soviet Union and China. The enormous losses in manpower during the Tet offensive had to a large extent been replaced with the conscription of the majority of fit men between the ages of 15 and 45.

During 1971 aid from the Soviets amounted to over a million tons, delivered in 350 ships into North Vietnamese ports. A large part of this aid was made up of main battle tanks and heavy artillery. The amount of equipment travelling down the Ho Chi Minh Trail was estimated to have increased to 14,000 tons a month. Two pipelines had been constructed between Haiphong and the Demilitarised Zone. Reconnaissance flights showed that large amounts of stores and equipment were stockpiled in the North and along the trail, and there were 8,000 trucks waiting in depots close to the border. American intelligence experts began to predict that an invasion of the South would occur during 1972.

Vo Nguyen Giap, the North Vietnamese Defence Minister, had defeated the French at Dien Bien Phu but had been thwarted by the Americans in the attempted take-overs of the South in 1965 and 1968. Giap was indeed planning another invasion of the South. He knew that there would be few American ground troops left by 1972, and that 1972 was a presidential election year in the United States. The calculation was that public opinion would stop the recommitment of ground forces to the war and force Nixon to negotiate. Even after 'Vietnamisation' the South's army was not seen as being capable of stopping a major invasion from the North. The North's politburo had not been unanimous in backing the invasion. One group, headed by Truong Chinh, wanted to wait and to try to strengthen the North economically, but the war faction headed by the Southerner Le Duan had its plans accepted.

President Nixon offered further proposals to the peace negotiations in October 1971. These included proposals for elections in the South and for President Thieu to stand down before these elections, but the negotiations once again came to nothing. Dissatisfaction with the war in the United States had reached an all-time high by the latter part of 1971. A poll showed that 71 per cent of the population thought that the war had been a mistake and that 58 per cent thought it morally wrong. A large part of the country was, after years of involvement in Vietnam, sick of the conflict. The never-ending cost in lives and money of a war that seemed to be unwinnable could not be sustained. Nixon knew that his actions were constrained as much by the political position in United States as by the situation in Vietnam.

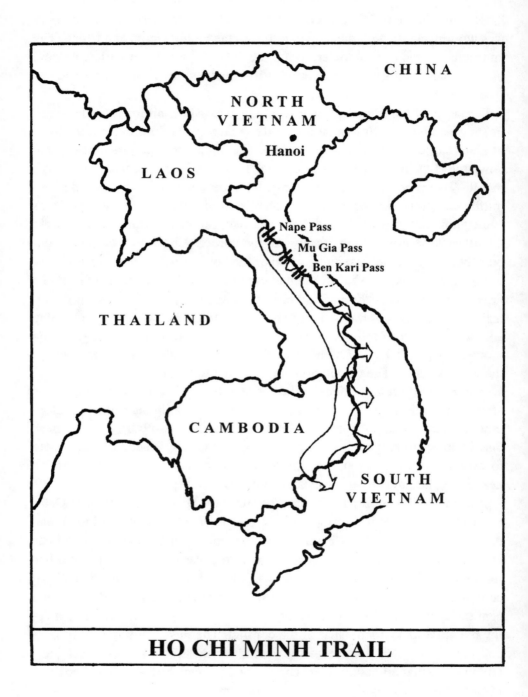

CHINA

NORTH
VIETNAM

Hanoi

LAOS

Nape Pass
Mu Gia Pass
Ben Kari Pass

THAILAND

CAMBODIA

SOUTH
VIETNAM

HO CHI MINH TRAIL

In reply to the build-up of supplies in North Vietnam and also the shelling of Saigon in December 1971, Nixon ordered the bombing of the North. This was called Operation 'Proud Deep Alpha' and was aimed at supply targets south of the 20th Parallel. Between 26 and 30 December 1,025 sorties were carried out by Air Force and Navy aircraft—the heaviest bombing of the North since the ending of 'Rolling Thunder' in November 1968. The aim was to disrupt or delay the preparations for the coming invasion of the South, and the longer any action by the North could be delayed the longer the South had to absorb the massive influx of equipment supplied by the United States under the 'Vietnamisation' policy. By the end of 1971 the numbers of American forces in South Vietnam had dropped to 155,000. In general the position in South Vietnam had improved. The pacification programme had to a large extent worked and many areas of the country were now reasonably safe. Large numbers of local armed forces had been created and had been successful in expelling what was left of the Viet Cong from many areas, although the North Vietnamese regular units were still active in the border regions.

At the start of 1972 supplies from China and the Soviet Union continued to flow into the North. After nearly twenty years of war the North Vietnamese economy was totally dependent on this support from abroad. Included in this aid were food and basic consumer supplies as well as military equipment. China was supplying 22,000 tons a month, delivered along the two rail lines that ran south from China into Hanoi. The Soviet Union and Eastern Europe were still using the port of Haiphong to provide North Vietnam with most of its more advanced military equipment, including SA-2 surface-to-air missiles, tanks and artillery.

On 25 January President Nixon announced the terms of his October 1971 peace proposals in a television speech, and the following day he revealed that secret talks had been taking place for over two years. The North Vietnamese reply was to request that talks take place in March, later asking to delay these until April. With hindsight it was obvious that they wanted to delay the start of the talks until after the invasion of the South had got under way so as to strengthen their position.

In February 1972 President Nixon made his historic trip to Peking. This was the first time that an American President had visited China. The visit signalled the end of the US policy of containment of Communist China. The United States had tried since the 1949 communist take-over of China to isolate the Chinese from world politics, but the visit led to an opening up of China's international relations and to the Chinese taking their permanent seat on the UN Security Council. The *rapprochement* with China was a major plank in Nixon's foreign policy and he hoped that it would give him some freedom of movement in Vietnam. He understood that the Chinese would continue to support the North Vietnamese, but he hoped that there would be limits to that support. His view was that the Chinese needed the United States more than the US needed China.

The details of the peace offer that Nixon made public concerned the withdrawal of all US forces within six months of the signing of an agreement. Internationally supervised elections would be held and President Thieu would step down before the elections took place so that he could not distort the results. Nixon hoped to build up pressure on the North Vietnamese to return to negotiations rather than turn to the military action that was seen to be coming. On 26 January Nixon sent letters to both the Chinese and the Soviet leadership stating that if North Vietnam attacked the South he would meet this attack with strong military countermeasures. The Soviets' reply amounted to a low-key continuation of support for the North, and Kissinger placed further pressure on the Soviet Union by telling the Soviet Ambassador Dobrynin that a North Vietnamese invasion would endanger the trip to Moscow by Nixon in May. The Chinese replied with a non-committal message which Nixon took to be a good sign. However, once they had supplied the equipment it was doubtful whether the Soviets or the Chinese had any control over North Vietnam.

The Americans had always maintained their right to carry out reconnaissance flights over the North. This was part of the settlement that President Johnson thought he had obtained in exchange for the ending of the 'Rolling Thunder' bombing campaign in 1968; the agreement also forbade the North from sending troops across the DMZ and attacking major cities in the South. The North Vietnamese had always claimed that no such agreement existed and had fired upon US reconnaissance aircraft, and in response the US had begun to carry out 'protective reaction strikes' (one of the war's many euphemisms) against the anti-aircraft sites responsible. The size and scale of these strikes continued to increase as North Vietnam gradually built up its air defences.

On 18 January an RA-5C Vigilante unarmed reconnaissance aircraft based on the aircraft carrier *Constellation* was sent to photograph the Quang Lang airfield after reports that MiG-21s were being based there and threatening operations over Laos. The RA-5 was escorted by A-6 Intruders and A-7 Corsairs carrying bombs, with F-4J Phantoms to provide a MiGCAP (combat air patrol) for the other aircraft. Altogether 35 aircraft were involved in escorting the RA-5. To create the impression that the aircraft were heading for a target in Laos the formation flew west across South Vietnam, then north through Laos, and then turned to enter North Vietnam from the west. Over the airfield the RA-5 was fired on by anti-aircraft guns and by SA-2 missiles. In reply the attack aircraft bombed the airfield and flak sites. One of the F-4Js was flown by Lieutenant Randall H. Cunningham, with Lieutenant William P. Driscoll as his radar operator. Cunningham claims that eighteen missiles were launched at his Phantom without success. After avoiding the missiles he spotted two MiG-21s at low level heading north. He closed behind the two MiGs and fired a Sidewinder missile at the lead aircraft. The MiG turned hard to the right and the Sidewinder missed. The Phantom turned hard right on the outside of the MiG's turn, and when the MiG reversed its turn to the left Cunningham fired another Sidewinder as the MiG passed in front of the Phantom. This time the missile guided and blew the tail off the MiG, and the aircraft crashed in a ball of flame. This was the first MiG shot down in 1972, but it would not be the last shot down by Cunningham and Driscoll.

On 21 February Major Robert A. Lodge and his weapon systems operator Roger C. Locher were the first Air Force pilots to shoot down a MiG in 1972. Lodge was part of the 'Triple Nickel' 555th TFS stationed in Thailand and was flying an F-4D. This was the first time a MiG had been shot down at night. Flying over north-east Laos about 90 miles south-west of Hanoi, Lodge was given vectors by the 'Red Crown' radar control service to contact a MiG in his area. After tailing the MiG at extremely low level Lodge fired three radar-controlled Sparrow missiles, one of which destroyed the MiG. Two other MiG-21s followed Lodge as he left the area low on fuel, but he managed to outrun them.

By the end of March 1972 the numbers of US forces in Vietnam had declined to 95,000. Of this total, 20,000 were Air Force personnel, and there were another 27,000 on the air bases in Thailand. By the end of April the numbers in Vietnam were down to 69,000. After three years of 'Vietnamisation' South Vietnam had over a million men under arms. Most of this total was made up of the local and regional militia forces, but the regular army had increased to 414,000 men. If North Vietnam did invade it was this force that would have to face the enemy on the ground. The numbers of American aircraft left in South-East Asia had also been reduced. In South Vietnam there were only 88 strike aircraft remaining. This total included three squadrons of

F-4s and five AC-119 gunships at Da Nang and one squadron of A-37s at Bien Hoa. The other airfields had been handed over to South Vietnam. In Thailand, stationed at Ubon, Korat, Udorn, U-Tapao and Nakhon Phanom, were 163 F-4 Phantoms, 16 F-105s, 15 A-1s, 10 B-57s and 52 B-52s. Although the numbers of aircraft in Thailand had been reduced, the infrastructure was still in place to receive any increase in forces. The last Marine aircraft had left Indo-China over a year earlier. Only two aircraft carriers were on station in the Gulf of Tonkin. Between them they carried about 170 aircraft. The USS *Constellation* had only just left to return home.

On 29 March 1972 the North Vietnamese finally launched their offensive against the South. The attack was a conventional invasion involving practically all of the Northern army. The aim was to confront head-on the South Vietnamese Army and to destroy it, or at the very least set back as far as possible the process of 'Vietnamisation'. It was also hoped to capture a large part of the South, in order to strengthen the position of the North in any talks that would follow. Besides the NVA regulars, what was left of the Viet Cong also took part in the invasion by disrupting as much of the countryside as they could.

There were three main thrusts to the invasion, one in the north across the Demilitarised Zone and from Laos aimed at the town of Quang Tri, one into the Central Highlands of South Vietnam from Laos to capture Kontum, and one from Cambodia only 80 miles north of Saigon to take the city of An Loc. Twelve of North Vietnam's fifteen divisions, comprising 150,000 troops, were involved in the invasion. Only one division was left in the North, while two were held in reserve in Laos. The fact that the North was left practically defenceless shows the total commitment to the invasion.

The first phase of the invasion to develop was the attack in the north. Three North Vietnamese divisions involving 40,000 troops crossed the DMZ, spearheaded by the T-54 tanks and 130mm artillery pieces they had obtained from the Soviets. The Americans and the South Vietnamese had not expected a direct crossing of the DMZ and the North Vietnamese easily defeated the 9,000 Marines and second-line South Vietnamese troops of the 3rd Division they encountered. The NVA forces were soon heading down the coastal highway towards Quang Tri. Bad weather had limited the amount of air support that could be used to counter the advance. Most of the South Vietnamese army had not been trained to operate against a conventional invasion, but after heavy losses on both sides the South's forces did manage to establish and hold a line north of Quang Tri. This gave time for the South Vietnamese Army to bring up reinforcements and by 14 April to start small-scale counter-attacks. But the North launched another major attack during a period of bad weather on 27 April. It was decided to pull the South's defence line back to Quang Tri, but during the move the morale of the troops collapsed and they fled in panic, abandoning the city. The 1st ARVN Division managed to re-establish a defence line north of Hue and again stopped the communist forces' advance.

In the Central Highlands the North Vietnamese Army attacked with two divisions, also well-supplied with tanks and artillery, in an attempt to capture Kontum and Pleiku. The capture of Route 19 and Route 14 would cut the links with the coast. Other Northern units pushed through to the coastal area in an attempt to cut South Vietnam in two. The NVA captured the fire-support bases around Kontum after extremely heavy fighting and Kontum itself was surrounded and cut off. The forces trapped in Kontum were obliged to rely on supplies airlifted in.

The communist attack in the South was aimed towards Saigon from the supply bases in Cambodia. The first objective would be the town of An Loc, the provincial capital. The main highway, Route 13, led down from close to the Fish Hook area of Cambodia into Saigon. The American 'incursion' into Cambodia two years earlier had been intended to capture supplies and disrupt the North Vietnamese build-up in that area. The communist forces first of all feigned a thrust towards the town of Tay Ninh, which was even closer to Saigon. After Southern forces had been drawn away from An Loc, the main thrust of the attack captured the town of Loc Ninh and then completely surrounded An Loc, although not before reinforcements had been rushed into the town. The supplies to the troops inside An Loc were maintained by helicopters and US C-130 Hercules flights. A number of helicopters were lost to the intensive ground fire while keeping the town supplied.

Captain Fred Olmsted shot down a MiG-21 on 30 March 1972. The aircraft was one of three that were trying to shoot down an AC-130 gunship operating over the southern part of North Vietnam. The combat occurred at night, and after following the MiG in his Phantom Olmsted finally had a chance to launch a Sparrow missile as the MiG turned into a head-on pass directly towards him. The first Sparrow missed but the second one hit the MiG and the aircraft exploded in a fireball. Olmsted destroyed a second MiG on 16 April. He was part of an escort protecting a strike over the North from MiGs. The North Vietnamese aircraft headed directly towards the Phantoms but a decision was

53

made to identify the aircraft visually before firing the radar-guided Sparrows. Once the MiGs were in sight Captain Olmsted turned behind one and followed it through a series of manoeuvres as it tried to escape. The MiG was finally hit by two Sparrows and destroyed.

By the end of April the position for the South Vietnamese Army was not looking good. The NVA had been generally successful in its carefully prepared invasion; the South Vietnamese Army stood on the defensive and still looked as though it could be on the brink of disaster. However, the Northern army had been subjected to constant attack from the air as soon as the weather had cleared. The Americans had always wanted the NVA to come out into the open and fight, and by the end of the first month large numbers of Northern tanks had been destroyed by air attack. The South Vietnamese Air Force had played a large part in slowing down the Northern invasion until more American aircraft became available.

It had been suspected that an invasion of the South would be attempted, but after the Tet holidays, when it was thought it would occur, had passed the actual timing of the attack came as a surprise to President Nixon. The news of the invasion seems to have made Nixon very angry and he immediately made his mind up to inflict a major defeat on the North Vietnamese. He viewed the invasion as a direct threat to his own policy in Vietnam and to his political position. Although he was determined not to allow South Vietnam to fall, it was politically impossible for him to move any ground forces back to Vietnam; indeed, the removal of US ground forces continued during the invasion.

The only option left open to the US President was the massive use of air power to stop the invasion. The North had come out into the open and tied themselves to a hugely increased logistics tail by adopting conventional warfare. Nixon seems genuinely to have believed that a major defeat could be inflicted on the North Vietnamese, even when the situation in South Vietnam was at its worst. On 4 April Nixon was recorded, by the tape system in the White House, speaking to the Attorney General John Mitchell. He said, 'The bastards have never been bombed like they're going to be bombed this time.'[1] Nixon now decided that he would send back to South-East Asia the necessary aircraft to mount a major air campaign against North Vietnam.

The first Air Force units moved to South-East Asia were the squadrons of the 3rd Tactical Fighter Wing stationed in Korea. On 31 March F-4Ds of the

---

[1] 'Nixon Bombing Recorded on Tape', *New York Times*, 30 June 1974.

3rd TFW were flown into the air bases at Da Nang and Ubon. Contingency plans for reinforcement already existed, and these were implemented under the code-name 'Constant Guard'. In the first of these movements, on 7 April, a squadron of extra F-105Gs and eight EB-66s were moved to Korat in Thailand. These were 'Wild Weasel' aircraft intended to attack anti-aircraft missile sites and radar-jammers that would be needed for a campaign against the North. Also part of 'Constant Guard I' was the moving of two F-4E squadrons from the United States to Thailand. The F-4Es were the latest version of the Phantom. These movements involved the airlifting of over 1,000 personnel and their equipment from the US to Thailand by 38 C-141s and four C-130s. On 6 April two squadrons of Marine A-4 Skyhawks also began to return to their old base at Da Nang, while two squadrons of F-4Js and one of A-6A Intruders of the Marine Corps moved on to the base at Nam Phong in Thailand. This base had never been completed, and Navy construction battalions had to be sent in to finish the runway. The Marines called Nam Phong 'The Rose Garden'.

'Constant Guard II' was the movement of two more squadrons of F-4Es to Udorn beginning on 26 April. This involved the 308th and 58th TFSs, both from Florida. Starting on 4 May, 'Constant Guard III' became the largest single deployment in the history of Tactical Air Command. Four squadrons of F-4Ds of the 49th TFW were flown from Holloman Air Base in New Mexico to Takhli in Thailand. The base in Thailand had been closed to US aircraft thirteen months beforehand and needed some work to bring it back to a reasonable condition. The move involved the transport of 1,350 tons of supplies and over 1,000 men to Takhli. Seventy-one of the wing's 72 aircraft arrived on time and some were in action within a day of their arrival. 'Constant Guard IV' was the movement of 36 C-130E Hercules in two squadrons, the 36th and 61st Tactical Airlift Squadrons, to the 374th Tactical Airlift Wing base in Taiwan. These aircraft operated over South Vietnam, moving men and equipment.

The B-52 was flown under the authority of Strategic Air Command, and SAC began to move more and more aircraft into the theatre under the code-name 'Bull Shot'. By the end of April there were 53 B-52s at U-Tapao in Thailand and 85 on the island of Guam at Andersen Air Base. By the end of May the number of B-52s on Guam totalled 117, with thousands of the extra personnel required sleeping in tents. To provide air refuelling for the huge numbers of strike aircraft and B-52s that were being amassed in South-East Asia the number of KC-135s in the theatre was also increased: strike aircraft from Thailand could not hit targets around Hanoi without air refuelling. The B-52s based at U-Tapao could bomb any where in Vietnam without refuelling, but those based on Guam did need to refuel in the air to give them the required range when carrying their maximum payload. SAC controlled all the tanker fleet and brought the number of KC-135s available up to 168. It was difficult to find bases for all these large aircraft and aircrews, and the KC-135s ended up scattered around six different locations from the Philippines to Thailand. By the middle of May the United States had over 1,000 aircraft ready in South-East Asia.

The US Navy had the aircraft carriers *Coral Sea* and *Hancock* in position on Yankee Station in the Gulf of Tonkin as part of Task Force 77. The USS *Kitty Hawk* arrived on 3 April and the recalled *Constellation* on the 8th of the month. These carriers had between them over 300 aircraft available. Two other carriers, *Midway* from the Eastern Pacific and *Saratoga* from the Atlantic, were given orders to join the four carriers already on station.

In support of their invasion the North Vietnamese had brought south as many anti-aircraft weapons as they could. SA-2 missile radars and mobile missile launchers were positioned in the DMZ and in Laos before the invasion started, and thousands of 23mm, 37mm, 57mm, 85mm and 100mm anti-aircraft guns were also brought into South Vietnam. It is alleged that seven full anti-aircraft regiments were moved into South Vietnam and another eight positioned along the DMZ. The Northern leadership knew that the major advantage the Americans and South Vietnamese possessed would be their control of the air, and they intended to make it as difficult as possible for the enemy to mount tactical air strikes. Over the DMZ SA-2s were fired in large numbers, and on 17 February 1972 81 SA-2s were fired and three F-4s were shot down. The Soviet SA-7 'Strela' was used for the first time in Vietnam during the invasion. This was a shoulder-launched, infra-red heat-seeking anti-aircraft missile which, although not particularly effective, was a threat to aircraft flying at up to 8,000ft at speeds below 450mph. The seeker could only home on to the exhaust of jet aircraft when the latter had passed over the operator. When the missile was fired from behind an aircraft it was very difficult for the pilot to spot the launch, although if the missile was seen it was possible for the pilot to turn hard and outmanoeuvre it. A number of aircraft were lost to the SA-7, especially the slow-flying FAC aircraft.

On 2 April an EB-66 of the 42nd TEWS from Korat Air Base was flying on station to jam the surveillance and guidance radar being used by a SA-2 battery to target a B-52 raid inside the DMZ. An SA-2 missile fired from within South Vietnam hit the EB-66 and shot it down. The only survivor of the crash was Lieutenant-Colonel Iceal Hambleton, the aircraft's navigator. The area in which Hambleton landed was held by the invading North Vietnamese Army, and over the next eleven days hundreds of bombing sorties were carried out and five aircraft and eleven lives were lost in failed attempts to rescue him. He finally made it to the Cam Lo river and was picked up by a party of Marines. A seventeen-mile exclusion zone had been placed around Hambleton, and South Vietnamese ground forces had been forbidden to fire their artillery into the area. The restricted zone was on the main axis of the North Vietnamese advance and thus the South Vietnamese 3rd Division was hampered in its attempts to stop the NVA.

President Nixon was determined to halt the invasion and he took the decision to resume the bombing of North Vietnam on 5 April. The operation was given the code-name 'Freedom Train', and bombing was to be limited to south of the 18th Parallel. Storage areas and supply lines were to be the main targets, although the missile sites just north of the DMZ were also to be attacked. On 9 April 'Freedom Train' was extended north to the 19th Parallel and later to the 20th Parallel. Kissinger had asked Nixon to restrict the bombing because of the President's forthcoming visit to Moscow that May. He hoped that the Soviets would continue to back, at least in public, a negotiated end to the war.

The North Vietnamese invasion had caught the end of the north-east monsoon season in South Vietnam, and low cloud and overcast skies restricted the use of aircraft; the south-west monsoon, lasting from May till September, gave better flying weather but still included heavy rain and thunderstorms. When President Nixon was informed of the weather restricting the Air Force response to the invasion he became extremely frustrated. He wanted to defeat the invasion and he knew that air power was his only weapon. The tape recording system in the White House shows Nixon making several disparaging remarks about the Air Force leadership in early April. On 6 April Air Force General John W. Vogt, who had shot down eight German aircraft in the Second World War, was appointed commander of the Seventh Air Force and had to listen to Nixon telling him to be aggressive and imaginative, like General Patton. But the weather did clear up by the second week in April, allowing the air strikes to go ahead. The commander of the Seventh Air Force had been General John D. Lavell. Liberally interpreting of the rules governing protective reaction strikes, he had authorised a number of attacks on North Vietnam that were thought by some to be outside the rules of engagement. When this was discovered he was charged with permitting over 20 unauthorised bombing missions against the North Vietnamese air defence system between 7 November 1971 and 9 March 1972. Early in April 1972 Lavell was removed from command, reduced in rank and forced to retire. Nixon was thus urging Lavell's replacement, Vogt, to be aggressive while at the same time removing Lavell from command for being too aggressive. The President had been authorising a secret bombing campaign in Cambodia for several years, but this, apparently, did not bother him.

On 8 April a B-52 was hit by an SA-2 anti-aircraft missile for the first time. The North Vietnamese had been trying to bring down one of the B-52s for years as it would have been a propaganda coup for them. Normally only operating over South Vietnam or Laos, the aircraft flew at too great a height to be affected by the anti-aircraft guns available to the North, and they were equipped with electronic countermeasures (ECM) to jam the radar-guided SA-2s. However, on this occasion the B-52 from U-Tapao, on a bombing mission over the DMZ, was damaged in the fuselage and left wing when the SA-2 missile's proximity fuse detonated the warhead close to the aircraft. The aircraft was forced to make an emergency landing at Da Nang, the nearest airfield in the South that was large enough to take it.

In order to signal his determination to the North Vietnamese leadership, Nixon granted permission for the B-52s to be used over the North, and during April five such missions were carried out. On 11 April B-52s carried out strikes close to the town of Vinh in North Vietnam, which was a transportation and storage centre on the road and rail lines from Hanoi to the DMZ. B-52s also attacked the airfield at Bai Thuong, close to Than Hoa. On 15 April, in Operation 'Freedom Porch Bravo', 20 B-52s from the 307th Strategic Wing from U-Tapao bombed oil and petroleum storage facilities at Haiphong. Speaking of the raid, the US President observed, 'We really left them our calling card this weekend.'[1] The Navy also launched 57 sorties in support of the B-52 raid on Haiphong. As the intensity of the fighting over the North increased, the North Vietnamese Air Force tried to stop the raids, but on 16 April three MiG-21s were shot down by US Air Force Phantoms from Udorn.

The Soviet reaction to the North Vietnamese invasion and the American bombing of the North was muted by the wish for the forthcoming trip to Mos-

---

[1] Nixon, Richard, *RN: The Memoirs of Richard Nixon*, Vol. 2, Warner Books (New York, 1978), p. 65.

cow by Nixon to continue. On 10 April the Soviet ambassador Anatoly Dobrynin invited Henry Kissinger to Moscow to discuss the situation in Vietnam. Kissinger stayed in Moscow between 20 and 24 April. The American negotiating position had been that all countries in South-East Asia must keep their armed forces inside their own borders, but in Moscow Kissinger stated that North Vietnam could be permitted to keep some troops in the South after a settlement provided that the bulk of the invading forces left. The North Vietnamese position was that Vietnam was one country and that they had a right to unify an artificially divided state. In the talks in Moscow Kissinger agreed that the public negotiations in Paris should re-start on 27 April and that he should have more secret talks with Le Duc Tho on 2 May. Although they wanted the Moscow summit with Nixon to go ahead, the Soviets refused to put any pressure on the North Vietnamese to end the invasion.

The military situation inside South Vietnam continued to deteriorate, but President Nixon only extended the bombing carried out under Operation 'Freedom Train' to 20° 25' N at the end of April; he was waiting until after the meeting on 2 May, which he saw as the last chance for any kind of negotiated settlement. When the meeting took place the North's delegates merely read prepared statements and boasted about the fall of Quang Tri the day before. They refused to respond to Nixon's peace proposals. Speaking about the talks, Kissinger said, 'What the 2nd May meeting revealed was Hanoi's conviction that it was so close to victory that it no longer needed even the pretence of a negotiation.'[1] From Nixon's viewpoint, his determination to stop the invasion of the South meant that he had no choice, now that the negotiating option had been closed off, but to turn to the military option. This could only mean a massive increase in the bombing.

Nixon wanted immediate B-52 attacks against Hanoi and Haiphong, but both Kissinger and General Alexander Haig, Kissinger's military adviser, suggested that an extension of the 'Freedom Train' operations to cover most of North Vietnam would have better results. It was estimated that 250,000 tons of supplies were imported by sea into North Vietnam each month and that the closing of Haiphong and other North Vietnamese ports would have a major effect on the war in the South—although not immediately, as the North had considerable stocks already inside the country. Nixon was assured that the ports could be closed using air-dropped mines. One of the main weaknesses of

---

[1] Kissinger, Henry A., *The White House Years*, Little, Brown (Boston, 1979), p. 1175.

the 'Rolling Thunder' campaign had been the decision not to close Haiphong, but the strength of Nixon's diplomatic position allowed him to take the decision to close the North Vietnamese ports and to launch an all-out bombing campaign. The day after the failure of the 2 May talks Nixon ordered Admiral Thomas Moore, the US Chief of Staff, to draw up the plans for what became the 'Linebacker I' campaign.

The plan to blockade the North Vietnamese ports started on 8 May 1972 (9 May in Vietnam). In Operation 'Pocket Money' Navy aircraft from the USS *Coral Sea* dropped mines in the approach to Haiphong harbour. The aircraft included A7s and A-6s, each carrying four 2,000lb mines. The leader of the strike was Commander Roger Sheets, and he reported that the last of the mines were in the water by 9.01 a.m. Other aircraft, including ECM radar-jammers and F-4 Phantoms, covered the aircraft carrying out the attack, and one MiG-21 was shot down by a Talos missile fired from a US cruiser stationed off Haiphong. The mines were fitted with three-day delays, to allow any ship that wanted to leave Haiphong immediately to do so before the mines became active. There were 36 ships in Haiphong harbour, and five left in time. Lieutenant Cunningham shot down a MiG-17 on the 8th while operating from the *Constellation* and Major Lodge shot down a MiG-21. In both cases it was the second MiG they had shot down.

In a television broadcast on 8 May Nixon announced his new bombing campaign against North Vietnam. In his speech he gave the aims of the bombing as being (a) to reduce the supplies being imported into North Vietnam; (b) to destroy the existing military supplies in North Vietnam; and (c) to stop or interdict the flow of troops and material from the North to the battlefields in the South. The targets would be much the same as they had been for 'Rolling Thunder' and included industrial sites, transport links, power plants and oil storage sites. Some of the lessons of 'Rolling Thunder' had been learned. Targets could be struck without specific permission from the President, the restricted zones were much smaller and permission to attack the latter was to be easier to obtain. The 'Linebacker' campaign started in earnest on 10 May 1972.

CHAPTER 3

THE HEAVIEST DAY

THE first day of the 'Linebacker' campaign, 10 May 1972, saw the heaviest day's fighting in the air over North Vietnam. The North Vietnamese Air Force rose to the challenge and did its utmost to stop the American aircraft bombing their country. During the day a whole series of air battles developed close to Hanoi and Haiphong.

It will be recalled that the Americans had begun to increase their air assets in South-East Asia during April and early May 1972. By the start of 'Linebacker' they had three aircraft carriers on line at Yankee Station in the Gulf of Tonkin. This was a notional point 100 miles east of Da Nang, although on occasions Yankee Station was moved much further north towards the main targets. The three ships were the USS *Constellation*, *Coral Sea* and *Kitty Hawk*, and between them they carried about 240 combat aircraft. The majority of the US Air Force units used to bomb North Vietnam were stationed at air bases in Thailand, principally Ubon, Takali, Udorn and Korat. The major units in Thailand included the 8th TFW (the 'Wolf Pack') at Ubon, the 388th TFW at Korat and the 432nd Tactical Reconnaissance Wing at Udorn. The 432nd was a composite wing that contained reconnaissance, strike-interdiction and counter-air squadrons including the 555th TFS (the 'Triple Nickel'), which became the leading air-to-air squadron.

American fighter aircraft operating over the North were under the control of 'Red Crown' or 'College Eye', and with large numbers of aircraft in the air they had to be given clearance to fire at any beyond visual range or had to identify enemy aircraft visually before opening fire. This seems to have demonstrated a lack of confidence in US IFF (identification friend or foe) systems and also cancelled out the longer range advantage of the Sparrow anti-aircraft missile, although some of the American aircraft were fitted with the 'Combat Tree' equipment which could trigger the North Vietnamese MiGs' IFF to give a positive hostile identification. Although US aircraft were under control it was not as rigid as the GCI (ground controlled intercept) used by the North

Vietnamese. The American pilots were given the opportunity to use their initiative where possible and could develop situations as they saw fit, the GCI acting more as an advisory service to provide information on the movements of the enemy aircraft.

On 10 May 'College Eye' was operating under the call-sign 'Disco' and 'Red Crown' was the cruiser *Chicago*, an *Albany* class guided missile cruiser with a full load displacement of 17,500 tons and armed with two twin Talos and two twin Tartar surface-to-air launchers. It was *Chicago* that had shot down a Vietnamese aircraft at extreme range using a Talos missile on 8 May. The most famous controller on board *Chicago* was Chief Radarman Larry H. Nowell, who was involved in helping the American pilots in the destruction of four of the North Vietnamese aircraft accounted for on 10 May. Nowell was the fighter controller for one in four of the aircraft shot down by the Americans in 1972. He was awarded the Distinguished Service Medal in August 1972, only the second enlisted man to win the DSM in Navy service.

As the bombing of North Vietnam resumed in earnest with the start of 'Linebacker I' on 10 May, the first North Vietnamese MiG was destroyed by Lieutenant Curt R. Dose and his radar operator Lieutenant-Commander James McDevitt, flying an F-4J Phantom belonging to VF-92 ('Silver Kings') operating from the carrier *Constellation*. The pair had taken off at 0830 hours as part of a naval alpha strike (major strike) of 35 aircraft to attack petroleum storage areas west of Haiphong. Aircraft from *Coral Sea* bombed the railyards at Haiphong and those from *Kitty Hawk* struck the bridges linking Haiphong to Hanoi. Dose was part of a two-aircraft flight that was to provide TARCAP (target combat air patrol: protection from enemy aircraft over the target).

'Red Crown' alerted the two fighters to MiG activity north-east of Hanoi around the North Vietnamese fighter base at Kep. The two US aircraft approached the airfield just as two MiG-21s were attempting to take off. The MiGs dropped their centre-line tanks and tried to accelerate away from the Phantoms. Dose lined up on the leading MiG and fired a Sidewinder, but the MiG turned hard inside the missile, which exploded on the outside of the turn. The MiG had turned so hard to avoid the missile that it had slowed down considerably, and a second Sidewinder fired by Dose homed on to the aircraft's exhaust and exploded. The wreckage landed close outside the circuit at Kep. This was kill no 1, at 0958 hours. The second US aircraft, flown by Lieutenant Vaughn Hawkins, fired three Sidewinders at the other MiG without success, and the arrival of more enemy aircraft forced him to leave the area.

Later in the morning the US Air Force launched a major strike from its bases in Thailand involving 32 Phantoms as the main strike elements. The force was divided between two targets, sixteen aircraft from the 388th TFW attacking the railway marshalling yards at Yen Vien north of Hanoi using conventional 500lb bombs, and sixteen from the 8th TFW attacking the Paul Doumer rail bridge on the outskirts of Hanoi using laser-guided and electro-optically guided bombs. The Paul Doumer bridge became one of the most bombed targets in the history of air warfare. It was a 19-span, 5,532ft long road and rail bridge that provided the main entry into Hanoi from the north and had been very heavily bombed during 'Rolling Thunder'. The bridge, named after one of the French governors of Vietnam, had been repaired and was again carrying the traffic from both the rail lines from China. Several of the American pilots bombing the bridge had also been involved in the bombing five years earlier.

The new 'smart' bombs that were to provide one of the main differences between 'Rolling Thunder' and 'Linebacker' were of two types. EOGBs (electro-optically guided bombs) used a television camera attached to the nose of a 2,000lb bomb. The back-seat crew member of the Phantom could view the picture from the bomb on a screen in the cockpit and designate the bomb's impact point. It was the contrast between light and shade on the target that became the bomb's aiming point. In clear weather these bombs could be very accurate, although it is thought that those aimed at the bridge on 10 May missed their target. Once they had been launched they were a 'fire and forget' weapon and the aircraft could then turn away. Describing the performance of the EOGBs, Alfred Price has written:

> After release several of these image-contrast weapons transferred lock-on from the bridge itself to the shadow of the bridge on the water. Others suffered guidance failures. Every EOGB missed the target, in some cases by a wide margin.[1]

The laser-guided bombs were basically ordinary bombs with a laser sensor mounted on the nose. In use the target was designated by a pod carried under the aircraft and the bomb homed on the reflected laser energy. The pod contained an optical viewing system that allowed the operator to continue to illuminate the target as the aircraft manoeuvred, and several aircraft could launch bombs to home on the same illumination.

Backing up the attacking aircraft were a considerable number of others. These included fifteen Republic F-105G 'Wild Weasels' for defence-suppres-

---

[1] Price, Alfred, 'Gap That Bridge', *Air International*, December 1997, p. 379.

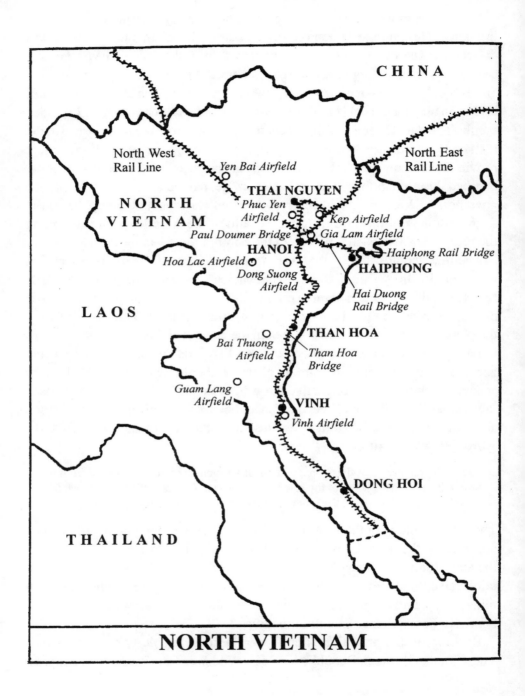

NORTH VIETNAM

sion from the 388th TFW based at Korat in Thailand and four EB-66s that would conduct ECM (electronic countermeasures) support by orbiting and jamming the North Vietnamese radar. There were eight other Phantoms from the 8th TFW that departed before the attack aircraft to lay a corridor of chaff through which the attack aircraft would fly, to confuse the radar network. There were also a large number of KC-135 tanker aircraft for refuelling the attacking aircraft in flight. The fighter cover (MiGCAP) for this fleet of aircraft was to be provided by the 555th TFS from Udorn, their task being to screen the attack aircraft from the two MiG airfields north of Hanoi. The flight of four F-4D Phantoms was under the control of Major Robert A. Lodge and was using the call-sign 'Oyster'. This one flight was to account for the next three MiGs destroyed. There was to have been an additional four-aircraft flight on MiGCAP, but this was delayed because of aircraft failures, so Lodge's flight was covering both areas.

As noted, Lodge had already destroyed two MiGs, the last one only two days before, and he seemed intent on becoming the first Air Force ace in Vietnam, along with his WSO Captain Roger C. Locher, who had already flown 400 combat missions. 'Oyster' flight crossed into Vietnam through the Gorilla's Head (viewed on a map the border at this point resembles such) on their way to their patrol line between Hanoi and the airfields at Kep and Yen Bai. After crossing the border the flight descend to 3,000ft and accelerated to 500kts. High speed gave some protection against ground fire and could always be converted into manoeuvrability. 'Red Crown' alerted 'Oyster' flight that there were no American aircraft north of their position, which meant that they could fire at any aircraft approaching from that direction without visual identification. North of Hanoi the flight turned north-west towards Yen Bai airfield. 'Red Crown' now provided them with the information that there was enemy activity north of their position. About 40 miles south of Yen Bai Captain Locher picked up on radar two pairs of enemy aircraft heading roughly towards them at between 13,000 and 15,000ft.

After crossing the Red River south of Yen Bai Major Lodge ordered 'Oyster' flight to climb towards the MiGs. The four Phantoms were divided into two elements of two aircraft, comprising a leader and a wingman. Lodge prepared to attack the leading MiG and told Captain Richard S. Ritchie and his WSO, Captain Charles B. DeBellevue (who would together become the first Air Force aces), the leader of the second element of 'Oyster' flight, to attack the third MiG. The MiGs were at a disadvantage as they had no missiles capable of homing head-on. At a range of eight miles Lodge fired a Sparrow missile at the leading MiG but this exploded too soon. A second Sparrow was launched at a range of six miles and seconds later what was described as a 'red/orange explosion' was observed and a MiG-21 was seen out of control with the left wing missing. This was kill no 2 , at 1043 hours.

Lodge's number two was crewed by Lieutenant John D. Markle and Captain Steven D. Eaves, and as the remaining MiGs continued to approach the Phantoms from ahead and slightly to the left they fired two Sparrows at the second MiG. The first missile guided correctly and exploded behind the MiG's cockpit, causing the aircraft to descend out of control (kill no 3, 1043 hours). The two remaining MiGs fired a salvo of 'Atoll' missiles at the American aircraft but, as they were not all-aspect-capable, they could not home on to the aircraft from the front and this gesture could only have been intended to distract the Americans.

As the remaining MiG-21s passed the flight of Phantoms the Americans turned to the right to follow them. Major Lodge found himself 200ft behind one of the MiGs—too close for him to fire either a Sparrow or a Sidewinder—and he attempted to continue to turn with the MiG while increasing the distance between the two aircraft. Ritchie had turned to the right behind the remaining MiG, and at a distance of 6,000ft he fired two Sparrows. The first missile passed within range of the aircraft but the proximity fuse did not detonate; the second Sparrow followed the turning MiG and caused it to detonate in a 'yellow fireball' (kill no 4, 1044 hours).

Lodge was still turning behind the third MiG, trying to fall back into a firing position, when the American aircraft were attacked without warning by four MiG-19s. The latter concentrated their attack on Lodge's aircraft, and even though he was warned by his wingman his concentration seems to have been fixed on the MiG he was following. He fired his third Sparrow at the turning MiG-21 but he was still too close and the missile did not guide. Lodge's aircraft was now hit by cannon shells from the MiG-19s and set on fire. Captain Locher described what happened:

> We immediately went out of control, flopping from side to side. Then fire started coming in the back of the cockpit. It seared my canopy with bubbles and I couldn't see out anymore. The airplane slowed down and went into a flat spin.[1]

---

[1] Futrell, Frank, et al., *Aces and Aerial Victories: The United States Air Force in Southeast Asia 1965–73*, Office of Air Force History (1976), p. 93.

Lodge was killed; there is one story that he had secret information that could not be allowed to fall into enemy hands and he elected to stay with the aircraft. It was claimed that Lodge was shot down by Lieutenant Le Thanh Dao flying a MiG-19, who, the North Vietnamese also claimed, later shot down five other US aircraft. Locher managed to eject from the burning Phantom. He landed in the Red River valley, in a heavily populated area only eight miles from the air base at Yen Bai. He spent the next 23 days living on rainwater and vegetables stolen from gardens while attempting to avoid capture. He was finally rescued after managing to contact American aircraft with his survival radio and he was lifted out by an HH-53 helicopter. The rescue involved 119 aircraft and was the furthest north that the Americans managed to rescue any of their downed aircrew.

The rest of 'Oyster' flight descended to low level and headed back towards Thailand. The main strike force had successfully cratered the marshalling yards at Yen Vien using conventional bombs and had damaged several spans of the Paul Doumer bridge with 'smart' bombs, rendering it unusable. The British consul-general in Hanoi sheltered under the stairs at the British residence while the bombing raid took place.

One other F-4 Phantom had been lost to an attack by MiG-19s. 'Harlow' flight, made up of four F-4Es from the 432nd TRW based at Udorn, had been covering the withdrawal of the strike aircraft. The four aircraft were close to Yen Bai airfield, flying at 8,000ft. This was near to where Major Lodge had been shot down earlier. With no warning a MiG-19 came in behind 'Harlow Four', flown by Captain J. Harris and Captain D. Wilkinson. Closing to within 500ft, the MiG opened fire and hit the Phantom in the left wing. Both the aircrew were killed as the burning aircraft hit the ground. The MiG did not stay to fight but left the area at high speed, pursued by the other aircraft of 'Harlow' flight. Missiles were launched at the MiG but failed to hit it, and the North Vietnamese aircraft escaped by diving away.

It was later estimated that around 100 surface-to-air missiles had been fired at the strike force and that 41 MiGs had been launched. Each of the attacking aircraft was equipped with a ALQ-87 jamming pod, and these seem to have been generally effective in countering the SA-2s. One of the post-strike photographic RF-4Cs was damaged by its own drop tanks and had to be flown back to Udorn on one engine by its pilot Don Packard.

The second Navy alpha strike of the day to become involved with the North Vietnamese MiGs was aimed at the railyards at Hai Duong. These were situ-

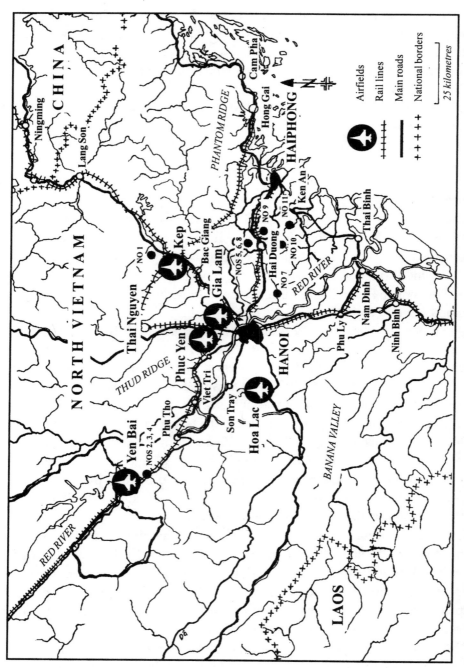

LOCATION OF NORTH VIETNAMESE AIRCRAFT SHOT DOWN ON 10 MAY 1972

ated half-way between Hanoi and the docks at Haiphong on the only connecting rail line between them, and included marshalling yards and storage areas. The strike comprised 27 aircraft from *Constellation* and at least two aircraft from *Coral Sea* and consisted of A-6s and A-7s with F-4s as fighter cover and flak-suppression aircraft. The North Vietnamese launched 22 MiGs, -17s, -19s, and -21s, against this strike force.

The attack group headed in over the Vietnamese coast north of Haiphong but overshot the target and the CAG (Commander Air Group), Commander Lowell F. Eggert, who had planned the strike and directed it from an A-7, was forced to turn the group and attack from west to east. As the A-6s and A-7s attacked the main targets, Commander H. L. Blackburn and his radar operator Lt. S. A. Rudloff, circling overhead as part of the TARCAP, were hit by 85mm anti-aircraft fire and their F-4J was destroyed. Both men ejected but only Rudloff came back after the war. The first group of attack aircraft destroyed the main target and the remaining aircraft attacked the secondary targets.

The American strike force attracted MiGs from all the surrounding airfields. Flying as part of the TARCAP, Lieutenant Michael J. Connelly and his radio operator Lieutenant Thomas J. J. Blonski, of VF-92 ('Fighting Falcons') and flying an F-4J, became involved in protecting the strike aircraft. As one MiG-17 approached the target area Connelly turned in behind it and destroyed it with a Sidewinder (kill no 5, 1400 hours). The story is that one A-7 pilot had dropped his bombs on the target and was leaving the area but, never having seen a MiG, returned to satisfy his curiosity. Two MiG-17s closed in on the tail of the A-7 and Connelly was forced to shoot one of them down with a Sidewinder to allow the A-7 to escape (kill no 6, 1400 hours). None of the strike aircraft were lost that day, and Connelly and his radar operator Blonski were subsequently awarded the Navy Cross.

As part of the MiGCAP for the strike on the Hai Duong railyards Lieutenant Kenneth L. Cannon and his radar operator Lt. Roy A. Morris of VF-51, flying from the carrier *Coral Sea*, were to screen the strike force from the airfields south of Hanoi. Cannon was flying an F-4B as part of a two-aircraft section. The two Phantoms were 30 miles away from Hai Duong, patrolling south-east of Hanoi, when they heard the main strike taking place over the radio. The two aircraft spotted a single MiG-21 heading towards Hai Duong, but, as they turned towards it, it left the area. A second aircraft, a MiG-17, was seen approaching and the second member of the two-aircraft element, Lieutenant-Commander Chuck Schroeder and his radar operator Lieutenant Dale Arends, moved on to the MiG's tail. The enemy pilot executed a high-g turn which forced Schroeder to overshoot him. Before the MiG could open fire Schroeder engaged his afterburner and pulled away from the following aircraft. Cannon manoeuvered his F-4 behind the MiG, which again attempted a high-g turn, but Cannon had already launched a Sidewinder which homed on to the heat from the MiG's exhaust and destroyed the aircraft (kill no 7, 1400 hours).

The next MiG to be destroyed in the general mêlée over Hai Duong was one by Lieutenants Steven C. Shoemaker and Keith V. Crenshaw, also from VF-96 flying an F-4J. Shoemaker fired one Sidewinder at a MiG-17 that was following a Phantom: the angle-off was too great and the missile failed to hit the target, but the MiG was forced to turn away from the American aircraft it had been following. Using a Sidewinder, the American crew destroyed another MiG-17 (kill no 8, 1401 hours.) The pair were then forced to break hard to avoid another MiG that was tailing them, and this violent manoeuvre lost them the use of their flight and navigational instruments, which had been overstressed. They descended to low level to return to the coast by visual navigation, but, having become disorientated, they nearly flew over the defences at Hanoi before reversing course to the correct direction. On the way out Shoemaker was forced to turn hard to avoid an SA-2 that was homing on to him from head on, but he waited until the last moment before breaking and the missile did not have the manoeuvrability to follow.

The last three MiGs destroyed that day were shot down by one crew, again from VF-96—a unit which had twice won the Clifton Trophy as the most outstanding fighter squadron. This crew comprised Lieutenant Randall H. Cunningham as pilot and Lieutenant William R. Driscoll as radar operator. Cunningham was a graduate of the Top Gun school and, as noted, already had two MiGs destroyed to his credit, and the three aircraft destroyed on 10 May would make Cunningham and Driscoll the first American aces of the war. The pair were launched from *Constellation* as part of the covering forces for the strike on Hai Duong. Their main role was intended to be flak-suppression around the target area, and their F-4J was loaded with Mk 20 Rockeye CBU-58 cluster bombs for this purpose, but they were also carrying four Sidewinders and two Sparrows. The main target was destroyed by the A-6 and A-7 strike force, and Cunningham and his wingman decided to attack the secondary targets instead of the surrounding flak emplacements. They attacked from a north-south heading, to vary their approach from the main strike group, aiming at what was described as 'a long, red-brick storage building'.

After pulling off the target Cunningham was warned by his wingman that they had MiG-17s on their tail. Cunningham turned hard to the left, followed by the MiG firing its cannon, his wingman, Lieutenant Brian Grant, dealing with a second MiG. Cunningham continued his break into the turning MiG, forcing it to miss. The MiG was travelling too quickly to continue turning with the F-4 and overshot above it. As the MiG moved in front of his aircraft Cunningham fired a Sidewinder well within minimum range, but the MiG was travelling so fast that by the time the missile reached the aircraft it was homing and destroyed the aircraft. This was kill no 9, at 1401 hours.

Another MiG attempted to follow Cunningham but he accelerated using afterburner up to 600kts and pulled away from it. Accompanied by his wingman, he executed an Immelmann turn to climb back to 15,000ft. Below them the two crews saw eight MIGs turning in a defensive Lufbery circle and three F-4s trying to break the circle. The Phantom's main advantages over the MiG-17 were its speed and power—and a better weapons system—but by slowing down to turn with the MiGs the F-4s had placed themselves at a disadvantage. As Cunningham and Driscoll dived towards the circling aircraft an F-4 broke away, followed by two MiG-17s and a MiG-21. They pulled in behind this string of aircraft, hoping to shoot the MiG-17 off the F-4's tail but the Phantom was using afterburner and this would have provided a more attractive target for a Sidewinder than the MiG's exhaust. Four MiG-17s and two MiG-19s now joined the chase behind Cunningham and tried to close to firing range. The leading Phantom turned hard to the right, allowing Cunningham to fire at the MiG-17 that had been following it. The missile guided correctly and the MiG was destroyed; the seeker head from the missile was described as 'travelling the entire length of the 17, blowing it to bits.'[1] This was kill no 10, at 1403 hours.

Four more MiG-21s now joined the fight and Cunningham attempted to head for the coastline at high speed. The last MiG destroyed that day, bringing Cunningham and Driscoll's overall total to five, is alleged to have been that of Colonel Thombs (sometimes spelt Toons—neither of which rendering is a Vietnamese name), the leading Vietnamese fighter pilot with 13 American aircraft to his credit, but there has never been any independent confirmation of this as the information is based on unnamed American intelligence sources. There is a famous photograph of a Vietnamese MiG-21 with markings for 13

---

[1] Cunningham, Randy, *Fox Two*, Champlin Fighter Museum (1984), p. 102.

American aircraft destroyed painted on it, but it is now known that this referred to the claims made by several different pilots while flying this particular MiG. It is quite possible that the Thombs story is completely apocryphal. However, the fight between Cunningham and 'Colonel Tomb' has become one of the most discussed and analysed air combats ever.

As Cunningham was heading for the coast a single MiG-17 was seen coming towards his aircraft. Cunningham guided the F-4 directly towards the MiG, forgetting the latter's forward-firing armament. The MiG opened fire and Cunningham pulled his aircraft directly into a vertical climb, thinking that the MiG would not follow as his experience had taught him that the Vietnamese preferred horizontal turning flight to vertical manoeuvring. He found the MiG climbing vertically with him, however, cockpit to cockpit at a distance of 300ft. The F-4 began to pull in front of the MiG and as the latter started to fire at him Cunningham pitched over and used his afterburner to pull away from the aircraft, which followed him. Cunningham pulled up into a high-g turn, forcing the MiG to overshoot. The MiG then went into a vertical rolling scissors, forcing the F-4 also to overshoot. For the next few minutes the two aircraft were locked into a series of manoeuvres as each attempted to gain a firing position on the other, the MiG pilot trying to remain close to the American aircraft inside the firing envelope of the F-4's missiles and Cunningham attempting to maintain the angle-off from Colonel Thombs's guns. The Phantom had a missile-only armament and the MiG a gun-only armament.

The two aircraft disengaged several times but returned to the fight. Cunningham described the MiG flyer as 'the best pilot I ever encountered, American or otherwise'. In a repeat of the manoeuvre that started the combat, the two aircraft were in a vertical climb when Cunningham dropped the speed brakes on the F-4 and put the engines to idle. This forced the MiG out in front in the climb and he pulled over the top and dived away, trying to clear the area, but Cunningham followed. The older models of Sidewinder did not work very well pointing towards the ground as they tended to home on to hot spots on the surface. Nevertheless, Cunningham launched a Sidewinder at the diving MiG and in this case the missile guided correctly and hit the descending aircraft, causing it to explode and crash into the ground—kill no 11, at 1408 hours. Cunningham did not see the pilot eject, but there is one story that Thombs did escape, landing with severe injuries that prevented him from flying again.

Cunningham was then attacked by four more MiG-17s, but these were scattered by a Sparrow missile fired by Lieutenant Connelly, who had destroyed two of the earlier MiGs. The American aircraft now headed out for the coast, followed at a distance by MiG-17s and -21s. Cunningham and Driscoll avoided two SA-2s fired at them by outmanoeuvering them, but they were finally damaged by a missile that detonated close to their aircraft. They had received no warning of this missile from their ECM equipment and it is thought possible that the weapon was one of the few electro-optically guided SA-2s.

The Phantom had been badly damaged, but Cunningham managed to nurse the aircraft, even though the hydraulics were failing, out over the coast. The crew were forced to eject when the aircraft went into a spin and the two men came down in the Red River estuary in sight of land. Several aircraft from their own squadron attacked North Vietnamese patrol boats that were attempting to pick them up, and they were finally lifted out of the water by a Marine helicopter, flown on to the deck of the USS *Okinawa* and then taken back to *Constellation.*

Later in the afternoon alpha strikes were mounted by aircraft from *Coral Sea*, *Kitty Hawk* and *Constellation* against the ports at Hon Gai and Cam Pha, north-east of Haiphong. Bridges at Cam Pha were damaged and the Soviet ship *Grish Akoyan* was damaged at Hon Gai. Although there was heavy anti-aircraft fire and missiles were launched, because of the heavy MiG losses earlier in the day only two MiGs were seen during the later strikes.

During the course of 10 May the Air Force had flown 120 sorties in the attacks on the North, 32 of these by bombing aircraft, and the Navy had flown 294 from the three carriers in the Gulf. American aircraft had destroyed eleven MiGs for the loss of two aircraft in air-to-air combat, with at least two others lost to AA fire and ground-launched missiles. Both the F-4s that had been lost, one F-4D and one F-4E, had been shot down by MiG-19s using 30mm cannon fire. The Navy had shot down eight of the MiGs without loss in air combat. Later on during 'Linebacker I' the Navy pilots managed to attain the 12:1 ratio they had achieved in the Korean War. Three of the pilots who shot down MiGs on the 10th had been through the Top Gun programme, and this would seem to have vindicated the Navy's policy in setting up the school.

CHAPTER 4

MAY 1972

THE bombing of the Paul Doumer bridge on 10 May had damaged it and prevented vehicular traffic from using it, but the bridge was still in one piece and none of the spans was down. It was decided that the bridge should be attacked again on 11 May. This time the strike force was made up of only four F-4s from the 8th FTW. One of the aircraft was armed with two M118 3,000lb laser-guided bombs and each of the other three with two Mk 84 2,000lb guided bombs. The flight was led by Captain Thomas Messett, who had also taken part in the raid on the day before.

It was only after the attack flight had crossed into North Vietnam that it was realised that because of an administrative failure the support forces had arrived much earlier. This meant that the chaff corridor had to a large extent been dissipated and that the covering fighters and 'Wild Weasel' F-105s were not there to keep the North Vietnamese defences at bay while the bombers hit the bridge. The North Vietnamese do not seem to have realised that the four aircraft were the main attack force, and although some SA-2s were fired at the Phantoms no MiGs were seen. The four Phantoms dived on to the bridge from the east. Messett's aircraft was carrying the designator pod and he chose to attack one of the spans close to the Hanoi side of the bridge. All eight of the bombs guided on to the bridge. The post-strike reconnaissance showed that three spans had been dropped into the river and three more damaged. All four of the attacking aircraft arrived back at Udorn without any damage.

The one bridge that had never been brought down in North Vietnam during the earlier bombing was the Than Hoa bridge. A rail bridge situated about 80 miles south of Hanoi, it was an immensely strong structure that had been over-engineered when it had been originally built in the 1950s to replace the earlier structure destroyed by the Viet Minh in 1945. It had a clear span of 540ft and provided a crossing of the Song Ma river. Two steel trusses provided the main support for the bridge, and these were carried on concrete piers; between 1965 and 1972 other concrete supports had been added. Over 1,000 sorties had been directed against the bridge and dozens of aircraft had been lost. Hits had been made on the bridge with Bullpup missiles and conventional bombs, but it had never been brought down, although the approaches to the bridge had been so badly bombed as to make them unusable for short periods.

On 13 May the bridge was attacked by 14 strike aircraft from the 8th TFW. The weather was 5/8ths cloud but was clear in the target area. Leading the aircraft was Captain D. L. Smith, and after crossing North Vietnam the Phantoms attacked the bridge from the east. No missiles seem to have been fired, but the anti-aircraft guns around the bridge put up an intense barrage. The F-4s were carrying nine 3,000lb and fifteen 2,000lb laser-guided bombs, plus forty-eight 500lb conventional bombs (used because of a shortage of guided bombs and laser pods). Diving through the flak, the Phantoms pressed home their attack and the western span of the bridge was brought down into the river. No aircraft were lost during the attack. To ensure that the bridge was not repaired the Navy carried out eleven further raids and the Air Force two more before the end of 'Linebacker I' in October.

Although the laser-guided bombs provided some spectacular results, most of the bombing of the North was still carried out with conventional 'iron' bombs. Two systems of laser guidance were available. In areas of lower threat in South Vietnam the Paveway system was used, but this required the laser-designating aircraft to circle the target while keeping the laser marker on the aiming point. In areas of higher threat in North Vietnam the Pave Knife system was used, but the Air Force only had six Pave Knife laser-designator pods available. In fact, only twelve pods were manufactured in a developmental programme: three were kept in the United States, three went to the Navy for use on A-6As and six went to the 433rd TFS at Ubon who had twelve F-4Ds wired to take them. Two of these pods were lost over the North and the remaining four became so valuable that General Vogt remarked, 'I gave orders to the pilots. Don't come back if you don't have that pod with you when you return.'[1] The banana-shaped pod was carried on the inner left wing pylon on the F-4D Phantoms with a 370-gallon fuel tank to balance it on the right wing. Two bombs could also be carried. The pod carried a low-light television camera in its nose and this was slaved to the laser marker. The TV screen was mounted in the rear cockpit of the aircraft and the camera could be tracked using the radar tracking handle to keep the laser pointing at the target. The

---

[1] Kohn, Richard H., and Harahan, Joseph P., *Air Interdiction in World War II, Korea and Vietnam*, Office of Air Force History, United States Air Force (Washington, 1986), p. 85.

camera could be pointed to the front of the aircraft, to the side and behind it to keep the aiming point illuminated with the laser. This meant that the attacking aircraft did not have to circle the target but could keep the target illuminated as it passed over it. Other aircraft could launch bombs at the same target provided that weapons were launched within a 500ft wide and 1,500ft long box created by the laser energy reflected from the target.

Besides creating minefields cutting off the harbour at Haiphong, Navy aircraft also laid mines around the smaller North Vietnamese ports. The locations included Hon Gay and Cam Pha north of Haiphong and the river estuaries at Quang Khe, Dong Hoi, Than Hoa and Vinh. Over 11,000 mines were dropped, and between May and December no merchant ships were able to use any North Vietnamese port. The North Vietnamese did attempt to bring in supplies from ships anchored in international waters by transferring the cargoes to lighters and smaller boats, but the US Navy, operating in the Gulf, attacked the lighters using aircraft, helicopters and destroyers. Although most of North Vietnam had been targeted for attack in 'Linebacker', including the transport system and storage areas for the supplies destined for the battlefields in the South, there were some targets that were still not available for attack by Navy and Air Force aircraft. These included the Hanoi thermal plant that had been attacked in the past during 'Rolling Thunder'; the airfield at Gia Lam, which was Hanoi's international airport and was used by the International Commission; the party headquarters in Hanoi; and the international radio station, also in Hanoi.

When the bombing started the decision was taken to reintroduce the route package system over the North. As stated earlier, this involved dividing North Vietnam into six areas, with RP 6 divided into two parts, A and B. The Navy controlled Route Packages 2, 3, 4 and 6B, with the Air Force responsible for RP 1, 5 and 6A. One of the major problems with the earlier 'Rolling Thunder' campaign had been the lack of an overall air commander. Both the Navy and Air Force had been in favour of this, but only if one of their own men had been in charge. Dividing North Vietnam into sections meant that there was no single headquarters controlling the targeting. Two of the advantages of air power are flexibility and concentration, but the division of command removes the edge from these advantages. Speaking on this point, General Momyer, who had been commander of the Seventh Air Force during 'Rolling Thunder', stated,

... the route package system was fundamentally wrong for the best application of all US airpower ... The route package system was a compromise approach to a tough command and control decision, an approach which, however understandable, inevitably prevented a unified, concentrated air effort.[1]

The Air Force and Navy were carrying out two separate campaigns over the North with only limited coordination between the two.

In simple terms, the stated aim of the campaign was to stop military supplies from reaching the South. To achieve this the main target was the North Vietnamese transport system, particularly the railway system. Most of this system had been built by the French early in the century. Two rail lines ran down from the Chinese border to Hanoi, the north-west and the north-east sections. A major rail line ran from Haiphong also into Hanoi, and a section of line then ran down from Hanoi to a point close to the DMZ. The bridges and marshalling yards on the railway system were attacked repeatedly to keep them out of operation. In reply, the North Vietnamese put enormous effort into repairing these facilities and keeping them running. Rail lines are easily repaired and air power has always found them to be frustrating targets: it was only the choke points that were worth bombing. Most of the major bridges were in RP 6.

It was estimated that North Vietnam had 5,800 miles of all-weather roads by 1972. There were eight main road crossings for supplies coming from the Chinese border. Military supplies either moved down to the DMZ or crossed into Laos through three main passes across the Annamite mountain range. Roads are an even more thankless target than rail lines, especially when there are 500,000 people dedicated to repairing and improving the transport system. Again, it was only bridges, choke points and storage areas that were worth bombing.

The USS *Saratoga* joined the other carriers on Yankee Station on 18 May. *Saratoga* was a 78,000-ton carrier and added another 80 aircraft to those already available. On 11 May a MiG-21 was shot down by F-4D Phantoms operating out of Thailand, but the action was so confused that the MiG could not be credited to any single one of the Phantom crews taking part. A day later two lieutenant-colonels from the 555th 'Triple Nickel' TFS shot down a MiG-19 close to Yen Bai airfield. MiG-19s were supplied to North Vietnam by China and in some ways were the best air superiority aircraft the North Vietnamese had. They had a higher thrust than the weight of the aircraft, which gave tham a good acceleration and climb rate. Lieutenant-Colonel Wayne T. Frye and his back-seater Lieutenant-Colonel James P. Cooney were part of a

---

[1] Momyer, William W., *Air Power in Three Wars*, US Government Printing Office (Washington, 1978), p. 95.

four-aircraft MiGCAP north-west of Yen Bai airfield when four MiG-19s were seen taking off. Frye placed his Phantom behind the last of the four MiGs, at 1,000ft, as they turned left after taking off. He fired three Sparrows at the MiG and the last one hit the aircraft, which crashed two miles south-west of the runway at Yen Bai from which it had earlier taken off. The two colonels claimed that they held the age record for a Phantom crew shooting down a MiG, their combined years being 85.

Two more MiG-19s were shot down on 18 May by Navy F-4Bs operating from the USS *Midway*. Lieutenants Henry Bartholomay and Oran Brown were in one Phantom and Lieutenants Pat Arwood and Mike Bell were in the other. They had launched to provide MiG cover for an alpha strike on Haiphong. They had difficulty receiving fuel from their tanker aircraft and were late in reaching their patrol line, which was five miles south of Kep airfield. They had intended to fly in behind a ridge line north of Haiphong known as Phantom Ridge, but because they were late they passed directly over Haiphong. The two aircraft were directed by 'Red Crown' to close on Kep airfield. When they arrived they found that two MiG-19s appeared to be lining up to land. After a turning engagement lasting several minutes both the MiGs were shot down by Sidewinder missiles. The missile fired by Arwood had been a AIM-9G, the first time that this advanced model of the Sidewinder had been used over North Vietnam.

Although the Phantom was an excellent aircraft, one its major drawbacks was its tendency to stall. Over the thirty years the Phantom was in service with air forces throughout the world, dozens of them have been lost as a result of the type's violent stall characteristics. The lightly loaded MiGs could turn inside the Phantoms and several F-4s were lost trying to turn with the MiGs. On 20 May Lieutenant John Markle, who had shot down a MiG on 10 May, was flying as wingman to Captain Ritchie, who had also shot down a MiG on the 10th. MiG-21s were vectored on to the two Phantoms and passed them on either side, and one of the MiGs turned behind Markle's aircraft and launched an 'Atoll' missile. Markle turned the Phantom to avoid the missile and he increased the turn until the Phantom departed into a deep stall and the aircraft crashed. Markle and his back-seater Captain Jim Williams ejected and were picked up by an American helicopter 30 miles west of Hanoi.

On 23 May another Phantom stalled while tying to turn with the MiGs. Lieutenant-Commander Ronald McKeown and his radar operator Lieutenant Jack Ensch were flying an F-4B from the USS *Midway* and were providing

MiGCAP for an alpha strike on Haiphong that was intended to stop MiGs from Kep interfering with the strike aircraft. 'Red Crown' that day was the destroyer USS *Biddle*, which ordered the Phantoms to intercept two MiG-19s close to Kep. As McKeown turned behind the MiG-19s he was attacked by a number of MiG-17s which had been following the -19s. While trying to turn away from one of the MiGs McKeown stalled the Phantom. He described the aircraft as falling end over end, but he did manage to regain control and shoot down two of the MiG-17s.

Two more MiGs were shot down on 31 May by the US Air Force. The first was despatched by Captains Bruce G. Leonard and Jeffrey S. Feinstein flying an F-4D of the 555th TFS, the second by Captains Steve Ritchie and Lawrence H. Pettit also from the 555th. Ritchie was leading a flight of four Phantoms on a MiGCAP north of Hanoi. 'Red Crown' notified the Phantoms of MiG-21s behind them at a range of fourteen miles and Ritchie manoeuvred the flight of Phantoms until it was behind the MiGs. Once his Phantom's radar had obtained a lock-on Ritchie fired three Sparrow missiles, which all missed, but the fourth Sparrow hit the MiG in the fuselage, breaking the aircraft into two.

The most advanced model of the Phantom in use by the US Air Force was the F-4E, which was the first to be fitted with an internal gun system. Many of the Air Force pilots had felt the need for a gun on the Phantom during the 'Rolling Thunder' campaign. When the lighter MiGs were able to keep close to the Phantoms they were safe because they were within the minimum range of the F-4's missile systems. It was for this type of close-in work that the internal gun was intended. The F-4E was a heavier aircraft than the earlier models of the Phantom but this was offset to some extent by the use of more powerful, 17,900lb thrust J79-GE-17 engines. Central to the F-4E was the 20mm Vulcan cannon, which could fire at a rate of 6,000 rounds a minute, and with both cannon and missile armament the F-4E became a very effective fighter aircraft. The Navy's most advanced model of the Phantom was the F-4J, which featured an improved undercarriage, better radar, improved ejection seats and a slotted, all-moving tailplane.

As the newer models of aircraft were introduced into Vietnam older types were retired. During May the last of the Martin B-57Gs left South-East Asia. These had been operated by the 13th Tactical Bomber Squadron at Ubon in Thailand. The B-57G was a specialised night attack variant of the Canberra with an array of sensors in the nose. Although it had not been used over Route Packages 4 or 5, the B-57 had been extensively employed over the southern part of North Vietnam. Since they were first introduced into Vietnam in the early 1960s the B-57s had flown over 50,000 sorties and 40 had been lost to enemy action.

In the South during May the North Vietnamese forces had launched their main attack on Kontum on the 14th. The main axis of the communist attack was from the north and north-west, led by large numbers of Soviet-built T-54 tanks. In reply American Cobra gunships armed with TOW (tube launched, optically aimed, wire-guided) missiles hit back at the tanks. Numerous attack sorties were flown close up to the South Vietnamese front lines. In most places the front held, and where the North Vietnamese broke through the South Vietnamese counter-attacked and drove them back. B-52s were used to bomb the actual front line as Southern forces quickly withdrew before the raid and then re-took the bombed positions. There was savage fighting for several days around Kontum as the NVA threw everything into an effort to force a way into the town. Another major assault was started on 24 May from the south-west, and the North Vietnamese were successful in breaking through in several places. A tactical emergency was declared and all available aircraft and helicopters were diverted to support the defenders. By the 26th the airfield had been taken and the only access was by helicopter into a local football field. During the 26th 1,000 shells were fired into Kontum. For the next three days it looked as though Kontum would fall, but the constant pressure from fighter strikes, B-52 raids and helicopter attacks brought the North's advance to a halt. On the 30th reinforcements managed to reach the town and the NVA forces slowly began to fall back.

In the north of South Vietnam the South Vietnamese Army had established a defence line north of Hue along the My Chanh river. Defending Hue were the 1st Division and the Southern marines, reinforced with airborne forces withdrawn from further south. On the 13th the marines made a limited attack north of the river line and on the 14th army units re-took positions they had earlier lost to the west of Hue. Northern forces launched a major attack on Hue on 20 May and succeeded in crossing the My Chanh river but were later forced back with the loss of 18 tanks. A second assault on the river line took place on 25 May and the river was crossed in several places, but with massive air support the Northern forces were pushed back after intense fighting.

The improved accuracy obtained by 'smart' weapons was demonstrated during the attack on the storage area at Son Tay on 26 May. The strike force involved only one flight of F-4s, and three warehouses were hit by three bombs.

If a target could be seen, which required good weather, the probability of hitting the target was thought to be between 80 and 90 per cent with laser-guided bombs. By utilising this increase in accuracy the numbers of bomb-carrying aircraft were reduced in the structure of the raids on the North. Speaking about the ratio of strike aircraft to support aircraft, General Vogt said,

> The ratio of attack airplanes to support airplanes has changed dramatically in the new environment I describe. We were typically running missions up in this high-risk environment over North Vietnam in which the total strike capability for that afternoon would be sixteen airplanes, but the force of airplanes providing the necessary technical support for them numbered 250. Jamming, anti-SAM, the Wild Weasel stuff, chaff dispensing, the MiGCAP ate up tremendous quantities of air operations just trying to keep a small strike force alive.[1]

While the ratio of 250 to 16 may be an exaggeration, enormous numbers of support aircraft were certainly used.

The large-scale use of chaff was one of the differences between the 'Linebacker' raids and the earlier 'Rolling Thunder' attacks. Chaff was a development of the Second World War 'window' that was used to confuse German radar. It is made up of strips of aluminium foil or coated glass fibre cut to half the length of the radar frequency that it is hoped to jam. The lightweight chaff floats in the air, reflecting the radar beams, and appears on the radar screen as a large blip that swamps all the other radar returns from that area while the chaff cloud lasts. Individual aircraft operating over North Vietnam had originally carried loose chaff inside their speed brakes that was discharged in a one-shot release when the speed brake was opened. Later chaff 'bombs' were used; these burst open in the air and were employed to produce 'chaff corridors' for use by strike aircraft (the timing for these was critical as the chaff soon dissipated, especially in high winds). Chaff dispensers were then introduced, ejecting a measured amount of chaff behind an aircraft as it flew along the required route.

Before the introduction of 'smart' weapons the most accurate aircraft operating in South-East Asia had been the Navy's A-6 Intruders. However, even though they had achieved highly accurate night and bad-weather bombing results these were not good enough to ensure that pinpoint targets like bridges could be destroyed. The fact that the laser and optical weapons were essentially clear-weather systems meant that the weather over the North was the controlling factor in the interdiction campaign.

---

[1] Kohn and Harahan, op. cit., p. 87.

While President Nixon was in Moscow between 21 May and 5 June bombing was forbidden within a ten-mile radius of Hanoi as a political gesture. In Moscow Nixon discussed the Strategic Arms Limitation Treaty with the Soviets, but he also discussed the situation in Vietnam. While the Soviets did not choose to upset the Americans, they would not do anything directly to assist them in their negotiations with the North Vietnamese.

By the end of May thirteen of the bridges on the rail lines between Hanoi and the Chinese border were down and four of the bridges between Haiphong and Hanoi. Other bridges were also down between Hanoi and the southern part of the country. During May the Air Force lost ten aircraft over North Vietnam and the Navy lost fourteen. The Navy had flown 3,949 sorties over North Vietnam in support of 'Linebacker I' and 3,920 sorties over South Vietnam. American pilots claimed 27 North Vietnamese aircraft shot down.

CHAPTER 6

JUNE 1972

THE weather on 2 June was good and more than 250 aircraft from both the Navy and the Air Force were active over North Vietnam. Operating northeast of Hanoi, Major Philip W. Handley and his WSO, Lieutenant John J. Smallwood, became the first F-4E crew to destroy a MiG using the internal 20mm cannon. Major Handley was the flight leader of four Phantoms providing fighter cover for a strike force. The flight became separated after avoiding SA-2 missiles that had been fired at them. Handley and his wingman, Captain Stanley C. Green, were leaving North Vietnam when they were attacked from behind by two MiG-19s. Handley manoeuvered behind one of the MiGs and from a range of 300ft fired a 300-round burst. The MiG started smoking from the wing root and crashed vertically into the ground.

On 8 June B-52s carried out their first bombing of the North as part of the 'Linebacker' campaign. An average of 30 sorties a day were flown by B-52s over the North between June and October. Most of the targets were in the southern part of North Vietnam and comprised mainly communications and storage areas.

The weather over the North was again clear on 10 June and aircraft from the 8th TFW attacked the Lang Chi hydro-electric plant. The North Vietnamese had often accused the Americans of attacking their extensive system of dykes, used to control the rivers, and there had been an international outcry on several occasions. There is no real evidence that the Americans did attack the dykes as a deliberate policy, although several were hit during the bombing campaigns over the North. The North Vietnamese did place stocks of supplies and anti-aircraft guns along the dykes where they knew they would be relatively safe, but the Americans claim that the dykes were never deliberately bombed; certainly, major damage was never caused, even though it was within the capabilities of the Americans to inflict such damage. The hydro-electric plant was close to a major dam and it was critical that no harm should come to the dam as this could have resulted in large numbers of civilian deaths downstream.

The strike force consisted of twelve McDonnell F-4D Phantoms flying from Ubon in Thailand and attacking in three flights of four aircraft. The first four, led by the wing commander, Colonel Carl Miller, blew most of the roof off the turbine house at the plant. The next four were targeted against the transformers but missed the target completely. The last flight of Phantoms dropped their laser-guided bombs through the hole in the roof and destroyed the plant. Heavy anti-aircraft fire was directed at the attacking aircraft, but by diving in from 23,000ft and levelling out at 11,000ft the latter were able to stay out of range of most of the AA guns and none was hit.

Navy F-4B Phantoms from the USS *Coral Sea* shot down two MiG-17s on 11 June. Both the Phantoms were from VF-51; Commander Foster S. Teague was the pilot and Lieutenant Ralph M. Howell his back-seat operator in one of the Phantoms, and Lieutenant Winston W. Copeland was the pilot and Lieutenant Donald R. Bouchoux the WSO in the other. On 13 June the USS *Saratoga* mounted an alpha strike on the Phu Ly bridges and transport staging area. This involved 33 aircraft and was led by Commander James H. Flatley. The targets were the rail bridge, the road bridge and storage areas within a 2½-mile radius of the bridges. The weather over the target area was clear. Six SA-2 missiles were fired at the strike aircraft but none was hit. Standard ARM missiles were fired at the North Vietnamese radar system by the attacking aircraft and the railway bridge was hit by two Walleye optically guided glide bombs. The highway and rail bridges were both heavily damaged and the storage areas were estimated to have been 75 per cent destroyed. Although the anti-aircraft fire had been heavy, all the aircraft returned to *Saratoga*.

The Russia politician Alexei Kosygin visited Hanoi between 14 and 18 June. The ten-mile restriction zone was again placed around Hanoi during the visit, stopping the bombing in this area while the party leader was in Vietnam. An F-4J Phantom of VF-214 from *Kitty Hawk* was shot down by North Vietnamese anti-aircraft guns on 18 June. Both the crew members, Lieutenant-Commander R. Cash and Lieutenant R. J. Laib, ejected safely and were recovered by helicopter. The day before an A-7E, also from *Kitty Hawk*, had been shot down by a missile and the pilot, Commander D. D. Owens, lifted out by helicopter.

On 19 June massive strikes were launched against the North Vietnamese air defence system. The 'Linebacker' sortie rate increased to over 300 each day. It was estimated that 76 SA-2 missile launchers were destroyed on 19 June and that another 46 were accounted for on the 21st. The mobile launchers were moved around a network of launch sites and it was difficult to know when a site would be occupied. Six missile launchers were used in each missile site along with the necessary radar and control equipment. The numbers of SA-2 missiles fired began to decline after the end of June as stocks of missiles were either fired or destroyed. The interdiction of the supply lines into North Vietnam meant that new stocks of missiles became increasingly difficult to come by.

Two MiGs were shot down on 21 June, one by the Navy and one by the Air Force. Commander Sam Flynn, the Executive Officer of VF-31 aboard *Saratoga*, and his back-seat operator Lieutenant William John shot down a MiG-21 with a Sidewinder missile while flying on a MiGCAP for a strike by other aircraft from the carrier. On the same day a flight of four F-4Es from the 469th TFS from Korat were escorting a flight of chaff-dispensing aircraft in Route Package 6. At least two MiG-21s attacked the chaff aircraft, one of them turning away to attack the escorting Phantoms. The American aircraft were operating below a layer of cloud and the MiGs came down through this layer without warning. The MiG fired two 'Atoll' missiles at one of the Phantoms, flown by Colonel Vojvodich, but by turning hard to the left the F-4 avoided the missiles. One of the other Phantoms, flown by Lieutenant-Colonel Von R. Christiansen and Major Kaye M. Harden, manoeuvred behind the MiG and after their Sparrow missiles failed to work shot it down with a Sidewinder. The MiG pilot ejected safely and a parachute was seen. Christiansen also damaged the other MiG-21 involved in the attack using the F-4E's 20mm cannon.

In June General Creighton W. Abrams was replaced by General Frederick C. Weyand as the new commander of MACV. Weyand had extensive experience of the Vietnam War from 1966 and had also been involved in the Paris peace talks. The mission given to Weyand by Nixon was to ensure that the communist invasion was defeated and to safeguard the continuing disengagement and withdrawal of American forces. In South Vietnam the situation on the ground began to turn in favour of the South Vietnamese forces and a series of successful counter-attacks began to take place from 28 June. The North Vietnamese offensive had began to run out of supplies as the heavy fighting and constant bombing in the South took its toll.

The North Vietnamese forces began to pull back from around Kontum during the early part of June after heavy bombing by B-52s. Large numbers of tanks were destroyed around Kontum by three UH-1B helicopters equipped with the TOW anti-tank missiles that had been delivered to South Vietnam in April. Out of the first 101 firings 89 were classified as hits, and by 12 June the helicopters had knocked out 26 tanks, including 11 T-54s. But heavy fighting continued to the north-west of Kontum and to the south of the town as the North Vietnamese tried to keep the road to Pleiku closed. A heavily fortified fire base had been constructed on Route 14 in the Kontum Pass by the Northern forces, and heavy fighting and bombing were needed before it was taken on 30 June.

The surrounded South Vietnamese garrison at An Loc had been kept supplied by Air Force drops. Most of these took place from high level (that is, above 6,000ft) using the Air Force GRADS (Ground Radar Aerial Delivery System). During May and June 3,000 tons had been dropped to the defenders. It was estimated that 90 per cent of these had been on target and recovered by the waiting troops, and enough supplies were delivered to enable the defence to continue. Several cargo aircraft were lost to ground fire during the operation to keep An Loc supplied. When the Southern troops began to expand their perimeter at An Loc they found 208 dead North Vietnamese in one area that had been hit by a B-52 strike.

The 21st Division of the South Vietnamese Army had been trying to break through to An Loc along Route 13 from Saigon. By 14 June the last of the NVA had been forced out of the town and the defenders' casualties had been airlifted out by helicopter. Over 1,600 fresh troops were also moved into An Loc and the seige was officially over by the 18th. The Northern troops were forced back, but heavy fighting continued in the area for several months.

The AC-130 gunships operating over South Vietnam had been obliged to fly at a higher altitude to avoid the SA-7 missiles. One AC-130 had been hit by an SA-7 close to An Loc but had only been damaged. However, an AC-130 was shot down on 18 June while operating in the area south-west of Hue. The crew thought they were at a safe enough altitude to avoid the missiles, but the missile was fired from the side of a hill and hit the aircraft in the No 3 engine. One of the crew, Sergeant William Patterson, had been hanging out of a door on the side of the AC-130 to watch for missiles and had reported the SA-7 being launched, but the pilot had been unable to avoid the missile and the aircraft crashed. Sergeant Patterson bailed out with his parachute only partially attached; only he and two others survived.

In the northern part of South Vietnam, around Hue, 18,000 sorties had been flown in support of the South Vietnamese Army. The Air Force had flown 45 per cent of these sorties, the Navy 30 per cent and the South Vietnamese Air Force 25 per cent. After one B-52 strike on 9 June 60 bodies and a large amount of equipment were found north of Hue. On 28 June the forces in Hue mounted a major advance to the North and crossed the My Chang river line that they had been holding for two months. The re-taking of Quang Tri was the next objective to the north of Hue.

By the end of June the 8th TFW claimed that they had destroyed 106 bridges in North Vietnam, mainly with the laser-guided bombs with which they specialised. It was estimated that no stretch of rail track longer than 50 miles without a break existed in the North. Speaking about the two rail lines north of Hanoi, General Vogt claimed, 'We did, in fact, keep an average of fifteen bridges out at any given time. The air operation virtually stopped the rail traffic on those two rail lines.'[1] The North Vietnamese were well practised in repairing bridges and rail lines, but the continual delays and the need for extra trucks in order to by-pass the damage reduced and delayed the movement of supplies.

It was estimated that by June North Vietnam's imports had been reduced to 30,000 tons a month, down from a pre-bombing level of 160,000 tons. Stock of some essential goods had been reduced to two months' supply. The main shortage concerned oil. Most of the oil had been delivered by tanker from the Soviet Union but the closing of Haiphong had shut off this route, while the pipeline from China down to the DMZ had been bombed and rendered unusable. This left the North Vietnamese dependent on the amount of oil they had stockpiled inside the country before the bombing started—an estimated 160,000 tons. The larger storage facilities had been attacked and destroyed by June, but this left nearly 100,000 tons stored in smaller dumps. Visitors to North Vietnam reported that they had seen thousands of 50-gallon oil drums spaced out along major highways. This extreme kind of dispersed storage was safe from any level of bombing, but it did mean that the movement and transport of these supplies was very difficult and haphazard. A limited guerrilla war could be mounted using such facilities, but not a major conventional war involving twelve divisions that needed massive amounts of supplies, munitions and oil every day.

On 29 June President Nixon called for a return to negotiations and an international ceasefire. He seems to have felt that the bombing was achieving its objective: 'The situation has been completely turned around,' he said. But he was not going to make what he saw as the mistake that Johnson had made of

---

[1] Kohn, Richard H., and Harahan, Joseph P., *USAF Warrior Studies*, Office of Air Force History, United States Air Force (Washington, 1986), p. 86.

stopping the bombing as an incentive to allow talks to take place. Referring to the Northern leadership, he also remarked,

> It has always been my theory that in dealing with these very pragmatic men . . . that they respect strength—not belligerence but strength—and at least that is the way I am always going to approach it, and I think it is going to be successful in the end.[1]

Although Nixon thought that the bombing was working and the situation in the South was under control, he intended to continue with it until the North Vietnamese agreed to a settlement he could accept.

Under the 'Bullet Shot' programme the numbers of B-52s in the theatre continued to increase, and by the end of June there were 206 in South-East Asia. This was the largest number of SAC bombers ever based in the area. Most of these aircraft were stationed at Andersen Air Base on Guam. The distance from Guam to Vietnam meant that they had to be refuelled in the air. To support this and to support the tactical aircraft strikes over the North the numbers of KC-135 Stratotankers had increased to 172, scattered on bases throughout the area. On their busiest days the KC-135s were carrying out 130 refuelling sorties.

During June the Air Force lost twelve aircraft over North Vietnam and the Navy lost nine aircraft in total. During the month seven Air Force aircraft were shot down by North Vietnamese MiGs for the loss of only two MiGs; none of the Navy aircraft, which accounted for three MiGs, was shot down by enemy aircraft.

There had been a collapse of morale in sections of the US ground forces in Vietnam during the late 1960s and early 1970s. As the war had dragged on and the number of American deaths increased, so morale had declined. The conflict had become more and more unpopular with the general public and huge demonstrations against the war had taken place. In some respects the decline in morale had increased after Nixon had announced the pull-out of American forces: no one wants to be the last man killed in a war, even less the last man killed in an unpopular war. This decline in morale had led to a massive drug-taking problem and even to troops murdering what they saw as 'gung-ho' officers who might get them killed.

These difficulties extended to a lesser degree to both the Navy and the Air Force. Drug problems existed in the Navy: in 1966 only 170 Navy personnel

---

[1] Nixon, Richard, 'Turning the Battle Around with Airpower', *Air Force Policy Letters for Commanders*, 15 July 1972, p. 1.

were discharged for drug offences but by 1970 this number had increased to 5,000. It was rumoured that in one destroyer over 10 per cent of the crew were found to be involved in a drug ring. The traditional, authoritarian naval life-style had become so unpopular that in 1971 only 13 per cent of sailors re-enlisted when they had finished their service. There were also race troubles in the Navy, and these led to fights between black and white sailors. Jeffrey L. Levinson describes one race incident: 'Late in a gruelling 282-day cruise, a race riot broke out on board the carrier *Kitty Hawk*, forcing the Naval aviators to take refuge in their squadron's ready rooms.'[1]

The morale of the Navy pilots was probably affected least, but there was pressure on all of them. In particular, there was constant pressure from senior Navy commanders to keep the sortie total as high as possible. Lieutenant Fred Knee, who flew A-7Es from *Kitty Hawk* in 1972, describes the problem:

> Then the North invades the South, and the wing starts getting guys shot down, plus negative events were occurring in the squadron from the JOs' [Junior Officers'] per-spective . . . More sorties, more sorties for no other purpose than to fly sorties. Guys were getting killed and the morale of the ship and our squadron plummeted. Some-how the magic was lost . . . we launched twenty attack airplanes on a suspected petroleum storage facility, and it's some sleepy fishing village along the river. More than once I'd just pull off, drop my bombs in the river, and say, 'This is crazy, this is insane.'[2]

The Navy pilots were flying at least one and sometimes two missions each day and risking their lives over the North. The missions were often flown in marginal weather with the threat of surface-to-air missiles, MiGs and anti-aircraft guns ever present. After all this the pilots had to fly back to the carrier and land on a tiny deck that could be rising and falling 30ft. It was found that night landings on a carrier made pilots' heart rates rise more than dodging missiles over the North. There was a steady loss of aircraft and pilots through deck accidents. This was also a time of shortage for airline pilots, and many left the Navy to double their wages flying Boeing 707s. However, the vast majority of the Air Force and Navy pilots continued to do everything that was asked of them.

---

[1] Levinson, Jeffrey L., *Alpha Strike Vietnam*, Presidio Press (California, 1989), p. 261.
[2] Ibid., pp. 268–9.

CHAPTER 6

JULY 1972

THE North Vietnamese Air Force had been winning the air-to-air contest against the US Air Force and at the start of July the North Vietnamese successes continued. On the 5th two F-4Es were shot down by MiGs. Captain Don Logan was flying one of the F-4s on a MiGCAP sortie protecting twelve bomb-carrying F-4Es on a strike mission close to Kep airfield. After carrying out the bombing attack the American aircraft turned for home. The F-4s were then attacked by at least two MiG-21s. Logan described what happened:

> I saw the number 2 airplane in our flight get hit by a missile which seemed to come from below the flight. The F-4 immediately burst into flames, and I saw the two crew members eject. We had completed the turn and had just rolled out when we got a radio telling us to break hard right. As we rolled I felt a violent jar, and looked out to see the outboard portion of the left wing, past the wing fold, badly damaged . . . I looked over my left shoulder and there was a North Vietnamese MiG-21 flying close formation on us! As soon as he saw me looking at him, he rolled over us and split S down behind us into a cloud deck . . . both his missile rails were empty.[1]

Captain Logan and his back-seat radar operator ejected and both became prisoners of war.

The ability of the North Vietnamese ground-based fighter controllers to vector the MiGs into an advantageous position to attack the American aircraft, usually from behind, meant that the US Air Force was now losing more aircraft than it was shooting down. But the North Vietnamese did not have everything their own way. On 8 July three MiG-21s were shot down by Air Force aircraft. The first of these was accounted for by an F-4E from the 4th TFS operating out of Da Nang and flown by Captains Richard F. Hardy and Paul T. Lewinski. On the way back from providing fighter cover for a flight of chaff dispensers operating in the Hanoi area, Captain Hardy's flight of four F-4Es was attacked

---

[1] Drendel, Lou, *Phantom II*, Squadron/Signal Publications (Warren, 1977), p. 46.

from behind by MiG-21s. Hardy fired two Sparrow missiles at a MiG-21 that had overshot his aircraft and destroyed it.

The other two MiGs lost on the 8th were shot down by Captains Steve Ritchie and Charles DeBellevue flying an F-4E from the 555th TFS operating out of Ubon Air Base. Ritchie was leading a flight of four F-4Es that had been on a MiGCAP operation covering a strike force over the North. The engagement took place over what was known as Banana Valley 30 miles south-west of Hanoi. As the F-4s were leaving they were warned by 'Disco', the call-sign of the EC-121s orbiting over Laos, that the F-4s were about to be attacked by MiG-21s coming from the north. Ritchie turned to meet the threat and passed the MiGs at a closing speed of over 1,000kts. Ritchie described the combat:

> I manoeuvered to 5 o'clock position on the number two MiG, obtained an auto-acquisition boresight radar lock-on, and fired two AIM-7 [Sparrow] missiles. The first missile impacted the number two MiG, causing a large yellow fireball as the MiG broke into parts. It continued to disintegrate until impacting the ground. I then unloaded again for energy and turned hard right in pursuit of the lead MiG-21, who was now in a rear-quarter threatening position on aircraft 4. I manoeuvered into a similar position on the lead MiG as was achieved on his wingman previously. Another radar auto-acquisition lock-on was obtained and one AIM-7 missile fired. The missile impacted the MiG, resulting in a large yellow fireball.[1]

Ritchie had now shot down four MiGs and had equalled the feat of Colonel Robin Olds, who had downed four MiGs during 'Rolling Thunder' five years earlier.

The Navy was also losing aircraft to MiGs. On 10 July an F-4J from VF-103 was shot down over North Vietnam. It was operating from the USS *Saratoga* and the crew, Lieutenants R. I. Randall and F. J. Masterson, ejected and became POWs. During July two of the six available Pave Knife laser guidance pods were lost, one on 5 July when the Phantom carrying it was shot down by an SA-2 missile over North Vietnam. The other was lost on the 10th at Ubon Air Base. Lieutenant-Colonel Brad Sharp, commander of the 25th TFS, was taking off from the runway at Ubon when his right main tyre burst. Parts of the wheel punctured the tank under the right wing, covering the runway with fuel. The aircraft left the end of the runway and hot engine parts ignited the fuel, the resulting fire destroying the aircraft. Both Sharp and Lieutenant Mike Pomphrey were lucky to get out before the bombs they were

---

[1] Futrell, Frank, et al., *Aces and Aerial Victories: The United States Air Force in Southeast Asia 1965–73*, Office of Air Force History (Washington, 1976), p. 99.

carrying exploded. The base was closed for several hours while the runway was cleared.

On 18 July Lieutenant-Colonel Carl G. Bailey, with Captain Jeffrey S. Feinstein, shot down a MiG-21 that tried to attack their MiGCAP flight from behind as they were leaving their patrol area close to Phuc Yen. Bailey manoeuvered the F-4E behind the MiG and fired four Sparrow missiles, all of which missed their target. Closing in on the MiG, Bailey fired a Sidewinder which hit the enemy aircraft, blowing off its right wing. Two more MiGs were shot down on 29 June. The first of these again fell to Bailey and Feinstein. Bailey was flying an F-4D of the 13th TFW as part of a MiGCAP for a strike on the north-east rail line, north of Hanoi and close to Kep airfield. 'Red Crown' vectored the four-aircraft flight towards two enemy aircraft close to Phuc Yen airfield. One of the MiG-21s was destroyed with a Sparrow missile. Later in the day another MiG-21 was shot down by Sparrow missile fired by Lieutenant-Colonel Gene E. Taft and Captain Stanley M. Imaye, flying an F-4E of the 366th TFS.

In reply to President Nixon's call for renewed discussions, the North Vietnamese agreed to re-start the open Paris peace talks on 13 June. The secret talks between Kissinger and Le Duc Tho started on 19 July, also in Paris, and there were three such meetings between 19 July and 14 August. Kissinger described these meetings as having a completely different atmosphere from the last meeting on 2 May, when the North Vietnamese had been boasting of their capture of Quang Tri in South Vietnam. Some headway was made at the talks as Le Duc Tho changed his demand for the immediate removal of President Thieu and for the unconditional removal of all American forces. But Tho was still adamant about the need for substantial representation for the North in any coalition government in the South.

In South Vietnam July was the month when the Southern forces began to advance on all fronts. It was obvious that the North Vietnamese invasion had failed in its major objectives. An offensive to re-take Quang Tri had started in June and continued into July. The offensive involved 20,000 South Vietnamese troops with support from B-52 and tactical fighter strikes; there were also seventeen Navy vessels on call for shore bombardment. By the end of the month, after heavy fighting, most of Quang Tri had been taken but some fighting in the area continued for several months. One US estimate put the number of North Vietnamese casualties in the invasion up to July as 100,000. American strength in South Vietnam had fallen to 49,000 by the end of the month.

The US Congress had requested that the State Department carry out an investigation into the accusations that the Americans had been bombing the North Vietnamese dykes. A report was presented at the end of July and concluded that only twelve cases of damage to the dykes could be found. A close examination of the evidence and target photographs showed that each of the twelve damaged dykes were close to what could be called legitimate military targets and were examples of 'collateral damage' caused by bombs that had missed their actual targets.

For a short period during July the US Navy had seven carriers on line at Yankee Station, *America, Coral Sea, Hancock, Kitty Hawk, Midway, Oriskany* and *Saratoga*—the most powerful force of carriers ever assembled on the station, with over 550 aircraft available. *Hancock* and *Oriskany* were older Second World War aircraft carriers with a full load displacement of 44,000 tons and a length of 894ft; too small to operate the F-4 Phantom, they carried two squadrons of late model F-8Js as their fighter aircraft, together with three light attack squadrons of A-4Fs or A-7Bs and small detachments of RF-8Gs, EKA-3Bs, E-1Bs and SH-3Gs to support the other aircraft. *Oriskany* was involved in a collision with an ammunition replenishment ship and the deck-edge elevator was damaged, although the ship was able to complete her cruise. *Midway* and *Coral Sea* were later, larger carriers and had a full load displacement of 62,000 tons and a length of 978ft. Two squadrons of F-4 Phantom replaced the F-8 Crusaders from the smaller carriers, and one squadron of A-6 Intruders was embarked for medium attack. E-2B Hawkeyes replaced the E-1Bs as the carriers' airborne early earning aircraft. *America, Saratoga* and *Kitty Hawk* were classed as super-carriers and had a full load displacement of 80,000 tons and a length of 1,062ft. The larger carriers operated the RA-5C as their reconnaissance aircraft rather than the RF-8.

The logistics effort necessary to keep these ships on station in the Gulf of Tonkin was enormous. The carriers had to be replenished with fuel, stores and munitions every few days and a trail of cargo ships streched back to the western coast of the USA. The seven carriers had a crew of around 30,000 between them. Supporting the task force of carriers was a full complement of other naval ships including anti-submarine destroyers and anti-aircraft missile-carrying cruisers. The command system for Task Force 77 was normally aboard one of the carriers in the Gulf. Targeting was organised by this command group and passed to the carrier air wings. Each carrier operated on a twelve-hour cyclic rotation, with flying for twelve hours and then twelve for maintenance.

During the flying period the carrier could launch three alpha strikes each involving up to 40 aircraft to attack one target. One alpha strike could be launched every four hours. Such a strike would include about ten fighter aircraft as the MiGCAP force to protect the rest of the aircraft from interference. The bombing force would comprise 10–15 light attack aircraft and 6–10 medium attack aircraft. The Navy did not have specialised 'Wild Weasel' aircraft and the strike would be supported by six A-7s or A-6s carrying Shrike missiles to launch at the SA-2 sites. This strike force would be supported by two E-2Bs to give radar coverage and up to five KA-6D tanker aircraft. After the strike two RF-8 or RA-5 photo-reconnaissance aircraft would provide bomb damage assessment photographs. If no large targets worth an alpha strike were available then the carrier could launch smaller strikes every 90 minutes, the first being recovered after the second had launched.

The Grumman EA-6B Prowler was introduced into Task Force 77 aboard the USS *America* during July. A version of the A-6 medium attack bomber, it was designed to jam the radar frequency used by air defence systems using ECM equipment. The Prowler's fuselage was increased in length by 40in over that of the A-6 and the crew of four included two jamming operators. Pods carried under the wings could jam eight frequencies simultaneously. The EA-6 was intended to carry out the same role as the Air Force's EB-66s by flying outside the range of enemy defences but monitoring his radar emissions and jamming them. The EA-6A, also based on the A-6, replaced the Marines' EF-10B, which had been operating from Da Nang since 1965.

Like the Air Force, the Navy used laser bombs and Walleye optically guided bombs. During July they introduced a modified Walleye which could be launched at a higher altitude, allowing the launching aircraft to avoid some of the anti-aircraft fire. The Navy used a hand-held designator for laser bombs. The back seat radar operator in an F-4 would hold the designator and focus it on the target through the Phantom's canopy. This meant that the aircraft had to be flown in a circle around the target. The laser-guided bombs were carried by other Phantoms or by A-7 attack aircraft and released over the target. The designating aircraft had to maintain a steady course around the target until the bombs impacted, which meant that it was very vulnerable in high-risk areas; thus this system was not used where the defences were thought to be to strong.

After the war it was generally thought that the Navy had developed better, more flexible tactical formations than the Air Force for their fighter aircraft. The formation still used by the Air Force was a development of the Second

World War 'finger four', which was itself a development of the German *Schwarm*. This was made up of two elements, or *Rotten*, of two aircraft. One of the two was the leader and the other the wingman. The leader was intended to do the shooting while the wingman was supposed to protect and support the leader. The variation of this formation used by the US Air Force in Vietnam was the 'fluid four'. The wingman was 1,000ft to the side and slightly behind the leader and the second element of two flew 3,000ft behind and 2,000ft above the first element. The Navy tactical fighter formation was the 'loose deuce', made up of two aircraft flying abeam of each other and between one and two miles apart. Although one of the aircraft was nominally the leader, either aircraft could take the lead role as the situation developed. Two others could be behind the first two or further out to the side. The wider separation with the Navy's 'loose deuce' gave more flexibility, especially with the wide-turning Phantoms, and the ability of the first person to spot an enemy aircraft to become the element lead made for faster reaction times.

Air Force losses to North Vietnamese MiGs showed that the the air defence system developed by the North had continued to improve and expand. It was based on the Soviet model, with a mass of interlocking ground-based radars feeding a control centre from where the MiGs were organised. The ground control intercept (GCI) operators had tight control of the MiGs, vectoring them on to the US aircraft and even telling the pilots when they could open fire. By using the tactic of hitting and running from the American fighters the MiGs made the best use of their limited resources. They knew that any attempt to meet the US fighters head-on was doomed to failure.

During the early months of 'Linebacker' many of the pilots involved were relatively inexperienced. It had been four years since the end of 'Rolling Thunder' and many men had left the services over that period. The Air Force policy was that all Air Force pilots had to be involved in the war. No pilot could be forced to fly a second tour (a tour was 100 missions over the North) in South-East Asia until all the Air Force pilots had flown one tour. Pilots could volunteer to fly a second tour and many did. However, many Air Force pilots had never flown tactical jet aircraft, which meant that they had to take part in intensive courses to learn skills that other pilots had spent years perfecting. On this point Steve Ritchie, the first Air Force ace in Vietnam has written,

Air Force policy during the war meant that no-one would be required to serve twice until everyone had been once. As a result many who had never flown fighters or even

95

knew the tactical mission, and who had not flown for years, were suddenly rushed through five to six months of combat crew training and sent to Southeast Asia. Quite often, on account of their rank these men found themselves in combat leadership roles for which they were unqualified. This kind of mismatch had some dramatic and tragic results.[1]

On 10 July, in an attempt to improve the dissemination of recent combat experience, General Vogt instituted mission critique conferences at Seventh Air Force headquarters, with the minutes of these meetings being sent to all field units.

At the end of July the Air Force established the Tea Ball Weapons Control Center, based at Nakhon Phanom in Thailand. The purpose of the centre was to give American pilots flying over North Vietnam all the information possible about the MiGs that were being operated by the North, based on a combination of signals intelligence (sigint) and radar information. Some aspects of the system are still secret. The airborne EC-121s operating over Laos were able to pick up the radio transmissions between the MiGs and their ground controllers and pass this back to Tea Ball, where they were translated and any relevant information was passed back to aircraft operating over the North. Once the system was in operation there was only a 40–60 second delay before information could be transmitted. With experience, the American operators came to know the Vietnamese pilots involved, and the ground controllers. With the use of ground radar in the north of Thailand and also of clandestine radar sites in Laos, the Navy's 'Red Crown' radar ships in the Gulf, the airborne radar circling over Laos or over the Gulf, the ability to trigger the MiGs' IFF systems and the monitoring of the MiGs' radio transmissions, a full picture of the way the North Vietnamese used their aircraft became available to the American pilots.This information was passed on in the form of a colour code. 'Blue Bandits' were MiG-21s, 'White Bandits' MiG-19s and 'Red Bandits' MiG-17s. The term 'Green Bandits' was used to warn that one of the North's small group of experienced pilots was in the air; the North did have a number of pilots who had shot down more than five US aircraft. 'Heads Up' was the warning code for MiGs very close to US aircraft. The position of the MiGs was relayed in relation to a notional point, 'Bull's Eye'. This was normally the city of Hanoi. The distance and bearing from 'Bull's Eye' was given, along with any height information, if available. It was possible for the position of

---

[1] Kohn, Richard H., and Harahan, Joseph P., *Air Interdiction in World War II, Korea and Vietnam*, Office of Air Force History, United States Air Force (Washington, 1986), pp. 71–2.

'Bull's Eye' to be programmed into the aircraft's inertial navigation system, and this allowed the position of the MiG in relation to the American aircraft readily to be calculated. The introduction of the Tea Ball centre did have an effect on the numbers of Air Force aircraft shot down. Speaking on this point, General Vogt said,

> . . . in essence it involved being able to have up-to-the-minute intelligence coupled to your operational command and control so that you could react . . . In July, as I say, we were less than one to one (our loss-to-victory ratio); in the month of August, the ratio shifted four to one in our favour and stayed that way right up to the end of the 'Linebacker' operations.

It was during July that the actress Jane Fonda visited Hanoi and denounced American policy towards North Vietnam. She also called on American serv- icemen to lay down their arms. There is no doubt that the visit affected the morale of some of the American service people. During July six MiGs had been shot down over North Vietnam and nine Navy aircraft shot down by the North Vietnamese defence system.

CHAPTER 7

AUGUST 1972

THE weather during July had been worse than expected, with considerable low cloud cover on most days. The weather during August was even worse, and the Air Force was able to fly only sixteen missions into North Vietnam. 'Smart' weapons, including the laser-guided bombs, needed good weather for the target to be clearly seen and the guidance systems to work. Although the bombing was evidently having an effect on North Vietnam, President Nixon seemed to feel that not enough was being done: although they were negotiating, the North Vietnamese still had not agreed to a settlement. On Nixon's direct orders early in the month Commander-in-Chief Pacific Command Admiral John S. McCain ordered that three of the six carriers on station should concentrate on bombing the North and that half the attacks on the North should be in Route Package 6. This increased the numbers of Navy sorties flown over the North by nearly 50 per cent. McCain also ordered the Air Force to carry out a minimum of 48 sorties a day into RPs 5 and 6. However, the bad weather prevented a number of Air Force strikes from being carried out.

Most of the MiGs shot down by Navy aircraft were destroyed by Sidewinder missiles and most of the those accounted for by the Air Force were destroyed by Sparrows. One of the rare Navy shoot-downs using Sparrows occurred on 10 August. The A-6 attack aircraft was often used to make single attacks at night, and the MiGCAP for these aircraft, which could be operating over a wide area, were either positioned on a patrol line or kept on board the carrier at five minutes' readiness to take off. During the evening of the 10th Lieutenant-Commander Gene Tucker and Lieutenant Bruce Edens were launched from the *Saratoga*'s deck to intercept a MiG in the vicinity of Vinh. After refuelling from a KA-6D tanker also launched from *Saratoga*, Tucker turned behind the MiG as it flew north towards Than Hoa. He managed to close to within two miles of the MiG and fired two radar-guided Sparrow missiles, the first of which hit the MiG and destroyed it. This was credited as being the first night-time destruction of a MiG by a Navy pilot using a Sparrow.

On 12 August a MiG-21 was shot down by an F-4E of the 58th TFS operating out of Udorn. The F-4E was flown by Captain Larry Richard, a Marines officer on exchange with the Air Force. The radar officer was Lieutenant-Commander Mike Ettel, a Navy officer also on exchange with the Air Force. Before strikes were flown into Route Packages 5 and 6 it was customary to check the weather in the possible target areas in order to ensure good visibility. These weather flights were flown by four Phantoms early in the morning of the planned raid. Captain Richard was leading a flight of three F-4Es and an RF-4C. The four aircraft took off from Udorn at 0730 hours and carried out a reconnaissance along the Red River and the north-east rail line. 'Red Crown' warned the F-4s that MiGs were manoeuvring to place themselves behind the Phantoms. Richard turned the flight to meet the MiGs. When the Phantoms and MiGs had closed to four miles the MiGs were spotted visually, turning to the left, and Richard began to turn with them. Although it was unarmed, the RF-4C was flying as Richard's wingman and turning with him. The other element of the flight had climbed above the MiGs to provide top cover. Captain Richard fired a Sparrow missile at the leading MiG but the latter tightened his turn and the missile passed over the top of him. The first MiG then dived away and out of the area. Continuing to turn, Richard fired another Sparrow at the second MiG and this guided correctly, destroying the aircraft by blowing its tail off.

The meeting between Henry Kissinger and Le Duc Tho that took place on 14 August showed that the North Vietnamese were still insisting that there should be a coalition government in the South, with members from all parties. Kissinger supported an electoral commission. No agreement was reached, and the next meeting was to take place on 15 September. President Nixon now seems to have decided that no settlement was possible before the election he was hoping to win later in the year. As it became more likely that he would be re-elected president, he did not need a settlement to increase his popularity. After leaving Paris Kissinger flew to South Vietnam for talks with President Thieu, who did not like any of the proposals put to him.

Another MiG-21 was shot down on 15 August by an F-4E Phantom of the 336th TFS flown by Captain W. Sheffler with Captain Mark A. Massen as his WSO. Sheffler was part of an eight-aircraft MiGCAP covering a strike on the thermal power station at Viet Tri, which was situated north-west of Hanoi on both the Red River and the north-west rail line. A MiG-21 attacked the F-4Es from behind and above. Sheffler broke hard right into the attacking fighter, and at a distance of 5,000ft he fired a Sparrow that hit the MiG on the left-hand side, causing it to descend trailing flames and smoke. Another MiG passed through the American aircraft at high speed but immediately left the area. This brought the number of MiGs destroyed by aircraft of the 8th TFW since 1965 to 38½.

An F-4J of VF-114 operating from *Kitty Hawk* and flown by Commander J. R. Pitzen with Lieutenant O. J. Pender was shot down by an SA-2 missile over North Vietnam on 16 August. Both crew members were killed. The bombing of the North continued by both night and day. During the night the technique was developed for specialist aircraft to drop flares to illuminate the target for other aircraft to bomb. These flare-dropping aircraft were known as 'Night Owl Fast FAC' aircraft. They were generally used to attack the transport links in the southern area of North Vietnam but on occasions were sent to attack targets close to Hanoi. On the night of 18 August Major B. V. Johnson was flying a Night Owl Fast FAC mission to attack a training area at Xuan Mai, twelve miles south-west of Hanoi. Johnson was flying an F-4D from the 497th TFS operating from Ubon, and flying with him as his WSO was Lieutenant Steve Johnson. The plan was for the crew, along with another flare-carrying aircraft, to mark the target with flares and for two flights of bomb-carrying F-4s to attack the target. From Thailand the attacking aircraft crossed the southern part of North Vietnam and refuelled from a tanker over the Gulf. Flying north, Major Johnson led the strike back into Vietnam across the mouth of the Red River, which showed up clearly in the dark. Anti-aircraft fire started as soon as they had crossed the coast. Two SA-2 missiles were fired at Major Johnson's aircraft and the second one exploded so closely that the Phantom was blown upside down though not damaged. When they reached the target Major Johnson fired flares from the SUU-42 flare dispenser. Only then was it discovered that the target was a school for anti-aircraft gunners, and an enormous amount of flak was fired at the attacking aircraft. Another SA-2 exploded close to the second Night Owl aircraft, damaging it, and it was decided to abandon the mission before the bomb-carrying aircraft had dropped their bombs. After flying back along Banana Valley and out over the Gulf, Major Johnson decided to attack the main coastal highway at Quang Khe close to Dong Hoi just north of the DMZ. A large number of trucks were found on the road and he released flares while the other F-4s bombed the trucks. The Night Owl Fast FAC missions were very wearing on the crews operating at night and often involved four or five refuellings, which gave a sortie time of 4–6 hours.

Another MiG was shot down on 19 August by an F-4E of the 4th TFS based at Takhli. The pilot was Captain Sam White, who was flying his 204th mission over North Vietnam, and the WSO Captain Frank Bettine. White was part of a flight of F-4Es acting as fighter cover for a flight of eight chaff bombers laying a corridor into North Vietnam above the port of Hon Gai, heading towards Hanoi. 'Red Crown' alerted the Phantoms that MiGs had taken off from Phuc Yen and were heading towards the chaff bombers. After passing the Phantoms at low level the MiGs positioned themselves behind the four MiGCAP aircraft. Captain White described the MiG attack:

> Not long after entering North Vietnam, the WSO in aircraft 2, Captain Forrest Penney, saw a MiG-21 in the flight leader's 6 o'clock position and called for a break. As the F-4Es broke, the MiG-21 faltered momentarily, then elected to disengage. We rolled off into the MiG's 6 o'clock and, following some maneuvering, fired an AIM-7 which tracked on the MiG and detonated. After the missile impacted, the MiG began to smoke and burn, followed by the ejection of the aircraft's pilot. Having reached minimum fuel, we egressed the area.[1]

The improved American control system did seem to be having an effect.

However, the North Vietnamese surface-to-air missiles and anti-aircraft guns were taking a steady toll of the attacking American aircraft. A F-4B from VF-161 operating from the USS *Midway* was shot down by an SA-2 missile on 25 August. The crew, Lieutenant-Commander N. W. Doyle and Lieutenant John C. Ensch, ejected and became prisoners of wars. Ensch had taken part in shooting down two MiGs on 23 May. The first Marine aircraft lost to a MiG was shot down on 26 August. This was an F-4J operating out of Nam Phong. Two F-4Js were flying as MiGCAP 40 miles from Hanoi when 'Red Crown' warned them that MiGs were approaching. The MiGs turned behind the F-4s and shot one down with an 'Atoll' missile. The pilot, Lieutenant Sam Cordova, was not recovered but the radar operator was lifted out of North Vietnam by helicopter. Another Navy Phantom was lost on 27 August when an F-4B from VF-151 based on *Midway* was brought down by a North Vietnamese missile. The crew, Lieutenants W. Triebel and D. A. Everett, ejected and became prisoners of war.

On 28 August Captain Steve Ritchie became the first US Air Force ace in the Vietnam War when he shot down his fifth MiG. He was flying as the leader

---

[1] Futrell, Frank, et al., *Aces and Aerial Victories: The United States Air Force in Southeast Asia 1965–73*, Office of Air Force History, (Washington, 1976), p. 102.

of four aircraft on a MiGCAP for a strike on the iron and steel foundry at Thai Nguyen, 40 miles directly north of Hanoi. Ritchie's WSO, Captain Charles B. DeBellevue, picked up a MiG south of Hanoi and the four-aircraft flight turned towards it. Ritchie passed the MiG and turned behind it. He described his victory thus:

> We converted to the stern and fired two AIM-7 missiles during the conversion. These missiles were out of parameters and were fired in an attempt to get the MiG to start a turn. As we rolled out behind the MiG, we fired the two remaining AIM-7s. The third missile missed, but the fourth impacted the MiG. The MiG was seen to explode and start tumbling towards the earth.[1]

Ritchie was never allowed to fly over the North again in order to protect him from the kind of treatment he would have received had he been shot down, considering the publicity there had been about his five kills.

By 12 August the last of the American ground combat troops had left South Vietnam. There were still 43,500 American military personnel in the South but these were advisers and support troops. On 25 August President Nixon announced that further reductions would take place and that numbers would be down to 27,000 by 1 December. The situation in the South continued to move in favour of the South Vietnamese Army. US intelligence reports put the number of North Vietnamese casualties caused by the use of air power at 120,000 by the end of August. With only one division left, the North Vietnamese Army simply had no reserves to hold the South Vietnamese advances in the South.

The amount of oil and petroleum available to the NVA engaged in the South also continued to decline. The destruction of the North Vietnamese power stations meant that the inhabitants were forced to rely on thousands of diesel generators to produce electricity. This put even further strains on the supply of fuel. Small amounts were still getting through to the South, but not enough to allow a major invasion to continue. Many of the North's tanks had been destroyed by August, but the thousands of trucks that were being used needed hundreds of tons of fuel every day in order to keep running. A bad harvest in the South meant that the Northern forces also had to bring in food supplies, even though they had planned to gain most of their food from the land they had captured in the South. North Vietnam's efforts to reorganise its supply routes were only partially successful. The Chinese restricted the amount of supplies

---

[1] Ibid., p. 103.

they delivered to North Vietnam in the early part of the bombing and did not allow the Soviets to transship anything into Vietnam for three months.

During the month of August the US Navy flew 4,819 sorties over the North—the highest monthly total flown by the Navy during the 'Linebacker' campaign. Seven USN aircraft were lost over North Vietnam during August.

CHAPTER 8

SEPTEMBER 1972

I N its continuing efforts to attack the North Vietnamese air defence system the US Air Force developed hunter-killer teams made up of two F-105G 'Wild Weasels' and two F-4Es. Using their specialised equipment the F-105s detected the active missile sites and attacked them with Shrike missiles, the F-4Es following the Shrike attack and bombing the SA-2 site with conventional bombs.

On 2 September a hunter-killer team was operating close to the airfield at Phuc Yen. Missiles were fired at an SA-2 site that had launched several missiles at the flight. The two F-4s attacked the site with cluster bombs, avoiding intense anti-aircraft fire. As they turned away a MiG-19 attacked one of the F-105s with an 'Atoll' missile. The F-105 turned hard right and the 'Atoll' missed the aircraft's left wing by only 20ft. The MiG then tried a gun attack on the second F-105, which also broke hard right. As the MiG tried to leave the area it passed over the F-4E flown by Major Jon I. Lucas and Lieutenant Douglas C. Malloy. Lucas turned behind it and obtained a radar lock-on. An AIM-7 Sparrow was launched and at the same moment an SA-2 missile was observed heading towards the F-4E; Lucas turned towards the SA-2 and managed to outmanoeuvre it. When the F-4E turned back to the MiG a parachute was observed and the aircraft was seen burning and spiralling downwards.

The services that had been organised to rescue aircrew shot down over the North continued to improve, and provided they did not land close to any major population centres downed crewmen had a good chance of being picked up. An A-4F based on board *Hancock* was shot down on 6 September by North Vietnamese anti-aircraft guns, but the pilot, Lieutenant W. F. Pear, was picked up. On 8 September an F-4J from VF-103 on board *Saratoga* was also shot down by gunfire, and, again, the crew, Commander P. P. Bordone and Lieutenant J. H. Findley, were picked up by helicopter.

The Air Force continued to improve its record against the North's MiGs and three were shot down on 9 September. Captain John A. Madden was leading a flight of three F-4Ds and one F-4E from the 555th TFS. Madden's back-seat operator was Captain Charles DeBellevue, who had already taken part in the destruction of four MiGs. The F-4s, which were providing fighter cover for another strike on the iron works at Thai Nguyen, established a patrol orbit west of Thud Ridge and waited to see if any of the MiGs would attempt to attack the strike aircraft. Madden received information that at least one MiG was heading back to Phuc Yen and would be short of fuel.

The four F-4s turned south-east and the MiG-21 was detected trying to land at Phuc Yen with his undercarriage and flaps down. Captain Madden pulled in behind the MiG and fired two AIM-7 Sparrows, but neither of the missiles guided. As the F-4 was travelling faster than the MiG it drew alongside at a range of 1,000ft. The MiG pilot spotted the F-4, cleaned up his aircraft and went into afterburner in an attempt to get away. Madden started to turn with the MiG but was too close. The leader of the second element of the F-4 flight, Captain Brian Tebbit with Lieutenant William S. Hargrove as his WSO, fired two AIM-9 Sidewinder missiles at the MiG but neither guided. Tebbit, who was flying the one F-4E in the flight, closed in on the MiG and fired on it with his 20mm cannon. Hits were seen on top of the aircraft and on the left wing. The pilot ejected and the aircraft crashed close to the perimeter at Phuc Yen.

As the flight turned away from Phuc Yen it was alerted to two more MiGs coming in behind. The Phantoms turned to meet them head-on and when they were sighted they were seen to be MiG-19s. The MiGs seem to have seen the American aircraft late and Madden had time to turn in behind them, firing one Sidewinder that exploded behind one of the MiGs and brought it down. Continuing to turn, he fired another Sidewinder and this, too, guided correctly, blowing the tail off the MiG, which crashed into a field and exploded. On the way back one of the four F-4s was hit by gunfire and crashed in northern Laos. The crew, Captains William Daelkey and Terry Murphey, were picked up by helicopter. These were the fifth and sixth MiGs shot down by Captain DeBellevue, making him the leading American ace of the Vietnam War.

On 10 September an A-7C of VA-82 operating from *America* was shot down by a missile and the pilot, Lieutenant S. O. Musselman, was killed.

As the weather cleared it was decided to attack the Paul Doumer bridge again. Attempts had been made to repair the bridge but it was still not carrying trains or vehicles. To ensure that the bridge was not repaired it was bombed on 10 September by four F-4Ds from the 8th TFW carrying laser-guided bombs and two more spans of the bridge were dropped into the Red River. The bridge would not carry supplies again until after the the Americans had signed the peace settlement and left Indo-China.

The first MiG shot down by a Marine crew in a Marine aircraft occurred on 11 August. VMFA-333 was operating as one of the F-4J fighter squadrons on board *America*. Two F-4Js were flying MiGCAP for a Navy strike that was hitting a target, a suspected SA-2 assembly site, close to the coast north of Haiphong. The pilot of one of the aircraft was Major Lee T. Lassiter, with Captain John D. Cummings in the back seat. After refuelling in the air the two F-4Js flew into North Vietnamese air space north of Haiphong, and at this point 'Red Crown' directed the pair of aircraft towards a group of MiGs circling above Phuc Yen airfield, nearly 80 miles away from the Navy strike aircraft that the F-4s were supposed to be protecting.

Flying at 3,000ft, the F-4s headed towards Phuc Yen and picked the MiGs up on their radar at a distance of nineteen miles. The MiGs had dropped down to 1,000ft in the circuit at Phuc Yen and it was difficult to keep a radar lock on them at this altitude. Major Lassiter engaged the MiGs in a turning combat and fired four Sparrows and two Sidewinders at one of the MiGs, all of which missed. As the MiG attempted to reverse its turn it passed in front of the F-4 and Lassiter fired another Sidewinder, which hit the MiG and destroyed it. Another of the MiGs tried to attack Lassiter's wingman and he fired his last Sidewinder at the MiG. This also missed, but is thought to have damaged the aircraft. On the way back to the carrier Lassiter's aircraft was hit by an SA-2 missile but the crew ejected into the Gulf and were picked up. The other F-4J ran out of fuel and the crew also ejected, ending up being lifted out of the water by a helicopter.

A strike against the La Danh storage caves was planned to take place on 12 September. A flight of four chaff bombers was laying a corridor into North Vietnam from the coast at the port of Hon Gay, just north of Haiphong. Protecting the chaff flight was a MiGCAP flight of four F-4E Phantoms from the 35th TFS. The flight leader was Lieutenant-Colonel Lyle L. Beckers, with Lieutenant Thomas M. Griffin as his WSO. The escort flight was positioned behind and slightly above the chaff bombers when it received warning of attacking MiGs. Two MiG-21s dived down on the chaff flight and Beckers fired a Sparrow missile that failed to launch. The chaff flight turned hard to the right but one of the MiGs fired an 'Atoll' missile that hit one of the rear section of chaff bombers. The crew tried to get the damaged aircraft back over the Gulf but they were forced to eject and became prisoners. The MiG dived away following the usual hit-and-run tactics. Colonel Beckers dived after the MiG and fired a Sidewinder that failed to function. Following the MiG, he fired another Sidewinder that guided and hit the aircraft in the wing, but the warhead failed to explode, whereupon Beckers closed in on the MiG and shot it down with 20mm cannon fire. The second MiG did not carry out an attack but was followed by Major Garry Retterbush and Lieutenant Daniel I. Autrey flying one of the F-4Es. Retterbush fired two Sparrow and three Sidewinder missiles which either missed or failed to explode. He was then forced to close with the MiG and open fire with the F-4E's 20mm gun. He observed hits on the MiG's fuselage and left wing, and it crashed.

Later the same day a strike force was attacking the Tuan Quan railway bridge close to the airfield at Yen Bai. Escorting the strike were four F-4s from the 388th TFW. Two MiG-21s attacked the strike force and one of the escorting F-4s fired two Sparrows and three Sidewinder missiles at one of the MiGs, but they all missed. One of the other F-4s, flow by Captain Michael J. Mahaffrey with Lieutenant George I. Shields as his WSO, attacked a second MiG with one Sidewinder that guided and hit the enemy aircraft in the tail. The combat had taken place at 16,000ft and the MiG was last seen at 8,000ft spiralling downwards.

Henry Kissinger met Le Duc Tho again on 15 September in Paris. The North Vietnamese seemed to think that they would be in a weaker position after Nixon was re-elected President, and it appeared increasingly likely that he would be. Le Duc Tho pushed for a speedy settlement. At a meeting on 20 September he produced a plan for an agreement within one month, but in reality both sides were still talking about different things and Le Duc Tho was still insisting that President Thieu should be removed from office before any elections could take place in the South. In a meeting on 26 September Kissinger presented a plan for a Tripartite Electoral Commission to oversee elections in the South. The North Vietnamese reply to this was to suggest a National Council of Reconciliation and Concord with much the same objective as the Commission. The two sides seemed slowly to be coming to some kind of agreement. However, President Thieu was not represented at the talks and did not like much of what he heard about them.

Captain Calvin B. Tibbett and his WSO Lieutenant William S. Hargrove shot down their second MiG within a week on 16 September. Tibbett was part of a flight of four F-4Es from the 'Triple Nickel' 555th TFS flying escort for an Air Force strike over the North. The flight followed a MiG-21 along the Red

River heading for Hanoi. The flight leader fired two Sparrows and four Sidewinders at the MiG, all of which missed. Tibbett then fired four Sidewinders, the last of which exploded near the MiG's tail, causing it to crash. The pilot ejected close to the ground.

The new F-4C Wild Weasel began to replace the old but well-liked F-105G Thunderchiefs when the first six arrived at Korat Air Base on 23 September. The F-4Cs normally carried two Sparrows, two Shrike anti-radar missiles, two wing tanks, an ECM jamming pod and either another fuel tank on the centreline hardpoint or four cluster bomb units. The electronic equipment carried by the aircraft detected the radar and a Shrike missile was fired. With a range of ten miles the Shrike could destroy or damage the air defence radar. In most cases the radar was switched off, causing the missile to miss, but this closed down the system, which was the main object of the mission.

Under the 'Constant Guard V' programme two squadrons of F-111As were moved to Takhli Air Base in Thailand on 25 September and replaced the four squadrons of F-4Ds from the 49th TFW which had been moved to South-East Asia under 'Constant Guard III' during May. The F-111A had been used before in South-East Asia, in 1968, but only in very small numbers and without great success. However, most of the 'bugs' had now been ironed out of the aircraft systems and the aircraft greatly increased the Air Force's all-weather capability. The advantages of the F-111 included its ability to fly at night 200ft above the ground at Mach 0.9, using terrain clearance radar. Launched at night against individual targets, by October the F-111 accounted for half the Air Force sorties in RPs 5 and 6.

In the South Quang Tri was finally cleared of North Vietnamese troops on 15 September when a fortified strongpoint inside the city was finally re-taken by South Vietnamese marines. The six Northern divisions in the northern region of South Vietnam were now being pushed steadily back by a smaller force of South Vietnamese troops. A general falling back was taking place in the South as the NVA fought to hang on to the territory it had earlier taken.

The shortage of laser guidance pods meant that around a third of the strike forces still carried conventional bombs. These were used on area targets like railyards or storage facilities. The F-4s carried up to 8,000lb of ordnance, including 500lb, 750lb and 1,000lb bombs. The technique used by the F-4Ds was to climb, or 'pop up', to 20,000ft, close to the target, then to dive on to the target at an angle of about 45 degrees and release the bombs at about 8,500ft. The F-4's attack system used the aircraft's radar in conjunction with the pilot's gunsight to provide aiming points and release times. The pilot held the correct heading and the ordnance was automatically released by the attack computer at the right moment. With experienced crews reasonably accurate bombing results could be obtained.

None of the F-4s had any genuine all-weather bombing capability without the laser-guided bombs. An attempt to give the Phantom the ability to bomb in bad weather was the use of the LORAN (Long Range Radio Navigation) system. This was a navigation system rather than a precision bombing system, and the best that could be hoped for was the placing of bombs within 500ft of the target. It worked by comparing the time between pulses transmitted from up to four ground stations to give the position of the aircraft. One of these ground stations was the master station and the others the slave stations. Once the position of the aircraft was calculated, the information was used constantly to update the F-4D's inertial navigation system, which provided data to the aircraft's attack computer. However, the distance between the ground stations and the targets in North Vietnam meant that some parts of the North were not covered. Bombing through cloud meant that 500ft was the best the system could achieve, but on occasions results were considerably beyond this figure.

During September the improved weather meant that more sorties were flown against North Vietnam than in any other month during 'Linebacker I'. The Air Force flew 111 laser-guided bomb missions, with good results—the pilots had built up the level of expertise available in the squadrons. On this point one Air Force publication stated that

> With Linebacker came the mission specialization of aircrews, even within the same squadron. In the past the fighter pilot had been a jack-of-all-trades—a bombing mission today, counter-air operation tomorrow, and a night attack another time. But because of the moves and counter-moves on either side and the increasing degree of sophistication involved in each area of expertise, specialisation became increasingly important to mission accomplishment.[1]

Air Force pilots shot down seven MiGs during September and the improved performance against the MiGs was due, at least in part, to the specialisation of the 432nd TRW, and in particular the 555th TFS, in fighter escort. Navy losses of aircraft involved in 'Linebacker' during September numbered ten. During the month the USS *Enterprise*, America's largest carrier, arrived in South-East Asian waters.

---

[1] Lavalle, Major A. J. C., (ed.), *The Tale of Two Bridges and the Battle for the Skies over North Vietnam*, U S Government Printing Office (Washington, 1976), pp. 151–2.

CHAPTER 9

OCTOBER 1972

MOST of North Vietnam's air defence system had been defeated by October. Very little anti-aircraft ammunition was left, nor SA-2 missiles, and the small quantities of supplies that were getting through were not sufficient to replace what had already been used. Moreover, a large number of North Vietnamese aircraft had been shot down. The American strike forces could operate practically at will as the air defence system ground to a halt, and most if not all of the important targets in the North had already been destroyed or damaged. In order to keep the North Vietnamese Air Force on the run a series of major strikes was carried out against the North's airfields on 1 October. Phuc Yen, Yen Bai, Vinh and Quang Lang were all attacked, and at least five MiGs were destroyed and nine damaged on the ground.

The first MiG of the month was shot down on 5 October. Captain Dick Coe was flying an F-4E of the 34th TFS out of Korat, with Lieutenant Omri Kenneth Webb as his WSO. Coe was originally leading a flight of four F-4Es but two of the other aircraft aborted the mission. The objective was to provide fighter cover for four strike aircraft attacking the north-east rail line with laser-guided bombs. The strike fighters flew into North Vietnam from the Gulf of Tonkin close to the Chinese border. The escorting fighters were behind the strike fighters and slightly above at 20,000ft. The F-4Es were attacked by two MiG-21s that seemed to come in from over China, and by two more flying north from around Hanoi. Coe managed to turn behind one of the MiGs and shoot it down with a Sparrow missile. At first the crew did not realise that they had shot the MiG down and it was only the next day that they received the credit.

As described earlier, the night Fast FAC (forward air control) mission was known as the Night Owl mission; the daytime Fast FAC was known as the Wolf FAC. In the Route Package 1 and 2 areas in the southern part of North Vietnam the Wolf FAC was used to control and mark the targets for the bombing aircraft. The normal load for an F-4D on this kind of operation was two wing tanks, four LAU-68 rocket pods on the inner pylons, two Sparrow missiles and an SUU-23 gunpod on the centre line. The Air Force Fast FACs marked targets using the white phosphorous rockets carried in the LAU-68 pods. Targets were mostly associated with the transport system, trucks, dumps or storage areas. Both Air Force and Navy aircraft used the Fast FACs to find and mark their targets. Lieutenant James Latham was flying an F-4 from Ubon, with Lieutenant Rick Bates in the back seat, on a Wolf FAC mission on 5 October. A four-aircraft flight of bomb-carrying F-4s from Ubon was being led by the wing commander, Colonel Carl Bailey, and expected to be presented with a marked target. Latham flew over an abandoned truck storage area to see if there were any trucks still in use parked there. The F-4 was hit by a 57mm anti-aircraft shell in the tail section. The crew lost control of the aircraft and it crashed less than a mile from the coast. Both crew members ejected and were taken prisoner.

On 6 October a hunter-killer team of two F-105Gs and two F-4Es was operating against the North Vietnamese radar system close to the iron works at Thai Nguyen. 'Disco', the call-sign of the airborne control centre, warned the flight that MiGs were approaching. The flight leader in one of the F-105Gs turned the Thunderchiefs away from the threat, leaving the 'killer' half of the flight to deal with the MiGs. One of the F-4Es was flown by Major Gordon L. Clouser with Lieutenant Cecil H. Brunson and the other by Captain Charles D. Barton with Lieutenant George D. Watson. The MiGs, one -21 and one -19, positioned themselves behind the Phantoms, which were forced to break away and jettison the bombs they were carrying. Barton went into a vertical dive, followed by the MiG-19, which began to open fire with its two 30mm guns. Clouser followed the MiG-19 into the dive and the MiG-21 followed behind. Barton levelled the F-4E out at 300ft above the ground in a valley surrounded by high peaks. The MiG-19 did not level out in time and crashed into the ground. The other Phantom pulled out of the dive into the valley, still followed by the MiG-21, which left the area at high speed. The two crews were each credited with the destruction of half the MiG-19.

On 8 October another MiG was destroyed by the crew of an F-4E Phantom from the 388th TFW. The leader of the flight of four aircraft, Captain Robert H. Jasperson, placed himself behind a MiG-21 after receiving warnings from 'Red Crown'. Jasperson tried to fire Sidewinder missiles at the MiG but none of them launched. Closing in on the MiG, he fired the F-4E's 20mm cannon and hits were observed on the enemy aircraft, which burst into flames and crashed. The MiG pilot ejected at approximately 1,500ft.

A major change in the command structure of US forces in South-East Asia took place when Admiral Noel A. M. Gayler became the new commanding officer in the Pacific, on 6 October. He issued a statement reiterating that the main targets for the 'Linebacker' operations were the transport system leading from China down into South Vietnam and the North's electrical generation plants. Admiral Gayler also made an attempt to introduce some changes to the Route Package system. The lack of real cooperation between the Air Force and Navy had been a limiting factor in the bombing campaign against North Vietnam since 1965. The inability to target all tactical aircraft operating in a theatre from one headquarters took away air power's strengths of flexibility and concentration. However, the changes made were only minor. Gayler said,

> . . . to improve efficient use of resources and to attain mass application of force where indicated, [a] geographical area which includes the NE/NW rail line and the Hanoi environs will be designated an integrated strike zone. This is the most vital area in North Vietnam. To bring the necessary weight to bear, CINCPACAF [Commander-in-Chief Pacific Air Force] and CINCPACFLT [Commander-in-Chief Pacific Fleet] will schedule strike missions into one another's geographical area.[1]

Had the bombing continued for much longer Admiral Gayler may well have created one overall air commander, as this seems to have been the way he was thinking.

The rotation of Air Force units into and out of the South-East Asia theatre continued with 'Constant Guard VI'. This involved the introduction of a new aircraft type to the war—the Vought A-7D. Three squadrons of the 354th TFW, equipped with the A-7D, were stationed at Korat in Thailand from 10 October. These were joined at a later date by the 3rd TFS, similarly equipped. Leaving the theatre to make room for the A-7s were the two squadrons of F-4Es that had arrived under 'Constant Guard II', the 308th TFS and the 58th TFS. The A-7D was a specialised ground attack aircraft based on the Navy's A-7E and the first combat missions were flown on 16 October. It was also intended to use the A-7 as a replacement for the A-1 in the combat search and rescue role as the A-1s were transferred to the South Vietnamese Air Force.

Captain John A. Madden and Captain Larry Pettit destroyed a third MiG on 12 October. Flying an F-4D from the 555th TFS, the two aircrew were part of a MiGCAP protecting a strike force bombing one of the bridges on the north-east rail line. A MiG took off from Phuc Yen and flew north-east to attack the

---

[1] Momyer, William W., *Air Power in Three Wars*, US Government Printing Office (Washington, 1978), pp. 98–9.

strike force. Madden passed the MiG head-on at 25,000ft, and the two aircraft then circled each other in a left hand-turn until the MiG dived away attempting to escape. Following the MiG, Madden passed through a layer of cloud and watched as the enemy aircraft continue to dive into a lower layer of cloud. It was later found that the MiG had failed to pull out and had crashed into the ground almost vertically. The credit for the MiG was given to Madden and Pettit.

The third Air Force ace of the war, Captain Jeffrey S. Feinstein, was also a weapons systems operator, as Charles Debellevue had been, rather than a pilot. On 13 October Feinstein was flying with Lieutenant-Colonel Curtis D. Westphalia as part of a MiGCAP near Kep airfield. 'Red Crown' warned the crew that MiGs were approaching, and the aircraft were picked up on the F-4's radar at seventeen miles and were seen visually at two. Westphalia launched three AIM-7 Sparrows at the MiG and the second one hit and destroyed it.

Three MiGs were shot down on 15 October. The first of these was destroyed by Major Robert M. Holtz with Lieutenant William C. Diehl. They were flying an F-4 protecting three flights of strike aircraft close to Viet Tri. After a series of engagements with several MiGs, Holtz fired a Sidewinder that blew the tail off a MiG-21. Later in the day Captains Gary M. Rubus and James L. Hendrickson from the 307th TFS carried out the destruction of the second MiG. Rubus described the combat:

> Northwest of Bullseye, while under Red Crown control, our flight vectored south against a pair of MiG-21s. A radar contact was established at a distance of 16 nautical miles, followed by a visual contact shortly thereafter. I fired an AIM-7 at a range of 4 nautical miles which detonated prematurely in front of my aircraft. A second AIM-7 was fired at a range of 4,500 feet which did not guide. I closed to cannon range and fired a burst from approximately 1,100 feet, followed by a second burst from approximately 800 feet. Both bursts impacted the MiG, and shortly thereafter I observed the pilot eject.[1]

The third MiG destroyed on the 15th was shot down by Major Ivy I. McCoy and Major Frederick W. Brown, who were operating as part of a MiGCAP of four F-4s. After being vectored by 'Red Crown' to close with MiG-21s that had taken off from Phuc Yen, McCoy fired three Sparrow missiles and then three Sidewinders. The third Sidewinder flew into the MiG's tail pipe and blew the tail off the aircraft.

---

[1] Futrell, Frank, et al., *Aces and Aerial Victories: The United States Air Force in Southeast Asia 1965–73*, Office of Air Force History (Washington, 1976), p. 110.

Meanwhile the peace talks in Paris seemed to be inching towards some kind of agreement. Kissinger felt that the real breakthrough occurred on 8 October when Le Duc Tho finally dropped the North's demand for a coalition government and accepted the idea of a ceasefire to stop the fighting in the South. Instead of the coalition government the suggested National Council for Reconciliation and Concord would supervise elections in the South. The original North Vietnamese position had been that the bombing must stop before any meaningful talks could take place; this stance had been abandoned, but Kissinger did tell Le Duc Tho that the bombing would be restricted during the final stages of the talks, prior to a settlement. President Nixon ordered a reduction to 200 in the number of strike sorties directed into Route Packages 5 and 6, although in reality this did not constitute a reduction as the number of sorties was already smaller than this. On 16 October, as Kissinger was starting another round of talks in Paris, Nixon ordered a further reduction to 150, but this still only reduced the number of Air Force sorties by 10.

After finally negotiating the basis of an agreement in Paris with the North Vietnamese, Kissinger now had to get the agreement of President Thieu. In South Vietnam Kissinger presented the proposals to Thieu on 19 October. When he learned what the negotiations had produced, Thieu, not surprisingly, rejected the idea of a National Council and the proposal to allow North Vietnamese troops to stay in South Vietnam, and as a result Nixon was forced to ask for further talks between Kissinger and Le Duc Tho. On 23 October, as a sign of goodwill, Nixon halted the bombing of North Vietnam north of the 20th Parallel, bringing 'Linebacker I' to a close. The North Vietnamese had asked that the agreement be signed on the 31st, and on 26 October Kissinger stated that 'Peace is at hand.'

By the end of October the numbers of Americans in South Vietnam had fallen to 32,000 and was continuing to fall. During the last few months of 'Linebacker I' large numbers of aircraft had been transferred to the South Vietnamese Air Force. The aim was to bolster the South's forces before the Americans had left. In three months 288 aircraft had been transferred under Operation 'Enhance Plus'. The South Vietnamese Air Force was now supposedly the third largest in the world, although in fact it had neither the pilots nor the infrastructure to operate these numbers of aircraft. The object of the rapid supply of aircraft was to anticipate any restriction that could come out of the Paris agreements and any limitation that could be imposed by the US Congress.

During the 'Linebacker I' campaign the US Navy had flown 23,652 sorties, almost a third of them at night, while the Air Force had flown 18,001 sorties over North Vietnam. The total tonnage of bombs dropped was 155,548, a figure greatly enhanced owing to the use of the B-52. The US Air Force had lost 44 aircraft, comprising five shot down by anti-aircraft guns, twelve by SA-2 missiles and 27 by MiGs. The Navy had lost 45 aircraft—27 to AA fire, seventeen to missiles and one to MiGs. Over 5½ months North Vietnam had lost 62 MiGs, or around 30 per cent of the establishment at the start of 'Linebacker I'.

CHAPTER 10

'LINEBACKER II'

ALTHOUGH the 'Linebacker' campaign had been halted on 23 October the bombing below the 20th Parallel continued and even increased as more aircraft became available. The agreement for which President Nixon had stopped the bombing became ever more elusive. Thieu's refusal to have anything to do with the agreement that Kissinger and Nixon thought was within sight meant that they could not deliver the settlement they had promised the Northern delegates at the peace conference. The North Vietnamese became obdurate and refused to discuss any renegotiation: after making what they saw as major concessions to get rid of the Americans, they felt that they had been duped when the latter came back with a new set of demands. The only reply the North Vietnamese would make was that the treaty should be signed on 31 of October as agreed, with no changes. As concessions to Thieu the agreement had stated that there would be no coalition government and that the Americans could still continue to supply arms to South Vietnam after the treaty had been signed, but Thieu saw the legitimisation of the North's army in the South as unacceptable and the National Council as a coalition government under another name. Any agreement that would remove the Americans from South Vietnam was seen as being not in the country's best interests, and Thieu's ideal would have been no agreement. Kissinger has since stated, 'We failed early enough to grasp that Thieu's real objection was not to terms but to the fact of any compromise.'[1]

Nixon supported Thieu's position and attempted to renegotiate with the North Vietnamese against Kissinger's advice. The ending of the 'Linebacker I' campaign was seen as a move to placate the North Vietnamese and give them the incentive to renegotiate. Kissinger's comment on 30 October that 'Peace is at hand' was his hope that he could keep the peace process moving. Thieu demanded that any settlement should define the DMZ as a national boundary,

---

[1] Kissinger, Henry A., *The White House Years*, Little, Brown, (Boston, 1979), p. 1393.

remove Northern troops from South Vietnam and ensure that the National Council did not become a coalition government. In total Thieu demanded 69 changes and then finally rejected the agreement on 22 October. Nixon was forced to ask for more negotiations on the 25th, and the North Vietnamese reply was to broadcast the terms of the agreement, including secret clauses, on Radio Hanoi and demand that the Americans keep to the agreed terms.

On 8 November Richard Nixon was re-elected President by a large majority of the votes cast. It was now obvious to the North Vietnamese that for the next four years they would have to negotiate with Nixon if they wanted a settlement (nobody foresaw the Watergate affair) or even if they only wanted to prevent the bombing from re-starting. The North wanted to keep the prospects of an agreement on the table and within sight but they did not wish to agree to anything.

On 20 November Kissinger was back in secret negotiations in Paris with Le Duc Tho, as he had been three years earlier. After they had been presented with Thieu's list of changes the North Vietnamese in turn presented a list of their own demands for changes and the talks achieved very little. To Kissinger it now appeared that the North Vietnamese did not want an agreement, as they had done during the summer, but were prepared to wait, without the pressure from the bombing, until the Americans simply left. As the talks again started to drag on with little sign that they were achieving anything Nixon told Kissinger to relay the message that if the talks broke down there would be 'massive force' used against the North. Nixon seemed to favour the immediate resumption of a modified bombing campaign but felt that a breakdown in talks should be clearly blamed on the North Vietnamese. In meetings with the Chiefs of Staff in late November he ordered them to prepare plans for the use of B-52s in a major bombing campaign in the Hanoi and Haiphong areas.

In the secret talks in Paris the North Vietnamese seemed to be offering concessions and then withdrawing them in an effort to keep the negotiations going. They finally seemed to be on the point of reaching an agreement, but on 13 December Kissinger found that they had inserted seventeen changes into the written proposal. Kissinger now passed the message to Nixon to 'turn hard on Hanoi and increase pressure enormously through bombing and other means.'[1] In a meeting involving Nixon, Kissinger and General Haig, who was Kissinger's military assistant, it was decided by Nixon to start the bombing campaign

---

[1] Ibid., p. 1445.

using the B-52s on 18 December. The military seem to have been surprised at the extent of the campaign ordered by Nixon. They had been ordered to prepare a plan for the bombing but had assumed that it would be a campaign *involving* the B-52s rather than one *based* on the B-52s. In passing this message on to the Chief of Staff Admiral Thomas H. Moorer, Nixon stated

> I don't want any more of this crap about the fact that we couldn't hit this target or that one. This is your chance to use military power effectively to win this war, and if you don't I'll consider you personally responsible.[1]

The only real constraints placed on the proposed campaign by Nixon was the avoidance of large-scale civilian casualties where possible.

Nixon hoped to force the North Vietnamese to negotiate seriously to allow him to achieve his goal of 'peace with honour'. He could see major difficulties with Congress when it reconvened in January. The bombing was ostensibly aimed the North's military capabilities but the main objective was to deliver a psychological blow against the Northern leadership's commitment to the war. There also seems to have been an element in Nixon's thinking that the North should be punished: the North Vietnamese had frustrated him in his attempts to extricate America from Vietnam, and the 'Linebacker II' campaign would punish them for their intransigence. 'Linebacker I' had been essentially an interdiction campaign intended to stop the flow of materials and equipment from the North to the South. Although many of the targets bombed during 'Linebacker II' were transport targets, the aim of the campaign was to break the will of the Northern leadership. It was thought that massive bombing and the destruction of targets in the Hanoi and Haiphong areas would place maximum pressure on the Northern leadership to reach an agreement. Both Hanoi and Haiphong had been bombed before but only intermittently, and there were targets in both cities that had never been attacked.

The North Vietnamese used the halting of 'Linebacker I' to begin to rebuild their military and transport infrastructure, but by December there was still massive disruption and damage to be repaired. The ports were still mined, but stocks of military supplies had entered the country overland from China, and these included anti-aircraft ammunition and SA-2 missiles. Having destroyed large parts of the North's air defence system during 'Linebacker I', the American pilots would be forced to face reinvigorated defences.

---

[1] Quoted in Morrocco, John, *Rain of Fire: Air War 1969–1973*, Boston Publishing Co (1985), p. 147.

In an effort to pressurise the North Vietnamese Nixon ordered the use of B-52s over North Vietnam—but south of the 20th Parallel—on 2 November. The North Vietnamese achieved their long-term goal of shooting down a B-52 on 22 November when a B-52D from the 307th Strategic Wing stationed at U-Tapao was was hit by an SA-2 missile while operating close to Vinh, the main trans-shipment point in the southern half of North Vietnam. After suffering heavy damage the B-52 crashed in Thailand and the crew were recovered. The destruction of the B-52 was a symbolic rather than a practical achievement for the North Vietnamese, who had destroyed thousands of American aircraft by this stage of the war, but the bringing down of a huge aircraft which had until then seemed invulnerable did boost North Vietnamese morale.

The original planning for 'Linebacker II' had specified a three-day campaign with the possibility of this being extended. After naming the new bombing campaign the Joint Chiefs of Staff issued a directive that called for 'A three-day maximum effort, repeat maximum effort, of B-52/TACAIR strikes in the Hanoi/Haiphong areas . . . Object is maximum destruction of selected military targets.'[1]

Admiral Moorer had passed the responsibility for the operations to General John C. Meyer, the head of Strategic Air Command (SAC) and the actual plans were drawn up by SAC headquarters at Offutt Air Force Base in Nebraska. These plans were then submitted to the Joint Chiefs of Staff for approval. The plans covered the choice of targets, direction of attack and bomb loads. It seemed that one of the major flaws of the 'Rolling Thunder' campaign was being repeated—the planning of raids far removed from the men who would have to carry them out.

All the B-52s in the Far East were under the control of the Eighth Air Force commanded by General Gerald W. Johnson with his headquarters at Andersen Air Base on Guam. The numbers of B-52s available for 'Linebacker II' included 150 on Guam and around 60 at U-Tapao in Thailand. Johnson was only told of the start of the bombing campaign on 15 December. He remarked,

> The first indication we had was late . . . on the afternoon of the 15th December and we were told it would be a maximum effort which would extend over a three-day period . . . And then on the third day, I knew it was going to continue, but I did not know how long.[2]

---

[1] Ibid., p. 148.

[2] Hopkins, Charles K., 'Linebacker II: A First Hand View', *Aerospace Historian*, September 1976, p. 134.

With the impending start of the bombing raids there does seem to have been some disagreement among the different military commands involved in Vietnam over who would command the raids. Pacific Air Command, in control of the Seventh Air Force in South-East Asia, wanted the final word on targets, as did the Military Assistance Command who controlled all US military activities in Vietnam. But General Meyer kept the B-52s under the command of SAC. The B-52s would be bombing targets in North Vietnam but would be ignoring the established Route Package system. However, they would be needing massive support from the tactical aircraft of the Seventh Air Force and from Navy aircraft from Task Force 77. General Vogt complained that SAC was supplying details of raids to the Seventh Air Force with little time for supporting raids to be organised. In the early part of the campaign SAC made certain that they would control the B-52s.

When General Johnson in Guam received the planning for the first raid of the campaign he was far from pleased. He had been asked to prepare a detailed plan for bombing the North in August 1972 but the plan supplied by SAC headquarters was completely different. The SAC plan called for three waves of aircraft attacking over a ten-hour period with all aircraft following exactly the same ingress and egress routes at the same heights and turning in the same places. It was thought that the stereotyped tactics could lead to heavy losses, but SAC refused to change the plans.

The view taken by SAC was that the loss rate would be 3 per cent of the attacking forces and that this would be acceptable. Nixon realised that losses would be inevitable. He wrote in his diary, 'We simply have to take losses if we are going to accomplish our objectives.'[1] Speaking after the campaign had ended, General Meyer said, 'I certainly do not look forward to another situation which would call on our SAC bombers to undertake such a mission.'[2]

The fact that no aircraft had been lost when B-52s had carried out five strikes in the northern part of Vietnam during April 1972 meant that many believed that the 'Linebacker II' campaign could be carried out with only light losses. Because the campaign was only supposed to last for three days there was no attempt to regain the air superiority that had been achieved by 'Linebacker I'. Ideally, the first part of a major bombing campaign should be focused on the enemy's air defences to destroy or at least weaken these, to allow the bombing to continue with the minimum of interference. With a cam-

---

[1] Nixon, Richard, *RN: The Memoirs of Richard Nixon*, Vol. II, Arbour House (New York, 1978), p. 244.
[2] Hopkins, op. cit., p. 134.

paign of short duration, effort diverted to the destruction of the defences would significantly weaken its main focus. Air defence targets were bombed during 'Linebacker II', but this was an attempt to suppress or harry the defences rather than to destroy them. The B-52s would have to face the North Vietnamese defences head on.

The defences in the North had to a large extent been rebuilt after the end of 'Linebacker I'. There were believed to be over 30 active missile sites in the Hanoi area, with adequate stocks of missiles. The altitude at which the B-52s operated, over 35,000ft, placed them above the range of the light and medium anti-aircraft guns, but the radar-directed 85mm and 100mm guns would be a significant threat. The North's MiG-21s and MiG-19s had originally been designed by the Soviets as point-defence interceptors to attack American bombers, and the MiG-21, armed with the 'Atoll' heat-seeking missiles, could be effective against the B-52s if the latter were operating without fighter cover.

The B-52 was a major component of the of the US strategic nuclear deterrent forces. It was a large aircraft powered by eight jet engines slung under the wings. With a maximum take-off weight of 500,000lb, it needed an enormous wing area of 4,000 sq ft to get airborne. The eight engines gave the B-52 a top speed of 650mph, and the aircraft possessed an extremely long range. By the early 1970s SAC had around 450 B-52s in service worldwide, and the fact that almost half of them were involved in 'Linebacker II' shows the degree of commitment to the campaign made by President Nixon.

The B-52s were equipped with a radar bombing system which gave them a genuine all-weather capability. This was not a precision system, but it did allow area targets to be hit by day or night, in any weather. The radar in the aircraft gave a picture of the ground underneath, and provided the target gave a distinctive return, or there was a distinctive feature in the area, the bombs could be dropped with reasonable accuracy. The two models of the B-52 involved were the D and the G. The older D model had been modified for use in the 'Arc Light' bombing over South Vietnam. The 'Big Belly' programme had increased the load of conventional bombs that could be carried to a maximum of 60,000lb. All the D models had also received structural strengthening and new, more advanced electronic equipment, including ECM equipment. The later G models were faster but could not carry the same bomb load and did not have advanced ECM equipment. Defensive armament was limited to one tail-mounted gun turret: in the D model this contained four 0.5in machine guns and in the G a 20mm cannon, both weapon systems being aimed by radar.

By the end of 'Linebacker I' the US Air Force and US Navy had created an effective system for bombing North Vietnam with tactical aircraft, but by December many of the personnel involved in the earlier bombing had gone home and had been replaced. Robert H. Connelly, who flew an F-4D from Udorn during 'Linebacker II', has written:

> The first four nights of Linebacker II I double-banged [two missions in one night] and the reason for that was that we were short on guys who were Pac Six flight lead qualified. Linebacker I had ended in October, and a lot of the experienced guys had left. We only had ten crews who were the primary crews to go 'downtown' [to Hanoi] during Linebacker I. When we got to Linebacker II everyone went . . . experienced or not.[1]

The combat experience in SAC at both pilot and command level was also extremely limited. B-52s had only carried out five raids in RP 6. There was experience of bombing in both the Second World War and the Korean War, and the 'Arc Light' bombing missions over South Vietnam had been going on for seven years. But nobody really knew how the bombers would succeed against the modern air defence system over the North. By 1972 the Americans had been bombing the North on and off for over eight years, and by the start of 'Linebacker II' the North Vietnamese were probably the world's most experienced air defence operators.

The B-52s were to operate over the North only at night, to lessen the chances of meeting enemy interceptors. On the afternoon of 18 December the crews were being briefed at both Andersen and U-Tapao Air Bases. On this first night the plan called for 129 bombers to attack the Hanoi area in three waves, with four hours between the first two waves and five hours between the second and third waves. For the aircraft from U-Tapao in Thailand it would be a four-hour mission, with no need for aerial refuelling, but from Andersen on Guam the mission would take up to sixteen hours, with the need to refuel on the way to and back from North Vietnam. The round trip to and from Guam was over 5,500 miles, making these some of the longest-range bombing raids in history. (The 1982 'Black Buck' bombing raids during the Falklands War were longer, as were the B-52 raids on Iraq from the United States during the Gulf War in 1991.) The route from Guam passed across the Western Pacific north of the Philippines and across South Vietnam into Laos. The B-52s would then turn north and cross into North Vietnam from the west. The return jour-

---

[1] Drendel, Lou, *USAF Phantoms in Combat*, Squadron/Signal Publications (Texas, 1987), p. 44.

ney would take them back the same way, but this time directly across the Philippines.

It was intended that the B-52s should fly in cells of three, which would maximise the effect of their ECM equipment. The bombers carried extensive ECM gear, with a specific crew member to operate it. The North Vietnamese air defence system was based on Soviet radars and the B-52s' ECM systems had been designed specifically to counter Soviet equipment. It was hoped that the bombers would therefore be able to counter the missile threat on their own.

Conditions at Andersen had been overcrowded with aircraft and personnel since the start of 'Linebacker I'. The numbers of people needed to maintain and fly the huge bombers were enormous. Every part of the base was full with parked B-52s. The first wave of bombers was to include 27 B-52s from Andersen. At 1451 hours the first bomber took off from the runway. There was a long line of B-52s nose to tail along the taxiway, waiting their turn to use the runway. Oriented west to east, the runway at Andersen is two miles long. Charles K. Hopkins, who watched the take-off wrote,

> Andersen's runways are quite uneven and just beyond their eastern extremity is a cliff and then a precipitous drop of several hundred feet into the ocean. The total effect to the eyes of the observer watching bombers launch is that the aircraft becomes airborne just before reaching the visible rim of the island, only to drop out of sight momentarily as if falling into the sea, then rising majestically into the sky in the airspace immediately beyond the edge of the island.[1]

Thousands of people watched the huge bombers struggle to become airborne and then climb away. The B-52s' engines were boosted with water-injection for take off and this left a trail of smoke through the sky behind the aircraft. After a number of B-52s had taken off the sky was full of smoke as there was not enough wind to clear it away. Off the coast at Andersen a Russian trawler counted the bombers as they took off and broadcast the information to North Vietnam.

The first wave was made up of 27 aircraft from Guam and 21 from Thailand. The two streams of B-52s came together over Laos as they formed into one long line of aircraft in groups of three, and with up to ten minutes between each three-aircraft cell the B-52s stretched over 70 miles of sky. After turning east into North Vietnam the bombers followed the same route that the F-105s had taken during 'Rolling Thunder', south over Thud Ridge and flying directly

---

[1] Hopkins, op. cit., p. 130.

over Hanoi. After dropping their bombs the plan was for the bombers to make a hard turn to the west and head back over Laos.

The B-52s were operating at their cruising height of 30,000ft. Targets for the first wave included the airfields at Phuc Yen, Kep and Hoa Lac. The other major targets were the railyards at Yen Vien, the Hanoi railway repair facility at Gia Lam, Radio Hanoi and the Kinh Ho storage area. As the bombers closed in on their targets the North Vietnamese defences began to react. The B-52 crews reported seeing anti-aircraft fire exploding in the air around them, but no B-52s were hit by gunfire during the campaign. Small numbers of MiG fighters were reported trailing the bombers and attempting to close in behind them. However, it was estimated that the North Vietnamese only managed to get 31 MiGs airborne during the whole of 'Linebacker II', and more effort was put into shadowing the bombers and reporting their position than attacking them.

The main defence against the bombers was the SA-2 missile, and an esti-mated 200 were fired at them during the first night. Holding in tight formations of three, the B-52s were forced to fly as straight and level as possible for four minutes before releasing their bombs to allow the radar bombing system to operate accurately. The first wave of B-52s reported dozens of missiles fired at the bombers as they approached their targets. The first bombs fell at 1930 hours (Hanoi is in a different time zone from Guam). The bombers had been flying with 100mph tail winds on the way to the target, giving them a speed of well over 600mph, but after they had turned to leave Hanoi they were slowed down considerably. The second wave of 30 bombers followed exactly the same course as the first and bombed at precisely midnight; the third wave followed the same course and bombed at 0500 hours. When the last aircraft of the final wave returned to Guam the aircraft taking part in the next night's strikes had already started their engines. During the course of the first night 121 of the 129 bombers committed to the raids, 42 from U-Tapao and 87 from Andersen, had bombed their targets—94 per cent.

In support of the bombers large numbers of aircraft had accompanied the B-52s. These had included radar-jamming EB-66s and Navy Prowlers, 'Wild Weasel' F-105s, F-4s as fighter escorts and chaff bombers. Tactical aircraft had attacked airfields and missile sites in the Hanoi area. On average, 85 Air Force aircraft were used to support the bombers each night. The Air Force was still involved in daylight operations over North and South Vietnam and the extra commitment needed to support the B-52s stretched its resources to the limits. As stated earlier, Robert N. Connelly flew two support missions during the night of the 18th, one with the first wave and one with the third. The first mission was as fighter escort for the chaff bombers laying a corridor into Hanoi. The chaff bombers were flying at 36,000ft and Connelly's flight of F-4s was at 20,000ft. He described the situation:

> I was the first guy over Hanoi on the first night of Linebacker II. There was an 8,000ft undercast that night, which covered most of North Vietnam. As the chaffers started their run, I could see the North Vietnamese start to fire SAMs. You could see the big glow that lit up the undercast as the first stage of the booster ignited, then the SAM would come up through the clouds heading your way.[1]

The hunter-killer 'Wild Weasel' teams were also busy that night attacking the active SA-2 sites. The 'hunters' were launching Shrikes and Standard ARMs (anti-radar missiles) at the emissions from the SA-2s' radar systems. The Standard ARM was an improvement over the Shrike, with a range of 25 miles and a larger warhead. The 'killer' part of the team attacked the active SA-2 sites with bombs and cluster bombs.

Navy EA-6B Prowlers and Marine EA-6As were involved in jamming the radars used by the North. The Marines had been using the EA-6A since 1966. This aircraft was only a limited modification of the original A-6 Intruder and kept the crew of two. The Marine squadron VMCJ-1 was stationed at Cubi in the Philippines, and to operate close to North Vietnam the EA-6As had to be refuelled in the air by the Marines' own KC-130 tankers. The North Vietnamese had changed the operating frequency of the 'Fan Song' radar used by the SA-2 system to the higher frequency 'I' band and the EA-6As were the only jamming system adequately to cover this waveband. A large fairing on the top of the Prowlers' fin held a receiver that picked up signals from the North's radar and communications systems. When signals had been analysed they were jammed by using one of the four active pods that were carried under the wings. The radio communications between the MiGs and their ground controllers were not usually jammed as these were use by the Tea Ball centre to provide intelligence on the movement of the MiGs. Prowlers were banned from crossing into North Vietnam and operated on 'racetrack' orbits off the coast.

The Navy's RA-5Cs had a passive ECM role during 'Linebacker II'. While the B-52 raids were taking place the Vigilantes would orbit at 35,000ft fifteen to twenty miles off the coast and record all the types of radar and radio fre-

---

[1] Drendel, op. cit., p. 46.

quencies being used by the North Vietnamese, while the raids were taking place. This information was then analysed to try to improve the coverage given by the Prowlers.

Even though the North Vietnamese defences had been degraded they still managed to fire off an estimated 200 missiles. Captain Robert E. Wolf, the pilot of one of the B-52s operating from Guam, described the missiles:

> SAMs were fired at the bomber stream in a shotgun pattern. The Vietnamese simply tripped off salvoes of six missiles from each site. From the beginning of the bomb run to the target, my gunner counted 32 SAMs fired at or at least passing close to our aircraft.[1]

During the course of the night three B-52s were shot down by the North Vietnamese missiles, two B-52Gs from Andersen and one B-52D from U-Tapao. Lieutenant-Colonel Don Rissi was the commander of a B-52G from Andersen and he was leading the fourteenth cell of three aircraft in the first wave. Making the turn after bombing the railyards at Yen Vien, the B-52 was hit by two missiles. Three of the crew ejected and became prisoners but Rissi and two others were killed as the aircraft exploded in a ball of fire. In the second wave another B-52G from Guam, flown by Lieutenant-Colonel Hendsley R. Conner, was heavily damaged by missiles after releasing its bombs. Conner managed to keep the aircraft flying until it was over Thailand, where the crew successfully bailed out. The third bomber shot down was a B-52D in the third wave.

The SA-2 had been in service with the Soviets since the 1950s and was the missile that had shot down Gary Powers' U-2. It was classified as a medium-range anti-aircraft missile. The system included a broad-band radar that de-tected the target and a narrow-band radar to track the target, known by the NATO code-name 'Fan Song'. Guidance was by radio command. The missile was fired from a special launcher and used a booster that burned for four seconds to get the missile into the air, whereupon the sustainer motor burned for a further 22 seconds, giving the missile a maximum speed of 2,000mph and a range of 30 miles. Large numbers of sites were used by the North Vietnam-ese and the semi-mobile missiles were moved around among them, which meant that the Americans were never sure which sites were active.

The inflexible and predictable routes used by the B-52s had been specified by SAC headquarters and played a large part in the losses that were sustained.

---

[1] Quoted in Berry, F. Clinton, *Strike Aircraft*, Bantam Books (London), pp. 136–7.

When making a hard turn after dropping their bombs the B-52s increased their radar returns as banking the wings increased the radar cross-section of the aircraft and degraded the ECM coverage. The ECM antennas were placed under the wings, and when the wings were banked during a turn the antennas were masked. The tactic used by the missile operators was to make certain where the post-target turn would take place and then to fire missiles into this area as the bombers passed through. The SA-2 was equipped with a proximity fuse and this was set to explode at the bombers' altitude. The 350lb warhead was large enough to destroy a B-52 even if it exploded close to the aircraft. The bombers' ECM operators reported that in a large number of missile launches they could not detect either the radio command signals to the missile or the down-link signals from the missile to the ground. This suggested that the missiles had been fired without guidance. This tactic, of course, neutralised the capabilities the 'Wild Weasels' and the jamming aircraft. MiG-21s were used by the North Vietnamese to shadow the bomber streams and report the exact height at which they were operating, in order to minimise the use of ground radars. With the long streams of B-52s approaching the target at exactly the same height, speed and course over a period of nine hours, the North Vietnamese had time to focus their response.

Chaff corridors had been laid into the Hanoi area three times during the first night to cover each of the three waves of bombers, but the 100mph winds that had increased the bombers' speed into the target area had also to a large extent dispersed the chaff. This led to a change of tactics, and rather than form corridors it was decided to create chaff clouds over the target, where the striking aircraft were most vulnerable. The chaff corridors also gave advance warning of the routes to be flown by the bombers, and larger clouds gave more room for manoeuvring by the bombers. The chaff was still at the mercy of the weather, and high winds could create holes or disperse the chaff. In any case, the North Vietnamese tactic of firing a proportion of the SA-2 missiles without guidance meant that the effectiveness of the chaff was limited.

Although three bombers were shot down, the B-52s managed to account for one MiG. In the B-52G the tail gunner sat in the front of the aircraft with the other five crew members and controlled the tail gun with radar, but in the B-52D the gunner sat in the tail of the aircraft, separated from the other crew members. Sergeant Samuel O. Turner was a tail gunner in a B-52D operating from U-Tapao and part of the first wave to attack. Turner described the destruction of the MiG:

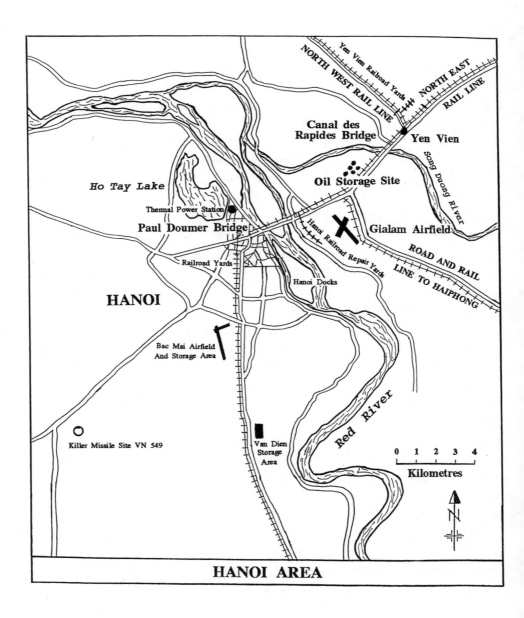

HANOI AREA

As we drew nearer to the target the intensity of the SAMs picked up. They were lightening up the sky. They seemed to be everywhere. We released our bombs over the target and had just proceeded outbound from the target when we learned that there were MiG aircraft airborne near a particular reference point . . . before long we learned the enemy fighter had us on its radar. As he closed on us I also picked him up on my radar when he was a few miles from our aircraft . . . A few seconds later, the fighter locked on to us. As the MiG closed in, I also locked on to him. He came in low in a rapid climb . . . As the attacking MiG came into firing range, I fired a burst. There was a gigantic explosion to the rear of the aircraft.[1]

Turner was credited with the destruction of the MiG.

The bombing campaign had started during some of the worst weather of the year, the middle of the north-east monsoon. Low cloud covered the Hanoi region for most of the day. During the whole of the 'Linebacker II' campaign the total amount of time when the weather was clear enough to allow visual bombing, including laser-guided bombing, amounted to twelve hours, occurring only during the afternoons of 21, 27 and 29 December. This did not affect the B-52s, the F-111s or the A-6s but it did restrict the other tactical bombers. Thus the campaign became almost exclusively a B-52 affair, the support given during the day by the tactical bombers being severely restricted.

In the evening of the 19th the B-52s were preparing to take off as the last aircraft that had bombed Hanoi the night before were landing. The planning for the raids had to be completed 42 hours before take-off time to allow the support forces to be organised. The second night's raid was to be a repeat of the first, with three waves of bombers following exactly the same course to the targets. The commander of SAC, General Meyer, considered that the three losses on the 18th were an acceptable total and did not deem it necessary to change the approach route.

The waves of bombers were again to strike at approximately 2000 hours, midnight and 0500 hours, and the targets were Yen Vien, Kinh Ho and the Hanoi radio station once more, plus the Thai Nguyen thermal power plant and the Bac Giang trans-shipment point. Included in the bombing were 96 B-52s. All the bombers hit their targets and no aircraft were lost, although two B-52s in the second wave were damaged by missile near-misses. It was estimated that a total of 180 SA-2s were fired at the attacking bombers during the second night.

---

[1] Futrell, R. Frank, et al., *Aces and Aerial Victories: The United States Air Force in Southeast Asia 1965–73*, Office of Air Force History (Washington, 1976), pp. 111–12.

The F-111s were used during 'Linebacker II' to attack the airfields just before the waves of B-52s arrived, to reduce the threat of the MiGs to the bombers. It had taken a long development period to get the F-111's attack system working correctly, but by December 1972 the aircraft were equipped with the Air Force's only tactical all-weather system. The terrain-following radar on the F-111 allowed the aircraft to cruise at 200ft above the ground, at 500mph, in any weather and at night. Provided the target gave a clear radar signature, the F-111 could attack from 200ft with little or no warning. At its operating altitude the F-111 was safe from the North Vietnamese radar and the SA-2 missiles. The attacks on the airfields destroyed few if any aircraft, but twelve 500lb bombs dropped on the airfield minutes before the B-52s arrived did disrupt North Vietnamese fighter operations.

On 19 December President Nixon extended the 'Linebacker' campaign indefinitely. The fact that that no B-52s had been lost on the second day was used to justify the planning and routes used during the first two days. The attack on the night of the 20th was again made up of three waves of aircraft following the same routes. This time 99 B-52s were to attack the Yen Vien rail yards, the Thai Nguyen thermal power plant again and the oil storage facilities at Kinh Ho and Hanoi. Also targeted were the Bac Giang trans-shipment point, the Hanoi storage area at Gia Thuong and three missile sites. The first wave of B-52s was made up of 33 aircraft in eleven cells. The first 27 bombers were to attack the railyard at Yen Vien. The pilots of the B-52s again reported that MiGs appeared to be shadowing the bombers and it was assumed that they reported the bombers' height, speed and direction to the ground controllers. Three aircraft in the attacking force were hit by missiles and brought down, two being destroyed over Hanoi and one making it back to Thailand where the crew ejected. Captain Rolland Scott, the pilot of one of the attacking B-52s, described the scene:

[The missiles] arrived in pairs, just a few seconds apart. Some, as they passed, would explode—a few close enough to shake my aircraft. I could see SAM activity ahead in the vicinity of the target. In fact, while on the run we saw a large ball of fire erupt and descend . . . and [I] was sure no one could survive what was apparently a direct hit. I later learned that what I saw was Quilt 3 [call-sign] going down in flames. Amazingly four crew members successfully ejected.[1]

---

[1] Quoted in Berry, op. cit., p. 139.

No 3 aircraft in the first cell, no 2 aircraft in the fourth cell and no 3 aircraft in the seventh cell had been shot down. All three of the aircraft destroyed were hit just before or just after the post-target turn. Two of the victims were B-52Gs with unmodified ECM equipment and one was a B-52D.

News of the losses was passed directly to SAC headquarters. There was an intense debate over whether or not to cancel the other two waves due to attack that night, but General Meyer finally gave the go-ahead for the raids to continue. He knew that if the raids were stopped then it would be difficult, if not impossible, ever to re-start them, and the whole existence of SAC and its mission would be called into doubt. If SAC could not bomb North Vietnam successfully, how could it claim to be able to bomb the Soviet Union?

The second wave of B-52 bombers attacked four hours after the first and consisted of aircraft fitted with the improved ECM equipment. Targets for this wave were the power plant at Thai Nguyen once again and the supply depot at Bac Giang. Both these targets were to the north and north-east of Hanoi and the bombers did not have to penetrate the main Hanoi defences. None of the bombers was destroyed or damaged. The third wave of B-52s approached its targets in the early hours and three of these were again in the Hanoi area. Following exactly the same route, the long line of bombers faced a waiting and prepared defence system dedicated to defending its homeland. Two B-52Gs were brought down over Hanoi and one B-52D was badly damaged and crashed in Laos.

During the night six B-52s had been shot down with one B-52D badly damaged. Three aircraft had been hit before bomb release and three in the post-target turn. It was estimated that 220 SA-2 missiles had been fired. It was obvious that the North Vietnamese had developed a crude but effective method of defeating the B-52s by firing a high proportion of their anti-aircraft missiles into the bomber stream without guidance but set to explode at their height. There was no way that SAC could sustain six losses a night, especially now that the campaign had been made indefinite.

Nixon was infuriated by the high loss rate. He had expected losses, but not at this level: it would send exactly the wrong message to the North Vietnamese. Nixon had wanted a crushing blow but the North Vietnamese could claim, with some justification, to be winning the campaign if they could continue to shoot down the bombers in such numbers.

The morale amongst the B-52 crews by the end of the third night had seen something of a collapse as they were forced to fly routes and schedules they knew were wrong. The numbers of aircrew reporting sick increased, and it was reported that some crews exaggerated maintenance problems with their aircraft in order to avoid flying. At U-Tapao, with the missions only lasting four hours, some of the aircrews were flying every night. Men began to complain bitterly to their commanders, demanding a change in tactics. They had been called upon to carry out a campaign for which they had been neither prepared nor trained. For the nuclear mission SAC pilots had been trained to act individually and had little experience of large-scale formation flying. However, even though morale fell, there was only one reported instance of a pilot refusing to fly.

The aircrew blamed the losses on the tactics being used by SAC headquarters. A special tactics panel was set up at U-Tapao on the 21st, chaired by Colonel Brown, to facilitate a discussion of the crews' views on the mission planning. Headquarters SAC now passed the responsibility for planning the raids to General Johnson, commanding the Eighth Air Force. The tactics panel recommended that the routes should be changed for every raid, that the bombers should be compressed in time in order to overwhelm the defences, that the altitude of the bombers should be varied with random changes and that post-target turns should be avoided. In 1942 the Royal Air Force had been forced to learn the same lesson about compressing bombing streams into as small a timescale as possible in order to pass through the German Kammhuber air defence line.

General Johnson accepted these recommendations, but they could only be implemented on the fifth day because of the delay involved in the planning process. The new tactics were almost exactly the same as the original plans submitted by Johnson in August 1972 but ignored by SAC. Johnson decided that the bombing on the night of the 21st would only be carried out by aircraft from U-Tapao using B-52Ds. This also allowed maintenance to catch up at Andersen after three days of sixteen-hour missions.

Taking part in the bombing on the 21st were 30 B-52Ds. Although the planning had already been prepared they were allowed to carry out all the bombing in a 15-minute period and the post-target turns permitted a course out of North Vietnam to the east, over the Gulf of Tonkin. Two of the bombers were shot down. One of the B-52s lost was flown by Captain Peter Giroux, who was leading a three-aircraft cell to attack the Bac Mai storage area. The radar in the B-52 failed and Giroux was forced to hand over the lead position to one of the following aircraft. As he tried to move to the rear position in the cell the aircraft was set upon by MiGs. In the manoeuvres to escape the attacking aircraft the ECM integrity of the three B-52s was lost and the aircraft flown by Giroux was hit by a missile and shot down. The crew ejected and were taken prisoner, although one crew member avoided capture until 3 January.

The second aircraft to be lost was flown by Lieutenant-Colonel Bill Conlee. As many as ten missiles exploded close to the aircraft as it approached the target, and following bomb release it was bracketed by two missiles exploding on either side. The B-52 crashed but the crew ejected. During the course of the night an F-4D from the 'Triple Nickel' at Udorn was credited with the destruction of a MiG. The pilot was Captain Gary L. Sholders, with Lieutenant Eldon D. Binkley as his radar operator. Sholders was flying a MiGCAP mission to cover the B-52s and after arriving in the Hanoi area he was vectored by 'Red Crown' on to a single MiG fighter. He pursued the MiG for nearly half an hour, never quite getting close enough to attack it. The MiG tried to land at Yen Bai airfield but was forced to break off its circuit and fly to the north. Sholders was finally forced to leave the area because of a fuel shortage. American intelligence later discovered that a MiG had crashed that night through lack of fuel, and its destruction was credited to Sholders 'due to continued pursuit which resulted in fuel starvation for the enemy aircraft'.

The new tactics were introduced in full on the fifth day of the campaign, the night of the 22nd. With the destruction of two more B-52s on the 21st General Meyer temporarily banned the bombing of targets in the immediate Hanoi area. Again it was only aircraft from U-Tapao that were taking part in the bombing on the 22nd, and the targets were the Haiphong railyards and oil storage tanks. Thirty B-52Ds were involved, and the route into North Vietnam was from the Gulf of Tonkin. In an attempt to confuse the defence system the bombers' course was made to appear to be heading for Hanoi but the aircraft then turned towards Haiphong. The B-52 stream divided into three and then divided again into six. Only 43 SA-2 missiles were counted as having been launched at the attacking aircraft, no aircraft were shot down or damaged and the target was claimed to be heavily bombed.

Haiphong being close to the coast, Navy aircraft had played the major role in supporting the B-52s, but one Air Force F-4E did destroy a MiG-21. Lieutenant-Colonel Jim Brunson was leading a flight of four MiGCAP F-4Es operating out of Udorn. When the flight arrived over North Vietnam it was vectored towards a flight of MiGs close to Hanoi. The MiGs were at 29,000ft, 10,000ft above Brunson's aircraft. 'Red Crown' would not give clearance to fire without visual recognition and Brunson was forced to close head-on with the MiGs. He saw a silver MiG-21 flying above him, obtained a radar lock-on and fired four Sparrow missiles. The first missile guided and hit the MiG, blowing off the tail section and sending the aircraft into an uncontrollable spin.

The targets for the sixth day of the campaign, 23 December, were to include missile sites to the north-east of Hanoi. This time twelve B-52s from Andersen joined eighteen from U-Tapao to carry out the raid. The bombers' course took them into North Vietnam from the Gulf of Tonkin, close to the Chinese border, before six of them attacked the missile sites and the remainder the railyards at Lang Dang. The bombers suffered no losses or damage, even though the support aircraft were late arriving because of a misunderstanding. The routes had again been varied, with random changes of height, speed and direction.

The raids on the 24th involved 30 B-52s from U-Tapao. The crews from Thailand had been flying most of the missions, and 22 crews from Guam were flown in to relieve the pressure. The targets for the seventh day of the campaign were the railyards at Thai Nguyen and Kep, both north of Hanoi. The bomber stream, supported by 69 other aircraft, entered North Vietnam from Laos and flew close to the Chinese border before turning south to hit the targets. No aircraft were lost and only one was damaged. The tail gunner in one of the B-52s attacking Thai Nguyen, Airman First Class Albert E. Moore, was credited with the destruction of a MiG-21 that had attacked his aircraft. He had picked up the MiG on his radar screen at 4,000yds and told his pilot to fire flares and chaff. As the MiG continued to close he opened fire at 2,000yds with his four 0.5in machine guns and the MiG was seen by another tail-gunner to be 'on fire and falling away'.

President Nixon ordered a halt to the bombing for 36 hours during the Christmas period; he also ordered that a resumption of the bombing on the 26th was to be a maximum effort. On 22 December Nixon had asked the North Vietnamese for a resumption of talks to begin on 3 January 1973 but had received no response. The bombers had been claiming that a high percentage of the B-52s had been hitting their targets and that most targets had been heavily damaged. However, some seem to have been attacked for several night running, indicating that the earlier attacks may not have been as successful as claimed. Commander Joseph Austley was the pilot of an RA-5C Vigilante reconnaissance aircraft operating from the USS *Ranger* during 'Linebacker II' which carried out photographic reconnaissance missions to record the damage after the B-52 raids. He described the damage caused:

... we'd go in the next day and not really find that much damage. I think the bombing damaged morale, but the way the North Vietnamese and Orientals work, they'd have fires out and everything out. There'd be no residuals, nothing.[1]

There were a few voices that maintained that the bombing was not as effective as claimed.

During the the day on the 26th the weather was too poor to allow visual bombing but the Air Force used LORAN to attack targets in Hanoi. The main target was a missile assembly site and this was attacked through cloud by sixteen F-4s. It was claimed that the site was destroyed, but there is some doubt about this.

The plan for the B-52s to bomb during the night of the 26th was a highly complex and detailed effort to make use of the experience gained by the earlier bombing. Involved in the raid were 120 B-52s, including aircraft from both Guam and Thailand. The raid was carried out on ten targets. These comprised seven in or close to Hanoi, two in Haiphong and the railyard at Thai Nguyen. The bomber stream was divided into seven waves, two waves of fifteen air-craft each to attack Haiphong, one of eighteen B-52s to attack Thai Nguyen and four totalling 72 aircraft to bomb Hanoi. All the waves of bombers approached their targets from a different direction and randomly varied their height and course. Two waves of bombers approached Hanoi from the west and two from the east. One wave of bombers attacked Haiphong from the north-east and one from the south-east. All the lead aircraft in each wave of bombers had the same initial time on target, 2230 hours. The entire fleet of bombers dropped 4,000 tons of bombs in a fifteen-minute period. Although this was a highly complex plan, it worked well in practice.

In support of the B-52s were 113 tactical aircraft from the Navy and Air Force. 'Iron Hand' and 'Wild Weasel' aircraft attacked 30 missile sites during the 26th to keep B-52 losses to a minimum, but the North Vietnamese had used the period after the 20th during which Hanoi had not been attacked to re-supply their missile sites around the capital and large numbers of SA-2s were fired at the B-52s. The commander of Wave I was Colonel James R. McCarthy, and he noted at least 26 SA-2s launched at his aircraft before he gave up counting. Two of the B-52s were lost to the North Vietnamese defences. One was hit over Hanoi and exploded in a ball of flame that 'lit up the sky for miles around', although four of the crew survived. The other B-52 to be lost was

---

[1] Levinson, Jeffery L., *Alpha Strike Vietnam*, Presidio Press (California, 1989), pp. 294–5.

badly damaged during the raid. The pilot managed to keep the aircraft in the air but crashed while trying to land at U-Tapao. Captain Brent O. Diefenback had flown one of the B-52s that had just landed at U-Tapao and he ran to the crashed aircraft and pulled the co-pilot from the burning wreck. He was awarded the Airman's Medal. The tail gunner had been thrown clear but the four other crew members died. Both the B-52s hit by missiles had been in two-aircraft cells, the third aircraft in each having aborted the mission, and it was thought that this had given insufficient ECM coverage. Hence it was decided that there should be no more two-aircraft cells: aircraft would join up with the cells in front or behind them in the bomber stream. The plan had been complex but was judged to have been a success. The loss of two B-52s from 120 was a loss rate of 1.66 per cent, within the acceptable limits. The attacks on the 26th have been called the most effective bombing raid in history.

The North Vietnamese notified President Nixon on the 27th that they would attend meetings in Paris on 8 January. Nixon insisted that there must be a time limit to the talks and that the North Vietnamese must be serious and not go back over agreements already reached. He promised the North Vietnamese that all bombing north of the 20th Parallel would cease within 36 hours of their agreement.

The weather during the afternoon of the 27th was clear and the F-4s operating from Thailand were able to carry out laser-guided bomb attacks in the Hanoi area. One of the F-4s, flown by Carl Jeffcoat and Jack Tremble, was lost over the North. They were part of a MiGCAP flight and as they released their wing tanks the Phantom exploded into flames. It is not known what hit their aircraft or even if their fuel tanks exploded. They ejected and were taken prisoner. The B-52 bombing continued on the night of the 27th as no reply had been received from the North.

The ninth day of the bombing involved 30 B-52s from U-Tapao and 30 more from Andersen, supported by 101 Navy and Air Force aircraft. Most of the targets were close to Hanoi, including three missile sites, except for the Lang Dang railyard close to the Chinese border. Haiphong was not attacked because it was thought that no worthwhile targets were left. The bombers operated in six waves against seven targets. The B-52s again followed various routes; the first aircraft dropped its bombs at 2259 hours and the last one ten minutes later. Two of the B-52s were shot down: one crashed close to its target and the other, flown by Captain John Mize, was hit after bomb release although Mize managed to keep flying until the aircraft was over friendly territory. Mize had bombed SA-2 missile site VN-243, but photo reconnaissance later showed no damage. As he was leaving the target area Captain Mize counted fifteen missiles aimed at his aircraft. It is thought that Mize's B-52 was hit by a missile launched from VN-549 (the 'Killer Site'), which was known to be the most effective of the Vietnamese sites. Mize's B-52 was hit in the left wing, knocking out all the engines on that side. He struggled to keep the aircraft in the air until it reached Laos, where the crew bailed out. All the crewmen had been injured and received Purple Hearts, and Captain Mize was awarded the Air Force Cross.

On the 28th President Nixon received a reply from the North Vietnamese to his message sent on the 27th. The reply was that Le Duc Tho had been ill, which had delayed the talks, and that the North Vietnamese were 'serious' about the negotiations, which could start between technical representatives on 2 January with the main talks beginning on the 8th. Nixon considered that this was a complete capitulation by the North Vietnamese and that the bombing had achieved its purpose. He ordered that all bombing should stop north of the 20th Parallel after 36 hours, which meant that the attacks during the nights of the 28th and 29th would continue. During the day on the 28th both the Navy and the Air Force shot down a MiG over the North. A Navy F-4J operating from *Enterprise* shot down a MiG-21, and an F-4 from the 555th TFS flown by Major Harry L. McKee with Captain John E. Dubler as his radar operator shot down a MiG-21 west of Hanoi at 2157 hours using an AIM-7 Sparrow missile. A MiG-21 shot down an RA-5C Vigilante reconnaissance aircraft during the day.

During the night of the 28th 60 B-52s again took off to bomb targets in the North. Thirty aircraft from U-Tapao and thirty from Andersen attacked missile sites and a missile storage area close to Hanoi and the Lang Dang railyard. The initial time over target was 2215 hours, eighteen minutes after the MiG-21 had been shot down by McKee and Dubler. The bombers were supported by 99 tactical aircraft. Very few missiles were launched at the bombers and no B-52s were damaged or lost. The tactics used by the B-52 and the fact that the North Vietnamese were running short of ammunition and missiles meant that the big bombers could now operate at will.

The eleventh and final night of the campaign was 29 December. The plan was for 30 bombers from Thailand and 30 from Guam to carry out the attacks, but one aircraft from Guam turned back with faulty refuelling equipment. The targets were two missile storage areas near Hanoi and, again, the Lang Dang railyard. The first bombs fell at 2320 hours and the last bomb at 2343. The crews reported that the few missiles encountered seemed to be fired erratically, and only one MiG was seen. All 59 B-52s claimed to have bombed their targets, and no aircraft were hit or damaged.

In eleven days of bombing fifteen of the B-52s had been destroyed by the North Vietnamese and nine badly damaged. These fifteen aircraft had carried a total of 92 crewmen. Of these, 26 were rescued by American forces, 34 became prisoners (one died in captivity) and 28 are listed as missing in action; four died on the runway at U-Tapao. The B-52s had flown 729 sorties over the North during the campaign, 340 from Thailand and 389 from Guam, and had dropped 49,000 bombs weighing 15,000 tons on to 34 targets. After the targets had been photographed it was claimed that 1,600 military structures had been damaged and 372 pieces of rolling stock destroyed. The transport system infrastructure was also claimed to have been heavily bombed, with roads and bridges badly damaged. The North Vietnamese power generation system had also been heavily damaged and a quarter of the North's oil reserves were thought to have been destroyed. Estimates put the numbers of SA-2 missiles fired at the bombers during the eleven-day campaign at 1,242. Original estimates on the bombers' loss rate had been 3 per cent of attacking forces and the final, actual loss rate was 2.05 per cent. The SA-2 missile system had only destroyed one B-52 for every 83 missiles fired. Seven MiG fighters were shot down during the eleven days. The Air Force had lost two F-4 fighters, two F-111s and fifteen B-52s; the Navy had lost one F-4, two A-7s, two A-6As, one RA-5C and one SH-3A rescue helicopter shot down over the North.

During 'Linebacker II' the Air Force had also flown 830 tactical sorties and the Navy and Marines 386. Together the tactical aircraft had dropped 5,000 tons of bombs on targets north of the 20th Parallel as part of the 'Linebacker II' campaign. President Nixon was certain that the bombing had achieved his original goals. When the North Vietnamese agreed to return to the talks he was quoted as saying, 'They can't take bombing any longer. Our Air Force really did the job.'[1] However, the response to the bombing among large parts of the American public was less enthusiastic. The scale and impact of the bombing had come as a shock to many people, especially as they had been told that 'peace is at hand' only a short time before. Nixon's popularity rating was instantly reduced to 39 per cent—and this was only weeks after he had been

[1] Colson, Charles W., *Born Again*, Chosen Books (New Jersey, 1976), p. 78.

elected with an enormous majority. The peace faction in Congress made it clear that it would oppose Nixon, and try to stop the bombing, when Congress reconvened.

The American press was highly critical of Nixon and the bombing, which was seen as an escalation of the war, at a time when everybody seemed to want peace. In other countries the press also attacked the bombing with comments such as 'a crime against humanity' and 'an attack on the peace process'. China's reaction to the bombing was much stronger than Nixon had expected. With the 'Linebacker I' bombing her response had been muted, but the 'Linebacker II' bombing was denounced in strong terms. Although the Soviets still wanted *détente* with the United States to continue, they joined the Chinese in strongly condemning the bombing.

The peace talks started in Paris on 2 January with the technical representatives taking part. The first meeting between Kissinger and Le Duc Tho was on the 8th. Although the feeling at the talks was strained, it became apparent that the North Vietnamese wanted a settlement. They had decided that they could not wait for the Americans to leave and they did not want a resumption of the bombing. In the South the North Vietnamese Army had reached exhaustion and would welcome a ceasefire to allow them to rebuild. The basic aims of the Northern leadership had not changed, but they had modified their short-term views about reaching a settlement. Le Duc Tho accepted the draft agreement that had been drawn up in late November. The DMZ was mentioned in the agreement but only as a 'provisional boundary'. Another change was the toning down of the description of the Council of Reconciliation and Concord in line with President Thieu's demands. However, the differences between the October agreement and the final agreement were minor. By 13 January the agreement had been drawn up, Nixon stopped all bombing of North Vietnam on the 15th and the final peace treaty was signed on the 23rd.

President Thieu had been told by Richard Nixon as early as 18 December that he, Nixon, was intent on reaching an agreement and that he would sign one with or without the South Vietnamese leader's approval. General Haig carried a letter to Thieu setting out the American position. Thieu was told that if he signed an agreement he would enjoy continued American backing and increased aid, but if he did not sign he would be on his own. Once it was expressed in these terms Thieu had no real choice but to sign. If this level of pressure had been put on Thieu to sign in October then 'Linebacker II' would not have been necessary, although the fact that Thieu was reluctant to sign a treaty that left 200,000 enemy troops within the borders of his country can be easily understood.

To bring Thieu into line Nixon promised that he would respond militarily if the North Vietnamese violated any of the agreements. In a letter to Thieu on 5 January Nixon wrote: 'We will respond with full force should the settlement be violated by North Vietnam.'[1] The fact that Nixon was forced to resign and in any case had his hands tied by Congress meant that he could never live up to the promises made to Thieu. Although the agreement was signed on the 23rd in Paris by Kissinger and Le Duc Tho, the ceasefire only came into force on 27 January. The Americans would get their prisoners back, but whether it was the 'peace with honour' that Nixon wanted is debatable. The South Vietnamese Government never formally ratified the agreement.

The Democrats in both the Senate and the House of Representatives voted amongst themselves on 2 January to cut off all funds for the war in South-East Asia, provided the prisoners were returned and all American personnel could be withdrawn. These were only internal party votes, but it was obvious that it was only a matter of time before the power to make decisions about the Vietnam War was taken out of Nixon's hands.

The last MiG 'kill' by the US Air Force was on 8 January. The bombing south of the 20th Parallel had continued and fighter aircraft were permitted to attack North Vietnamese aircraft north of the Parallel. Captain Paul D. Howman and his WSO Lieutenant Lawrence W. Kullman were flying a MiGCAP in the area south-west of Hanoi when they were alerted by 'Red Crown' that a MiG was airborne from Phuc Yen and heading south towards the American aircraft attacking targets south of the 20th Parallel. Howman was flying an F-4D from the 4th TFS at Udorn and was vectored towards the MiG at 0230 hours. Howman described the events leading up to the destruction of the MiG:

At 10 miles I got a visual on an afterburner plume 20 degrees right and slightly high. I called him out to the backseater and put the pipper on him. At 6 miles Lt Kullman got a good full-system lock-on. Range was about 4 miles and overtake 900+ knots when I squeezed the trigger. The missile came off, did a little roll to the left, and tracked towards the 'burner plume.' It detonated about 50 feet short of his tail. I squeezed another one off at 2 miles' range. This one just pulled some lead, then went straight for the MiG. It hit him in the fuselage and the airplane exploded and broke into three big flaming pieces.[2]

---

[1] Hung, Tien Nguyen, and Schecter, Jerrold L., *The Palace File: Vietnam Secret Documents*, Harper & Row (New York, 1986), App. A.

[2] Drew, Middleton, *Air War Vietnam*, Arms & Armour Press (London, 1978), p. 290.

No other airborne MiGs were detected that night.

The last occasion on which Navy aircraft shot down a MiG occurred on 12 January. This was also the last aircraft shot down by the Americans in the Vietnam War. Lieutenant Victor T. Kovaleski was flying an F-4B from the USS *Midway* on a BARCAP mission with his radar operator Lieutenant James A. Wise. Using a Sidewinder, Kovaleski shot down a MiG-17. Two days later he was himself downed by anti-aircraft fire over North Vietnam while escorting a reconnaissance aircraft near Than Hoa. This was the last aircraft shot down in the war. Both crew members were recovered.

The B-52s continued to bomb North Vietnam below the 20th Parallel before the bombing was stopped completely on the 15th. The B-52s carried out 532 sorties, during which they bombed mainly transport targets, including transshipment points, storage areas and truck parks. The B-52 'Arc Light' missions continued over South Vietnam until the ceasefire on 27 January. The tactical aircraft of the Air Force and Navy also carried out 716 sorties over the North before the 15th.

CHAPTER 11

THE NORTH VIETNAMESE REACTION

NORTH Vietnam did not prove to be the ideal candidate to receive the attention of a strategic bombing campaign. During 'Linebacker I' over 155,000 tons of bombs had been dropped on North Vietnam and during 'Linebacker II' 20,000 tons had been dropped during an eleven-day period. But North Vietnam had not collapsed under the bombing. Although massive damage was done to the North's transport system and industry, the North Vietnamese had managed to maintain a movement of stores and equipment to the South. The NVA in the South had not collapsed but had maintained its position until driven back by the South Vietnamese Army and had continued to hold on to some territory. The North Vietnamese had been bombed for 3½ years between 1965 and 1968 and had learned the hard way how to survive under a strategic bombing campaign. All the systems and techniques they had developed to allow them to continue to function were again put into operation during the 'Linebacker' campaigns.

North Vietnam had been created by the 1954 peace settlement that ended the French Indo-China war. At the Geneva Conference Vietnam had been divided into North and South, with the Viet Minh, victors of the war, controlling the North. Ho Chi Minh did not want the division but knew it was the best settlement he could have achieved from the peace talks. The two halves of the country were supposed to be re-joined after democratic elections had decided the wishes of the people. But the elections never took place because it was thought, in the South, that Ho Chi Minh was popular enough to have a good chance of winning. Originally Ho thought that the regime in the South would collapse of its own accord, and all he had to do was wait for the country to be reunited. After the agreement in 1954 at least 90,000 Viet Minh from the South moved North, as part of the settlement, after burying their weapons in the South. It was these people who formed the origins of the Viet Cong.

Diem, the South's president, started a programme to return large sections of land that had been taken over by the peasants to the original landlords. This was enormously unpopular and caused considerable unrest. In order to control this movement against him Diem ordered a massive campaign against anyone who was suspected of being a communist sympathiser. Hundreds of thousands of people were arrested and thousands killed. Although Ho Chi Minh had originally thought that the regime in the South would collapse, the killing of thousands of communist followers in the South and the worsening position of the peasant class meant that, from the Northern viewpoint, he was forced to support the communists in the South.

The communist party of North Vietnam was known as the Lao Dong party, and the Fifteenth Plenum of the Party Central Committee meeting in 1959 was the crucial moment when the Party decided that the North would support the communists in the South, in order to reunify Vietnam. The Northern leadership was a closely knit group who had known and worked with each other for many years. There were disagreements amongst the leadership, but these were always kept within the group, and a policy was finally agreed upon that all would support. Even during the height of the bombing there was no real threat to the leadership. All the members of the Politburo had spent time in jails, either French or Japanese. They had dedicated their lives to an independent Vietnam. The overall leader was Ho Chi Minh (real name Nguyen That Thanh), a life-long communist and Vietnamese nationalist. Ho's position was that of Chairman: he chose the goals and the direction the North would take, and the other members of the Politburo would devise the policies that would be followed in order to attain these goals.

Amongst the eleven members of the Politburo the most influential were the following. The North Vietnamese Prime Minister was Pham Van Dong, a long-time supporter of Ho Chi Minh. He had been born in the South of the country but had spent most of his life in the North. Vo Nguyen Giap was the major military figure in the war against the French, and his name is always connected with the defeat of South Vietnam. Giap was a former history teacher whose wife had died in prison. He had been fighting against the French since his early teenage years. Le Duan was a Southerner and had led the war against the French in the South of the country. When he became a member of the Politburo he was the leading protagonist for the war in the South against Diem, and then against the Americans. Le Duc Tho was awarded the Nobel Peace Prize along with Kissinger, but, unlike Kissinger, he never accepted it. Tho was born in the North of the country close to Hanoi but worked with Le Duan in the South. He was a leading supporter of the war in the South.

The eleven men in the Politburo were a closed group of people held in position by an autocratic political system; the same system produced in the Soviet Union a leadership that only changed with death and bred inefficiency. The North Vietnamese leaders had been involved in a war for most of their adult lives, and this had removed any traces of incompetence. The Politburo organised and ran the war against South Vietnam and the United States as well as could be expected of a third-world country fighting a superpower. Whether they ran the peace after the war as efficiently is another story. The Americans had a view of the North Vietnamese as being part of some worldwide communist conspiracy, aiming for world dominance, but although the North Vietnamese received aid from the Soviets and the Chinese they can better be seen as militant nationalists who took aid from wherever they could find it.

The North Vietnamese held their Third Party Congress in 1960. The final outcome of the Congress was that the overall strategy should be, first, to carry out the socialist revolution in the North, and secondly to liberate the South from the rule of the American imperialists and their henchmen and achieve national reunification and complete independence and freedom throughout the country. For the next fifteen years the North Vietnamese followed this strategy until they destroyed South Vietnam in 1975. Although the two points agreed at the Congress do not seem to be in conflict, there was considerable disagreement amongst the North Vietnamese leadership over which should be given the greater weight. There was no disagreement over the general direction of policy but only over which aspect should come first—the creation of a strong, stable North Vietnam, or unification, possibly using force, with South Vietnam.

The members of the Politburo who supported the building of a strong North Vietnam first had originally believed that South Vietnam would collapse without any outside help from the North and that the popularity of Ho Chi Minh would carry the South into the control of the North. But after Diem, with the help of the Americans, had strengthened his position this did not seem likely to happen. The 'North-firsters' contended that the development and the industrial and social strengthening of North Vietnam would be a better long-term strategy than even a small-scale involvement in a war in the South.The other view was that the insurrection that was beginning in the South should be supported, even if this would delay or slow down the development in the North. There was very little support for the fighting in the South from the North during the late 1950s and early 1960s. The fighting was basically a reaction to

Diem's policies and used the arms and equipment stored after the 1954 settlement. The 'North-first' faction is believed to have included General Giap and Prime Minister Dong, while the leading advocates of the war in the South were Le Duan and Pham Hung. Ho Chi Minh seems to have take a neutral position and left the discussions to his lieutenants. By 1960 the Southern faction had gained dominance in the Politburo.

General Giap is always credited in the West with being the architect of the military side of the Vietnam War, and to a large extent this is true, but he was never one of the original supporters of the war in the South. He had been modernising the armed forces and did not want to see them committed to a conflict of unification. However, as a loyal member of the Politburo he carried out the decisions of the majority. The Viet Minh forces, 90,000 strong, that had moved North after the end of the war with France provided the first contingent sent from the North to the growing insurrection in the South, and a force of North Vietnamese regular troops established a presence in Laos to aid the passage of the forces returning to the South. However, the majority of the people and the arms came from within South Vietnam during the early years of the war.

The North Vietnamese government seems to have followed the same slow process of escalation into the war that the Americans followed. Gradually more and more effort was committed to the South, and as this effort increased the North Vietnamese were forced to turn to both the Soviet Union and China for the hardware and money to continue. In 1960 the Chinese were the major suppliers of arms to North Vietnam but by 1964 the Soviets had supplanted the Chinese and were furnishing large amounts of aid to the North. This aid included industrial machinery, oil and petroleum, ships and military equipment. The Soviets continued to increase their aid throughout the war, and did so even after President Nixon had visited Moscow in 1972. Although they were no longer the major supplier the Chinese continued to provide small arms, ammunition, artillery and food. The Vietnamese were quite willing to take aid from the Chinese but were reluctant to take any advice. For most of Vietnamese history China had been the country's natural enemy and a border war was fought between the two in 1980. There are still major differences between Vietnam and China, including sovereignty of the Spratly and Paracel Islands. After the Vietnam War many ethnic Chinese were forced out of Vietnam. Even though China supplied Vietnam with aid this gave them very little leverage with the Vietnamese, and despite the North Vietnamese' total dependence on

Soviet aid the Soviets told Kissinger in 1971 that they had very little influence over the conduct of the North Vietnamese either. The Northern leadership had not been fighting all their lives for an independent Vietnam to hand control over to anybody.

Ho Chi Minh's view was that the war would be a long one and that this would favour the North Vietnamese. He thought the Americans would not be committed to a long, inconclusive conflict and that without American help the regime in the South could not survive. Speaking in 1966 Ho Chi Minh said,

> The war may last another five, ten, twenty years or longer. Hanoi, Haiphong and other cities may be destroyed, but the Vietnamese people will not be intimidated. Nothing is more precious than independence and freedom.[1]

The Northern leadership were prepared to wait until the Americans had had enough. Pham Van Dong, the Prime Minister, supported the 'long war' view and he observed that 'Americans do not like long, inconclusive wars . . . thus we are sure to win in the end.'[2] Although they did plan for a 'long war', it is doubtful whether the Northern leadership realised how long and how destructive the conflict would be. It was part of their tactics to prepare the population for the privations and the horrors of the war that would be inflicted on the North.

As the war in the South developed the numbers of people and the amount of aid sent from the North also increased. At the Ninth Plenum meeting of the Central Committee in December 1963 the faction within the Northern leadership that believed in achieving the unification of the country by armed intervention became the dominant force. Le Duan, who had become First Secretary, carried the Central Committee with him in stressing the need to bring the war in the South to a conclusion, as a first priority. He believed that the continuation of the revolution, and the development in the North, could wait until the country had been unified.

It was estimated that by 1964 all of the Southern Viet Minh who had moved to the North after the 1954 settlement and had wanted to return to the war in the South had gone. Between 1959 and 1964 around 20,000 infiltrators had been sent from the North to the South down the Ho Chi Minh Trail. The vast majority of the Viet Cong operating in the South at this time were still were Southerners, fighting against what they saw as corrupt governments. Although

---

[1] Hai Thu, *North Vietnam against US Air Force*, Foreign Languages Publishing House (Hanoi, 1967), p. 9.

[2] Van Dyke, John M., *North Vietnam's Strategy for Survival*, Pacific Books (California, 1972), pp. 30–1.

the Diem regime had been removed in 1963, the following military govern-ments were no more representative. The first regular Northern Army unit to be infiltrated into the South was the 95th Regiment of the 325th Division in De-cember 1964. From that time the Northern Army would play an increasingly important role and the part played by the Southern Viet Cong would slowly decrease. The final take-over of the South in 1975 was a conventional inva-sion by regular Northern forces.

The Northern Army slowly increased in size to provide the manpower needed. In 1959 conscription was extended to all males between 16 and 45, for a pe-riod of two years in the armed forces, increased in 1964 to three years and in 1965 to an indefinite period. By 1965 the size of the North Vietnamese Army had grown to 250,000 and by 1975 it was 650,000. As late as 1980 the North Vietnamese had one million men under arms, making it the fourth largest army in the world. In the early 1970s the North Vietnamese had 190,000 youths reaching the required age and 120,000 of these were taken into the Army each year. The militia was also increased in size, and those able-bodied people not in the Army were conscripted into the militia. Each village and factory had its own unit.

The Americans started bombing North Vietnam in 1964 in individual at-tacks and continuously in the 'Rolling Thunder' campaign in 1965. The main aim of the bombing was to stop the North Vietnamese support for the war in the South. The bombing continued for 3½ years, but during this period the North Vietnamese increased the number of men and the amount of supplies provided for the war in the South. With the massive Tet offensive in 1968 nobody could doubt that the North Vietnamese had still managed to continue their support for the war in the South, even after three years of bombing. By the time President Johnson stopped the bombing in 1968 the North Vietnam-ese had developed considerable knowledge and expertise in how to continue military operations, and when the 'Linebacker' bombing campaigns began in 1972 they were already well experienced in keeping their country running under aerial attack.

During 'Rolling Thunder' the North Vietnamese had developed an active and a passive defence to the bombing. The active aspect was massively to increase the North's air defence system to include fighter aircraft, SA-2 mis-siles and large numbers of anti-aircraft guns, controlled by radar systems. This active defence managed to shoot down over 900 American aircraft during 'Roll-ing Thunder'. The air defence system had been strengthened and modernised

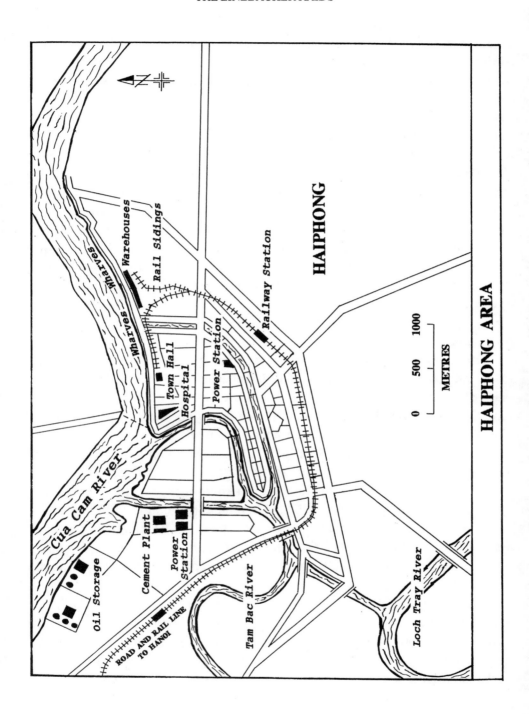

HAIPHONG AREA

by the start of 'Linebacker I', but so had the American reaction to it. The passive aspect of the North Vietnamese reaction to the bombing was the development of air raid shelters, a civil defence system, evacuation, rationing, the dispersal of industry and the construction of alternative transport routes. While the damage caused by the bombing was enormous, the North Vietnamese managed to change their society to allow them to contain the effects of the bombing, and learned to live with it. All these measures were again used when the 'Linebacker' campaign started.

The North Vietnamese character was one of the main assets available to the Northern leadership. The essentially stoic attitude to the bombing shown by the people of North Vietnam allowed them to continue to live and operate under the bombing. The country had an overwhelmingly agrarian society, and the expectations of the people were modest and their aspirations limited. The Vietnamese had a long history of struggle going back hundreds of years. Prime Minister Pham Van Dong is quoted as saying,

> What is our history? There is nothing else in our history except struggle. Struggle against foreign invaders, always more powerful than ourselves; struggle against nature—and we've had nowhere else to go, we've had to fight things out where we were . . . And whatever new situation arises, our people say, 'Ah, well, there it goes again.'[1]

There were times when the morale of the North Vietnamese did slump, but it never came near to cracking.

The main components of the North Vietnamese transport system were the rail lines into China in the North and the port of Haiphong, and the major proportion of the aid coming into the country arrived via these links. During the war with the French most of the transport system had been destroyed, so the North Vietnamese had already had the experience of rebuilding their roads, bridges and rail lines. A system to keep the roads repaired was created, building materials being placed every few hundred yards at the sides of major routes. Many of the roads were only dirt roads, surfaced with crushed rock, and bomb craters only required infilling and the surface re-covering with gravel. In the more lightly bombed areas the local people were made responsible for keeping the roads repaired, although where the bombing was heavier government organisations were used to keep the traffic moving. The rail system was of a lighter, narrower gauge than western railways. Extra rails and sleepers were

---

[1] Quoted in Maclear, Michael, *Vietnam: The Ten Thousand Day War*, Thames Methuen (London, 1981), p. 331.

placed along the tracks to replace any damaged in the bombing. It was thought that there could be a shortage of oil and petrol, and as the rail system burned coal and wood considerable effort was directed towards keeping the rail lines running, in case petrol for road transport ran out.

The North Vietnamese developed a whole industry to keep the country's bridges repaired. In any interdiction campaign the bridges in a transport system are the first targets as they are the ones most likely to cause delays and the most difficult to repair. All the major bridges on the transport system were bombed by the Americans. Before the bombing had begun all the smaller rivers had been surveyed and all possible crossing sites had been listed for every area. If larger bridges had been damaged they were repaired using removable sections of steel or bamboo; if bridges were completely destroyed, then in some cases they were reconstructed below water level in an attempt to hide the new structure from American reconnaissance aircraft. The North Vietnamese became adept at building pontoon bridges across rivers. During daylight hours such a bridge would be broken down and the pontoons hidden along the river banks. These pontoons were built to a common specification in village workshops and stored close to all the main bridges. Waterways could also be crossed by barges hauled across by means of pulleys. Even railway engines and coaches were taken across rivers on barges pulled by tugs. All these methods greatly added to the cost and time of transport, but they did keep supplies moving. A western visitor to North Vietnam, John Gerassi, described how quickly bridges could be re-built:

> I looked at it [the bridge]: it was completely destroyed. I was certain we'd be stuck all night. Less than two hours later, however, the officer returned. 'You may cross now,' he said. A whole new bridge, forty feet long, had been built out of bamboo. And was sturdy enough for two loaded trucks which were ahead of us.[1]

Hundreds of thousands of North Vietnamese laboured every day to repair the damage that had been inflicted by the bombers the day before. The Ho Chi Minh Trail in Laos and Cambodia was the main conduit for supplies going south. In the early days of the war considerable amounts of material were sent south by sea to South Vietnam or by sea into Cambodia and then overland into the South, but later on these routes had been effectively cut and the major supply route was down the Ho Chi Minh Trail. Running down the western side of North Vietnam is the Annamite mountain range and the entry to the trail was

---

[1] Gerassi, John, *North Vietnam: A Documentary*, Allan & Unwin (London, 1968), p. 86.

through three major passes in this range, the Na Pe , the Mu Gia (the largest) and the Ben Kari.

The trail was not one path but hundreds, spread out across Laos. Supplies coming south were stockpiled around Vinh in North Vietnam and then taken through the Mu Gia pass into Laos and down the Ho Chi Minh Trail. The proliferation of tracks made it virtually impossible for bombing to close the route completely, and large numbers of regular troops and construction workers were based in Laos to keep the traffic moving. It was estimated that only two per cent of the personnel travelling South were stopped by the bombing: more North Vietnamese soldiers died of malaria on the trail than were killed by bombs. The troops were split into small numbers, and in the early years most of them walked to South Vietnam.

During the course of the war the Soviets and Chinese provided tens of thousands of trucks to the North Vietnamese, and most of the material moved to the South went in these trucks. Trucks moved during the night and parked up during the day. There were hundreds of parking areas and no more than a small number of trucks waited in any one area for the next night—any large collection of vehicles was almost certain to be attacked from the air. In the early years of the war human labour was used to carry aid to the South and it was claimed that bicycles could carry up to 600lb of materials. Even though the trail was heavily bombed the North Vietnamese still managed to increase the numbers going South.

The North Vietnamese created several organisations specifically to keep the transport system working. Youth Shock Brigades were formed out of the small numbers of young people not in the army. By 1965 there were over 100,000 members, mostly women, providing labour to repair roads and bridges. The brigades were mobile and moved to any part of the country that needed extra help to keep the system working. Members of the Youth Brigades were aged between 15 and 30 and enlisted for specific periods. They were rewarded by easier access to higher education after they had left the brigades. Some of the brigades specialised in bomb defusing and disposal. Local militias were also involved in road repairs and members of farming communes had to give a number of days each month to road and bridge repairs.

During periods of heavy bombing men and equipment in North Vietnam only moved at night. Everything was geared to be dispersed and hidden under prepared camouflaged positions during the day, and to move on the trail during the night. Jacques Decornoy visited North Vietnam during 1966:

I saw lines of lorries that leave the main towns at night. They are countless, in spite of the destruction of convoys. Their headlights are kept on as far south as Than Hoa. Then, farther towards the South, the journey goes on slowly, obstinately, in the dark.[1]

The Americans developed techniques for carrying out bombing at night but they had very little true all-weather or night attack capability. The Ho Chi Minh Trail was covered in sensors dropped by aircraft, but this highly expensive network to detect movement on the trail never really worked. The Americans claimed to have destroyed large numbers of trucks on the trail, but the numbers claimed over the years were more than North Vietnam ever possessed. Although trucks were destroyed, the losses were never enough to stop the flow of material.

An elaborate alarm system was created to give advance warning of bombing attacks. Soviet ships were following the American aircraft carriers in the Gulf of Tonkin and reporting when strikes were being mounted, and Soviet intelligence-gathering vessels were stationed off the coast of Guam and could report when flights of B-52s were taking off. It is thought that the North Vietnamese had a comprehensive spy network operating around all the American air bases in South Vietnam and Thailand. All these sources of information gave general warning of attacks on the North, though not the specific targets. The North Vietnamese radar network could follow the American raids when they came within range and estimate their targets; even when heavy jamming was taking place the position of the jamming and its existence were enough to allow a raid to be plotted. The whole of North Vietnam was also covered by a observer system to give warning of aircraft operating too low for the radar to follow, the observation points being linked by land lines to command centres.

Warnings of the bombing raids were issued to the population when the aircraft were within twenty miles of a town or possible target. These warnings were given over the radio for the general population and air raid sirens were used when the aircraft came closer. Along the roads used as part of the transport network a system of coloured lights was used to warn the trucks using the roads: yellow lights meant that there was a possibility of a raid and red lights indicated that a raid was close. Bechir Ben Yahmed, who experienced the air raid warning system in 1967, remarked, 'I never experienced an alert without bombing, or bombing without an alarm. The system works perfectly, it seems.'[2]

---

[1] Decornoy, Jacques, 'Eye Witness Report of the Bombing: How North Vietnam Survives', *The Observer*, 1 January 1967, p. 6.

[2] Yahmed, Bechir Ben, 'Report from North Vietnam', *The Times*, 17 April 1967, p. 9.

The air raid alarm system allowed the population time to gain protection in the numerous air raid shelters. The North Vietnamese had created a large number of various types of shelters. In the southern region of North Vietnam whole villages disappeared underground and large numbers of people lived their entire lives there, with schools, hospitals and living quarters beneath the surface. Further north, out of reach of the really heavy bombing, each village had covered trenches to provide emergency shelter. In the cities concrete shelters were constructed close to residential areas and to factories and offices. Along the streets in built-up areas individual shelters were constructed by sinking concrete pipes into the pavements. These were just large enough for one person and were covered by a concrete lid. The North Vietnamese government claimed to have constructed 21 million of these shelters.

As part of their passive policy against the bombing the government placed great weight on the responsibility of each individual to ensure that he or she had shelters available at home and work. These shelters had to be well maintained and well equipped, and kept clean. The government's slogan was, 'The shelter is your second home.' The relatively small numbers of people killed by the bombing can in some measure be credited to the effective warning system and to the emphasis placed on the air raid shelters.

The North Vietnamese also carried out a policy of both political and economic decentralisation in an attempt to cancel out the effects of the bombing. Classic communist theory led to most communist governments being highly centralised, and North Vietnam was no exception to this way of thinking. However, under the pressure of the bombing the North Vietnamese leadership was forced to disperse many of the functions of central government to the provinces and the village communes. It was thought possible that the bombing was a prelude to an invasion of the North, and that the area of the Red River Delta might have to be abandoned. To counter this the powers of the local communist parties were strengthened to provide the local leadership that would be needed if the central government were moved from Hanoi.

Although North Vietnam was still essentially an agricultural country, it had managed to create a small industrial base. This included the iron works at Thai Nguyen and the cement works at Haiphong. These two facilities used equipment that was too big to be moved elsewhere, but medium-sized and smaller workshops were evacuated into the countryside. The factories were broken down into smaller units, their machinery being distributed to different locations; in some cases each individual piece of machinery was in a different place. This was a highly inefficient way of working, but it did allow some production to continue, and, with the factories moved into the countryside, American aircraft would have to attack each individual machine to stop production completely. With the destruction of a number of the North Vietnamese power plants, power for the dispersed machine tools was provided by thousands of individual generators imported from the Soviet Union. The aim was to create local self-sufficiency as far as possible, and by encouraging the establishment of a village-based 'craft workshop' economy the Vietnamese government moved a certain amount of the country's industry beyond the reach of the bombing.

Government offices were moved at least 24 miles away from Hanoi by order of the Politburo, and to maintain its control in the regions the government increased the numbers of Party members and cadres. With the increase in importance of the regions and the moving of production out of the towns and cities the central government hoped to use the extra party members to provide the local leadership. The party members did receive extra rations and privileges, but they were expected to carry out the central government's policies without question. The party workers provided the local administration, schoolteachers, factory organisers and community leadership, and, with large numbers of men in the Army, many of the new party leadership were women.

Much of the population was also evacuated from Hanoi, Haiphong and the larger towns. The Politburo was forced to order the evacuation since many people did not want to leave their homes. The first people affected were schoolchildren and the elderly, these groups being thought of as non-productive. In Hanoi the population was an estimated one million and at times as many as half this number were evacuated. Schools were set up in the countryside to take the evacuated schoolchildren and village families were forced to provide accommodation. In some ways this helped the government as it enabled them to carry out more indoctrination of the children, without the strong Asian family background.

Many hospitals and health centres were also moved into the countryside away from the towns. This meant that there was some loss of services, but many country areas had their first local health facilities as a result of the moves. Many of the evacuation orders were unpopular and as soon as the bombing slackened off people moved back home to the towns, so to enforce the evacuation the government would only issue ration cards to people in the areas to which they had been sent. As the government controlled the food supply most people had no choice but to comply. In general, the morale of the people in North Vietnam remained relatively high during the bombing.

In some ways the bombing strengthened the position of the North Vietnamese government. The attacks on the North allowed the Politburo to present the Americans as evil imperialists trying to destroy the country. Once the bombing had started the government had a ready-made excuse for its own failings—everything was the fault of the American bombing. Other major bombing campaigns have had the effect of strengthening the commitment of the people to a war, at least until the bombing becomes very heavy and kills large numbers of people, and the bombing of North Vietnam does seem to have brought the people together and to have increased support for the war in the South.

With both their active and passive defence the North Vietnamese had developed a whole range of strategies to cancel out the effects of the bombing on their society. By late 1968 President Johnson had stopped the 'Rolling Thunder' bombing campaign with very little to show for it, and when the 'Linebacker' campaign started in 1972 the Vietnamese had a great deal of experience of how to minimise the effects and continue the war in the South. After the bombing had stopped in 1968 the North Vietnamese leadership had attempted to reconstruct the country's industry and shattered infrastructure. They believed that it was quite possible for the Americans to re-start the bombing, and they focused the rebuilding on smaller, dispersed units when they could; there was an attempt to increase production by introducing a small degree of competition into the economy; the peasant farmers were allowed to keep for themselves a higher proportion of the food they grew for the communes; and higher prices were paid by the government for farm produce. In the factories a type of piecework system was introduced on a small scale, also in an attempt to boost production. The attempt to restructure the economy was only partly successful as the managerial and administrative skills were not available to carry this through. The North Vietnamese Communist Party were trying to revitalise the economy without loosening the political control of the party, and by the early 1970s the attempts to boost the economy had been only partially successful.

The North Vietnamese people seem to have become less disciplined after the end of the 'Rolling Thunder' bombing. In an attempt to boost production the government had called for a increase of 16 per cent in industrial output but less than 8 per cent was achieved. Production targets for light industry were set at 26 per cent but only a 2 per cent increase took place. Large-scale electrical production had been heavily bombed, but by 1971 this had been restored to

60 per cent of the original total. Even after the changes that were introduced for the agricultural communes, North Vietnam still could not produce enough food to feed itself. Before the war the rice harvest had been 3½m tons and in 1971 this had only increased to 4m tons, but with the population increasing 5.9m tons were needed each year. The Lao Dong Party carried out a massive propaganda campaign to exhort the people to work harder and produce more. This seems to have had only limited success.

The rebuilding of the physical damage caused by the bombing was more effective than the economic restructuring. Many of the communes and individuals had rebuilt their houses themselves. Michael Maclear visited Hanoi in 1968 and 1971. Commenting on the rebuilding, he said,

> Everywhere the landscape gleamed with the bright red of brick and tile—new homes, schools, factories standing out like beacons in towns which had seemed permanently extinguished. Evacuees had returned to rebuild their own homes, and a common sight was thousands of galvanised citizens moving acres of stacked bricks.[1]

But Maclear also observed that there were posters on the walls of Hanoi stating, 'The Bombers Will Return'.

The American reconnaissance flights had continued over North Vietnam. This had been allowed under the agreement that President Johnson thought he had obtained to end the bombing in 1968. The North Vietnamese saw this differently and did fire on the reconnaissance flights, leading to the 'protective reaction' bombing raids on the North. In this respect the bombing had never ended completely, and the sporadic raids did allow the Northern leadership to keep alive the threat of renewed heavy bombing in the minds of their people. Wilfred Burchett, who visited the North on several occasions, described the Northern leadership thus:

> They believed from the outset that, as a last card, a Nixon or some other president would attempt to wipe out Hanoi and Haiphong. Ho Chi Minh prepared the North Vietnamese people for this from the very first bombing raids.[2]

The North Vietnamese leadership had psychologically prepared the North Vietnamese people for the bombing to re-start, as it did with the 'Linebacker' campaigns. With a people prepared and even ready for the bombing, morale was much easier to sustain.

---

[1] Maclear, op. cit., p. 347.

[2] Burchett, William, *Grasshoppers and Elephants*, Urizen Books (New York, 1977), p. 167.

Ho Chi Minh died in 1969 and his testament to the people of Vietnam, published after his death, contained the phrase 'The American invaders defeated, we will rebuild our land ten times more beautiful.' The leadership of the party devolved to Le Duan, who had been the leading member of the 'South-first' faction of the party. The war in the South had been relatively quiet after the heavy fighting during the Tet offensive, but with Le Duan becoming the party leader it was only a matter of time before he would renew the attempt to reunite the country.

The Ho Chi Minh Trail had been constantly upgraded since the beginning of the war. An oil pipeline had been laid from North Vietnam through the Mu Gia pass, along the trail and into the A Shau valley in South Vietnam. The roads had been improved and the number of all-weather roads increased. Large numbers of extra trucks had been obtained from the Soviet Union and China to move the supplies needed for the military build-up. The trail was no longer a rough track used by human labour carrying supplies on backs or on bicycles but a large number of efficient roads used by thousands of trucks. The Americans carried out more bombing in Laos than in North Vietnam, and this bombing continued for eleven years. But the supplies coming South down the trail were never stopped or significantly reduced. Preparations for a renewed major attack in the South became obvious. The South Vietnamese offensive Lam Son 719, in February 1971, was an attempt to disrupt the build-up of troops and equipment that were coming down the Ho Chi Minh Trail. South Vietnamese troops were hoping to reach the major staging area around the town of Tchepone inside Laos. However, Giap committed the North Vietnamese reserves and the South Vietnamese were driven back in disorder. This attack would not have been necessary had the bombing been able to stop the traffic using the trail.

The North Vietnamese leadership's warnings were proved correct when the Americans started bombing the North again in early 1972, and before the end of the year the bombing had reached levels never seen before during the course of the war. As 'Linebacker' developed and expanded, the North Vietnamese brought back into use all the ways of minimising the effects of the bombing they had used before. They attempted to continue the support for the war in the South and to keep the supplies moving. The bombing did cause enormous damage, especially to the transport system, and the amount of materials moving was greatly reduced, while the closing of the port at Haiphong made the delivery of equipment from the Soviet Union extremely difficult. Nevertheless, by using enormous effort a minimum level of supplies did continue to move.

Life for the ordinary citizens living in the towns and cities in the North was completely disrupted. In the southern regions of North Vietnam the population moved back underground as the area around Vinh was heavily bombed. The shelters had been kept in good repair, and living in them became a way of life. Families were divided as the children and old people were evacuated away from the towns—almost half the population was under the age of 15. Even though heavy damage was suffered and the economy, the industry and the lives of the people were disrupted the country continued to operate as an economic and social unit. The effects of the bombing were absorbed and the people adapted their way of living to wait for the bombing to end.

Some of the North Vietnamese even had respect for the professionalism of the American pilots and their efforts to avoid civilian casualties. Master Sergeant Nguyen Van Mo, who was in Hanoi during the bombing, described the accuracy achieved:

> In the beginning, the Americans carried out their attacks very carefully—the attacks on the Long Bien bridge [Paul Doumer bridge], for example, and the Gia Lam airfield, and on Van Dien. We used to watch them, to see how accurate the bombers were, and to judge how good the pilots were at avoiding anti-aircraft fire and rockets. We had to admit that during the early attacks they hit proper military targets and their flying techniques were pretty good . . . Later, because the anti-aircraft fire had gotten so heavy, the pilots had to escape themselves, and they dropped their bombs carelessly, without paying any attention to the lives of the people.[1]

The bombing during 'Linebacker I' did cause civilian deaths but this was not the primary reason for the raids. It is also obvious that the military targets were being hit and damaged.

The Paul Doumer bridge (re-named the Long Bien bridge), across which most of the supplies entering Vietnam through Haiphong and from China passed, was bombed on the first day of the 'Linebacker I' campaign, 10 May 1972, and damaged. Although the bridge was put out of action on the first day, at least two temporary bridges were constructed to carry some of the traffic. A pontoon bridge called the Paul Doumer by-pass was constructed downstream and a ferry was in use even further downstream. Wilfred Burchett visited Ha-

---

[1] Chanoff, David, and Van Toai, Doan, *Portrait of the Enemy*, I. B. Tauris (London, 1977), p. 126.

noi in January just after the end of the bombing and passed over the pontoon bridge. He described this trip by saying,

> Our car bump-bumped its way across one of the several pontoon bridges with the ruins of the big Long Bien bridge in the background, one span drooping into the river, a great gap where another had been—twinkling blue flashes testifying that welders were at work.[1]

Although the bridge had been described as the premier transport target in North Vietnam, and had been badly damaged on the first day of the 'Linebacker campaign', this had not stopped some supplies still crossing the Red River.

The international airport for Hanoi was the airfield at Gia Lam, across the Red River from the capital. One of the targets bombed by B-52s during 'Linebacker II' was the Hanoi railway repair yards next to the airport. William Burchett also described the destruction of these two targets:

> There were ugly gaps in the walls and missing roofs and windows at Hanoi's Gia Lam civilian air terminal . . . Gia Lam itself, an industrial suburb on the northern side of the Red River from Hanoi, was a mass of rubble, the big railway repair depot reduced to twisted steel and collapsed roofs through which one saw rusted wrecks of burned-out trains. Rubble choked the footpaths and where façades of houses and shops still stood there were gutted ruins behind.[2]

There is no doubt that heavy damage was caused to the targets given to the bombers, but there were inevitably times when bombs were dropped in the wrong place. The hospital at Bac Mai, close to the airfield, was hit by bombs from a B-52. On 11 October 1972 targets close to the centre of Hanoi were attacked and the French delegate-general Pierre Susini was killed when the French Embassy was hit by bombs; during the same bombing raid the Albanian Chargé d'Affaires was injured. The Algerian and Indian Embassies were also damaged, with four Egyptian and French members of staff killed. Later, during the 'Linebacker II' Christmas raids, the Hungarian and East German diplomatic missions were hit by bombs from B-52s. However, large numbers of the citizens of Hanoi still thought the diplomatic district of the city the safest place to be, and camped out every night in the streets around the embassies.

During the 'Linebacker II' raids the city of Hanoi was again evacuated by as many people as possible. The Mayor of Hanoi, Tran Duy Hung, claimed

---

[1] Burchett, op.cit., p. 172.
[2] Ibid., pp. 171–2.

that the evacuation started on 4 December after Henry Kissinger had issued what were taken to be threats to bomb Hanoi if the talks did not progress. Children were moved from Hanoi first and then a general evacuation order was issued. However, large-scale evacuation only took place after the 16th when Kissinger gave a press conference in Washington. Although it was a Sunday, the transport system of buses was used to move people out of the city. People also left in trucks and on bicycles into the surrounding countryside. The villages and farming communes were made responsible for looking after the evacuees. In two days it was claimed that the population in Hanoi had been reduced from one million to 500,000.

When the bombing started on the 18th the Mayor of Hanoi described the shooting down of the first B-52:

> The first bombs were already crashing down on Gia Lam when a blip in one of the leading waves disappeared. I rushed out of the command bunker—and there it was, like a great torch, coming down quite slowly it seemed. People had come out of their shelters to cheer . . . Later that night a second one was downed over Hanoi and a third on its way here.[1]

The North Vietnamese claimed to have shot down three B-52s on the first night and the Americans admitted the loss of three aircraft. The North Vietnamese seem to have expected the bombing to re-start and to have prepared for this as far as possible.

The North Vietnamese also claimed to have captured information on the ECM systems carried by the B-52s which enabled them to improve their anti-aircraft system. The B-52s were completely dependent on ECM to enable them to penetrate the North Vietnamese defences. The Mayor of Hanoi, speaking in January 1972, stated,

> The pockets of the chief pilot shot down were stuffed with technical data on the model he was flying. He would never have been carrying it had there seemed the slightest risk of being shot down. It was very precious documentation for us because these were the latest B-52Ds and B-52Gs with no fewer than 17 electronic jamming devices to fool our radar warning system and especially conventional missile guidance systems. By the time the sun was up our electronic experts were working on how to counter those of the jamming systems which could affect the efficiency of our missile batteries.[2]

---

[1] Ibid., pp. 162–3.
[2] Ibid., pp. 164–5.

Above: A Boeing B-52 dropping bombs over South Vietnam.
Below: McDonnell F-4D Phantoms from the 4th TFW carrying laser-guided bombs and Sparrow missiles, September 1972.

Left, top: *A McDonnell RF-4C Phantom from the 11th TRS.*
Left, centre: *A Republic F-105G Thunderchief 'Wild Weasel' aircraft.*
Left, bottom: *A Douglas RB-66 Destroyer electronic warfare aircraft.*
Above: *A Vought A-7E Corsair II from VA-147.*
Below: *Grumman A-6 Intruders of VA-145 from the USS* Ranger, *15 January 1973, dropping some of the last bombs to fall on North Vietnam.*

Above: A Vought F-8D Crusader from VF 111 pulling out from an attack over North Vietnam. The high G is creating vortices from the aircraft's wing tips.
Below: General Dynamics F-111As over Thailand.
Bottom: The Douglas A-1E Skyraider was used by the US Air Force to escort rescue helicopters over North Vietnam. This 'Sandy' mission was one of the most dangerous.

Top: A Sikorsky HH-53 Super Jolly Green Giant helicopter used by the rescue forces.
Above: The Sikorsky HH-3E dedicated rescue version of the Sea King.
Below: A Kaman HH-43 Husky helicopter used for search and rescue during the Vietnam War.

Above: Randy Cunningham (left) and Willy Driscoll shown back on board the USS Constellation *on 10 May 1972 after they had shot down three North Vietnamese MiGs and had their Phantom shot down by an SA-2 missile. They were the first American aces of the Vietnam War.*
Below: The F-4J flown by Cunningham and Driscoll on 10 May 1972, shown here earlier in the year.

Above: Captain Richard S. Ritchie of the 555th TFS ('Triple Nickel') was the first US Air Force pilot to shoot down five North Vietnamese aircraft.
Below: An AIM-7 Sparrow radar-guided air-to-air missile in the process of being loaded on to an F-4 at Cam Ranh Bay.

Above: AIM-9 Sidewinder infra-red guided air-to-air missiles.
Below: Douglas A-4 Skyhawk light attack bombers from VA-155.

Above: The USS Constellation.
Below: A North Vietnamese MiG-21.

Above: *SA-2 ground-to-air missiles. The SA-2 shot down fifteen B-52s during 'Linebacker II'.*
Below: *An SA-2 launch. If the missiles could be seen the American pilots had a good chance of avoiding them.*
Right, upper: *North Vietnamese MiG-17s photographed in revetments on Kep airfield.*
Right, lower: *The Paul Doumer bridge, North Vietnam's premier transport target, photographed in 1968.*

HANOI RR/HWY BR OV RED RIVER

27 MAY 68

FLOATING CRANE

REPLACED SPANS ←

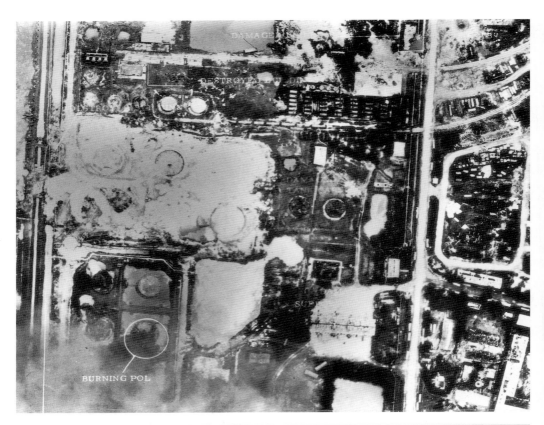

DAMAGE

DESTROYED OIL DR

DESTROYED

SUP

BURNING POL

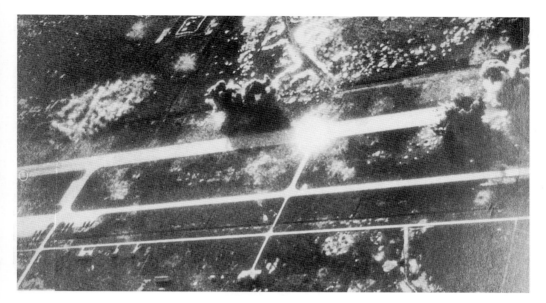

Left, upper: The Hanoi oil storage facility bombed on 18 May 1972 by Phantoms of the 8th TFW using laser-guided bombs. It was claimed that 5.5 million gallons of oil products were destroyed.
Left, lower: The highway bridge at Lang Met, 45 miles north of Hanoi—typical of the bridges bombed in North Vietnam.
Above: Phuc Yen air base under attack. Bombs can be seen exploding on the runway.
Below: Thai Nguyen power station showing bomb damage.

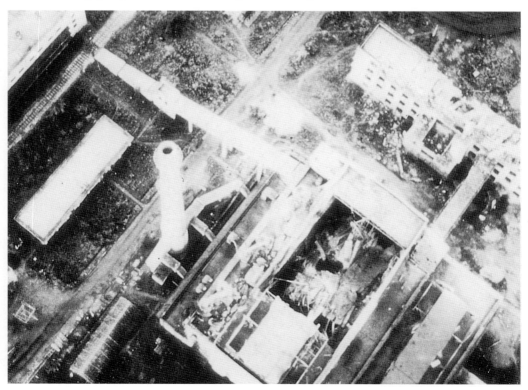

Above: Haiphong docks under attack.
Below: Than Hoa bridge. This photograph shows one of the early, unsuccessful attacks on the bridge, which was finally brought down on 13 May 1972 by laser-guided bombs.

Above: Oil storage facilities at Haiphong burning after an attack.
Below: Bombed rail trucks close to the Than Hoa bridge.

Above: Thai Nguyen railyards, showing bomb damage.
Below: An RF-101 Voodoo photographed over Kep airfield.

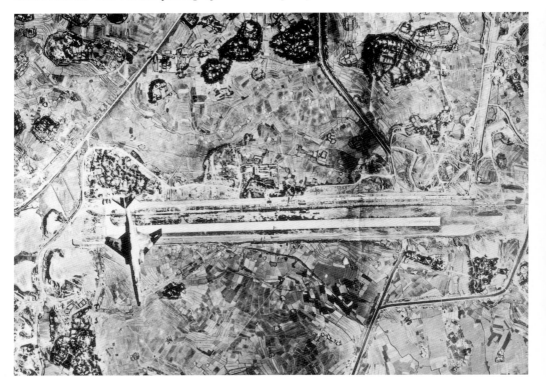

If this assertion is true it represented a major breakdown in American security, and would have given the North Vietnamese, and the Soviets, access to information they would have found difficulty in obtaining elsewhere. As 'Linebacker II' lasted only days it is unlikely that the North Vietnamese would have been able to make any major changes to their defence system because of this information, but even if after reading the documents they realised that there was no way of breaking the American jamming, it at least allowed them to change their tactics to try to counter it.

The Mayor of Hanoi confirmed the American suspicion that the North Vietnamese were firing missiles in salvos, without guidance, into the bomber stream:

> They [the North Vietnamese technicians] made the accuracy of the missiles independent of ground radio control by firing them in salvos in the path of oncoming aircraft, with proximity fuses which exploded the warheads when they were in effective range. So most of the enemy's complicated jamming devices were neutralised . . . Our Soviet comrades were very astonished at this . . . [1]

The Soviets were certainly astonished (although perhaps not in the way the North Vietnamese thought) and had described the North Vietnamese as firing the SA-2 missiles like machine guns. Standard proximity fuses on the SA-2s were command detonation, which could be jammed, but the missiles were set to explode at the altitude at which the bombers were flying—which is not really a system of proximity fusing. Regimented American tactics, in the early days of the campaign, did allow the North Vietnamese to achieve some measure of success against the B-52s, by making the best of what they had.

North Vietnamese morale did not break in any major way, but the bombing did have a psychological impact on the population directly subjected to it and on the government in general. American prisoners of war were concentrated in Hanoi after the attempted raid on the prison camp at Tan Son. All the prisoners spoke about hearing the bombing raids taking place, and several prisoners commented on the change in attitude of their guards after the bombing. Air Force Lieutenant-Colonel Jon A. Reynolds was in Hanoi during the bombing:

> There was no joking, no laughing, no acts of defiance or reprisal. They simply headed for their shelters . . . For the first time the United States meant business. We knew it, the guards knew it, and it seems clear that the leaders of North Vietnam knew it. Some, perhaps most, will suggest that the negotiations did not result from the B-52

---

[1] Ibid.

strikes. From my vantage point, however, the reason the North Vietnamese negotiated was obvious.[1]

There seems little doubt that the bombing did have an impact on the North Vietnamese in Hanoi.

Another prisoner in Hanoi at the time of the bombing was Lieutenant-Colonel Robinson Risner, who was an ace from the Korean War. He had been shot down on 16 September 1965 while leading an 'Iron Hand' mission against a North Vietnamese missile site in an F-105D. In the 7½ years he spent in captivity Risner became one of the leaders of the American prisoners of war. He described the Vietnamese reaction to the bombing:

> We knew that they were B-52s and that President Nixon was keeping his word. We saw a reaction in the Vietnamese that we had never seen before under the attacks from the fighters. They at last knew that we had some weapons they had not felt, and that President Nixon was willing to use those weapons to get us out.[2]

Risner was a long-time member of the US Air Force and a career aviator, who was released from captivity only weeks after the Christmas bombing. It is possible that he was seeing the event from a particular point of view.

A third American prisoner of war in Hanoi when the bombing took place was Commander James B. Stockdale. He described how the prison guards cowered and hid against the walls of the prison as the bombs fell. Writing after the war, Stockdale mentioned that the North Vietnamese showed

> . . . accommodation, hopelessness, remorse, fear . . . all that separated Hanoi from doomsday was an American national order to keep the bombs out on the hard targets. We prisoners knew this was the end of North Vietnamese resistance, and the North Vietnamese knew it too.[3]

Stockdale seems have no doubt about the effects of the bombing. He saw at first hand the Vietnamese reaction to the B-52s' attacks close to the centre of Hanoi. However, since he was locked up in prison, the number of people with whom he came into contact was restricted to the prison guards, who were not a representative group of the general population.

Visitors to the airport at Gia Lam reported that after the sustained bombing of the airport employees were seen wandering around completely disoriented

---

[1] Reynolds, Jon A., 'Linebacker II: The POW Perspective', *Air Force*, September 1979.

[2] Quoted in Morrocco, John, *Rain of Fire: Air War 1969–1973*, Boston Publishing Co. (Boston, 1985), pp. 160-1.

[3] Stockdale, Jim, *In Love and War*, Harper & Row (New York, 1984), p. 184.

and apparently out of control. Visitors were able to walk around the airport without any one stopping them and visit areas where access was normally restricted for foreigners. Normal control mechanisms at the airport seem to have broken down completely under the bombing: the psychological impact of the continuous bombing had been too much for some of the population to bear. How widespread this effect was is difficult to ascertain, but the overall control of the North Vietnamese government was not affected and the Lao Dong Party, with cadres active down to the local level, maintained its position.

Also present during the 'Linebacker II' raids was the American jurist Telford Taylor. He had been a prosecutor at the Nuremberg Trials in Germany after the Second World War and had an international reputation as a lawyer of some standing. Taylor was a strong critic of the Vietnam War but has since stated that the American bombing was not intended to cause civilian deaths. He wrote:

> Despite the enormous weight of bombs that were dropped, I rapidly became convinced that we were making no effort to destroy Hanoi. The city remained largely intact and it seemed quite apparent that if there were an effort to destroy Hanoi it could have been done very rapidly in two or three nights.[1]

The bombing during 'Linebacker I' and 'II' had been extremely heavy and had caused enormous damage to North Vietnam, but the targets hit had been, in the main, military or transport targets. Civilians had been killed, but the numbers perishing were fewer than the numbers of civilians killed in the South by the North Vietnamese during the Easter offensive. The effect on the North Vietnamese government had not been as shattering as had been hoped, although there is no doubt that the bombing had been more extensive and effective than it had expected. The Americans had certainly got the attention of the North Vietnamese when they agreed to a return to the talks.

The North Vietnamese view of the peace talks had always been totally different from that of the Americans. By late 1972 the Americans only wanted an agreement that would allow them to leave South-East Asia with some measure of the 'peace with honour' position taken by President Nixon still intact. The view taken by the North Vietnamese of the talks was the Marxist 'talk/fight' strategy. They viewed the conflict as having both a military and a political dimension. The military aspect was fought on the battlefield and the political aspect in the minds of the population in the South. As part of the political

---

[1] Taylor, Telford, 'Reports and Comments—North Vietnam', *Atlantic Monthly*, May 1973.

aspect of the war the peace talks were viewed as part of a propaganda offensive against the Americans. This was summed up in the phrase used by Le Duc Tho, 'We can only win at the conference table what we have won on the battlefield.' The North Vietnamese had no intention of negotiating anything that would prevent them from achieving their long-term goals. On the other hand, they were prepared cynically to agree to anything they could safely ignore later.

As the Christmas bombing continued the Americans asked the North Vietnamese to return to the Paris peace talks and offered to stop the bombing if they negotiated with a 'serious attitude'. The North Vietnamese leadership stated categorically that it would not negotiate while the bombing continued. Even after the heavy bombing the will of the Northern leadership had not been broken. It seemed to be prepared to accept further bombing rather than give way to the Americans. On 28 December the North Vietnamese sent a telegram to the Americans maintaining that they had always operated a 'consistently serious negotiating position'. This was enough for Nixon to order an end to the bombing. In concrete terms this phrase, in one telegram, was all that had been achieved by the bombing.

The Vietnamese view when Kissinger and Le Duc Tho met in Paris on 8 January was that they had now weathered the worst the Americans could do, and they had come through it. After the storm of international protest at the bombing it would be nearly impossible for the Americans to re-start the attacks. The North Vietnamese felt that their position at the talks was now stronger than it had been in December. When the final treaty was signed on 27 January it was only cosmetically different from that agreed in October. Nixon had forced Thieu to sign by threatening to cut off all American aid if he did not. If Nixon had compelled Thieu to sign in October then the 'Linebacker II' campaign would have been unnecessary.

The North Vietnamese did not make any major changes in their negotiating position between early December and early January. It could be said that the bombing forced the North Vietnamese back to the negotiating table but had not changed their views when they arrived there. Ha Van Lau, who became Vietnam's first ambassador to the United Nations, claimed that the bombing was a North Vietnamese victory: 'It was this decisive victory—an aerial equivalent to Dien Bien Phu—which obliged Nixon to sign the accords.'[1] Although

---

[1] Quoted in Maclear, op.cit., p. 423.

some North Vietnamese viewed the 'Linebacker II' bombing as a victory, this is probably an overstatement. They had not defeated the B-52 bombers—by the end of the eleven-day campaign the US Air Force could have bombed any target they wished—but they had reorganised their society to absorb the bombing and had learned to live with it. The bombing during 'Linebacker I' had helped to cripple the North Vietnamese offensive in the South and helped the South Vietnamese recover most of the territory that they had lost. However, the bombing had not crippled the North Vietnamese and had not forced them to change their long-term goals.

CHAPTER 12

CONCLUSION

'**L**INEBACKER I' and 'II' had both involved enormous effort by the US Air Force and US Navy. Large areas of North Vietnam had been devastated by the bombing. The pilots had been given targets in the North and most of these targets had been hit. If they had not been successful the aircraft returned again until the targets had been destroyed. But had all this destruction achieved everything that had been expected of it? Had the strategic bombing theories been proved correct? Could aircraft win wars on their own when directed against an enemy's homeland?

The United States Air Force had been created in 1947 out of the bombing campaigns in the Second World War, and had been based on the idea that strategic bombing could win wars. In essence, the theories stated that aircraft could pass over the heads of army and naval forces and attack an enemy's homeland, that there were 'vital targets' within an enemy country that could be destroyed and that the enemy could not continue to operate without these targets. If these selected targets were hit, then the enemy would be forced to surrender as his industry, his morale and his ability to continue the war would be destroyed. The application of these theories in the Second World War, in Korea and during the 'Rolling Thunder' campaign in Vietnam had at best proved inconclusive. The air power theorists, who had by this time reached the highest levels of the military, looked upon the 'Linebacker' campaigns as a last chance to prove the theories correct.

From its creation in 1946 Strategic Air Command had been given priority over both Air Defence Command and Tactical Air Command. Within the restricted budgets after the Second World War, most of the Air Force's money had been spent on SAC. Although this bias was based on the use of nuclear weapons, it was also predicated on the idea that air power could win wars. The overall American strategy during this period was one of 'massive retaliation', involving the early use of nuclear weapons, but in reality no president would have allowed the use of nuclear bombs except as a last resort. It would seem that SAC was created only to be used as a threat, rather than to be used directly.

When faced with the war in Vietnam it would seem that the American military leadership made the classic mistake of trying to make a particular conflict fit the available weapons and thinking, rather than the other way round. For most of the war the B-52s were used for bombing South Vietnam. When North Vietnam was bombed the Air Chiefs had chosen a poor country to put their theories to the test. North Vietnam was basically a agricultural society with a small industrial base. The factories producing the weapons used by North Vietnam were in China and the Soviet Union. The number of genuine 'vital targets' in North Vietnam was extremely small, if there were any at all. Attacking the general population was specifically excluded by Presidential directive, so the morale of the population could not be targeted. However, having based their military careers on the strategic bombing theories, some of the Air Force commanders still believed that North Vietnam could be defeated by bombing alone.

As stated earlier, in simple terms the use of air power can be divided into three forms, close air support, interdiction and strategic bombing. Taking these three together there is little doubt that air power has come to dominate warfare. Close air support is the use of aircraft in the area of the ground battle as a form of flying artillery—essentially aircraft used as support for the army. Interdiction is the destruction of the enemy's men and equipment while they are being transported between the his homeland and the battle front. Strategic bombing is the bombing of the enemy's homeland, including the centres of industry and government. The supporters of the strategic bombing theories held that only the bombing of the enemy homeland was needed and that any other use of aircraft was a diversion from the essential. In practice the theories have been difficult to demonstrate as correct.

The classic formulation of the strategic bombing theories by Giulio Douhet in the 1920s stated that only two steps were needed. The first was to achieve what he called command of the air by bombing the enemy's air bases and aircraft factories, to destroy his air force. This allowed the second step to be put into effect, namely the destruction of the enemy's war-making capacity including both morale and industrial targets. In reality, winning wars through air power alone has proved considerably more difficult than first envisaged, even when command of the air has been achieved. Forcing an enemy to surrender by bombing has proved difficult, if not impossible.

In Vietnam the Americans had in general achieved command of the air. The North Vietnamese Air Force had never been completely destroyed, and it continued to shoot down American aircraft, but was never effective enough to stop the bombing taking place. The destruction of North Vietnamese governmental and industrial centres had occurred. In terms of Douhet's theories the two stages had taken place, but were the outcomes the ones that were expected? The use of American aircraft in close support of the South Vietnamese Army inside South Vietnam had practically destroyed the North Vietnamese force that had invaded South Vietnam. By carrying out a conventional invasion the North Vietnamese had given the Americans what they had always wanted—for the North Vietnamese to stand up and fight. It was the use of guerrilla tactics and elusive hit-and-run methods that the Americans had found difficult to combat. The Tet offensive had been a massive tactical victory for the Americans, as had the attack on Khe Sanh. When the North Vietnamese attempted a conventional battle with the Americans they invariably lost.

The Soviet tanks and artillery that North Vietnam had used to spearhead the attack on the South were soon destroyed by American helicopters and aircraft. Hundreds of sorties a day were used to support the South Vietnamese Army and B-52s even dropped bombs within a hundred yards of South Vietnamese forces. The American aircraft tore the heart out of the North Vietnamese Army and by October 1972 it was estimated that the North Vietnamese had suffered 100,000 casualties. Some sources state that their morale was close to collapse. The South Vietnamese Army had played a large part in this defeat of the North and had also suffered heavy casualties, but there can be little doubt that the use of American aircraft, in close support, was the decisive factor.

The interdiction that took place during the campaign is less easy to assess. Supply routes through Laos and Cambodia were heavily bombed, as was the transport system in North Vietnam, but the Ho Chi Minh Trail had been bombed for many years with little general success. During the 1960s it was estimated that the outside needs of the Viet Cong amounted to as little as 15 tons a day, and it proved to be impossible to stop such small quantities of supplies getting through. In any case, the Viet Cong held the initiative in the South and could scale up or scale down their activities to suit the supplies available. However, when the North Vietnamese regular army became the principal force in the South, especially after the Viet Cong had been largely destroyed in the Tet offensive, the volume of logistics needed increased and the supply lines became more vulnerable. With the spring invasion in 1972 the amounts of fuel,

168

ammunition and supplies that had to be brought in from the North were enormous. This reliance on conventional forces, needing large amounts of supplies each day, with fixed supply routes, made the interdiction of these routes more effective, but it is still hard to quantify the level of success that the interdiction of the supply routes achieved.

The history of interdiction has shown how difficult it is to stop the movement of supplies. Before and after the D-Day landings the Allied air forces attempted to cut off Normandy and tens of thousands of sorties were flown, but the German Army still made the Allied armies fight for every inch of territory until it was finally defeated. The situation in Italy during the Second World War again showed how difficult it is to stop the resupply of a resourceful enemy. Even though Italy is a narrow peninsula which is mountainous in the centre, it proved impossible to stop the movement of supplies by bombing. In Korea the experience was the same—the complete air interdiction of the enemy's supplies proved to be impossible. In all these cases the amounts of supplies reaching the front line was restricted but not stopped.

The bombing during 'Linebacker I' was successful in that targets were destroyed, but how much this restricted the flow of supplies and the effect it had on the fighting in the South are still debatable. One of the major transport targets in the North was the bridge at Than Hoa. The bridge had been bombed for the first time in 1965, and hundreds of sorties had been flown against it and dozens of aircraft lost. As noted earlier, it was finally destroyed by laser-guided bombs on 13 May 1972. However, sections of a pontoon bridge had been in place waiting to be used, and a ford in the river was available five miles upstream. Was the amount of effort put into destroying the bridge worth the effort? In financial terms it had cost over a billion dollars to do it. North Vietnam's transport system also contained massive redundancy, and new bridges, new sections of road and by-passes for any bottlenecks in the system were continually being constructed. This redundancy meant that only 15 per cent of the North's transport system was in use at any one time.

The North Vietnamese, moreover, had access to what was for practical purposes unlimited aid from the Soviet Union, China and Eastern Europe. Although both China and the Soviet Union had improved their relations with the United States, they both continued to supply North Vietnam, despite some interruptions in the supply from China. These allies were prepared to furnish all of the North's needs, the only limiting factor being the amount of resources the North Vietnamese could absorb. The mining of the harbours and the bombing of the rail lines from China meant that it was considerably more difficult to import supplies into the country, but it was not impossible. With the amounts of materials and equipment coming into the country it is hard to see what level of bombing would have been necessary to have stopped them completely.

There are occasions when bombing can only achieve just so much, and it is in the final analysis up to the ground troops to decide the conclusion. Air Marshal John Slessor, writing in 1954 about the Korean War, observed,

> The idea that superior air power can in some way be a substitute for hard slogging and professional skill on the ground in this sort of war is beguiling but illusory.'[1]

Although bombing can be effective, in that the targets given to the bombers are hit, the actual results can prove to be less effective than originally thought.

The bombing of the Ho Chi Minh Trail had not stopped the North from moving fourteen divisions, practically its entire army, into position to attack the South. The massively increased bombing after the invasion did restrict the movement of men and supplies but did not stop it. With massive amounts of aid available, at least in theory, and with the North devoting its entire national effort to the war in the South, it was possible for at least some of the supplies to continue moving. But fourteen regular army divisions need truly enormous amounts of logistic supplies each day to continue to operate in a conventional role, and this amount was at least restricted. The evidence given to a US Senate committee in September 1972 estimated that the quantity of imports into North Vietnam and the amount of supplies transported to the South was reduced by 50–65 per cent between May and September 1972. This reduction in materials reaching the front line and the massive close support bombing did damage the North Vietnamese invasion forces enough to allow the South Vietnamese Army to regain most of the territory it had earlier lost.

It is considerably more difficult to reach a conclusion about the effectiveness of the strategic bombing of the North. The theories were predicated on the model of an advanced, highly industrialised nation involved in total war. Fighting between these nations was seen as intense, continuous and involving large amounts of military equipment and supplies. Large armies locked into high-intensity combat would become vulnerable to any loss of supplies that could be caused by bombing. North Vietnam did not meet this model. For most of the war the fighting was low-key and the industries feeding the war

---

[1] Armitage, A., and Mason, R. A., *Air Power in the Nuclear Age*, University of Illinois Press (1983), p. 45.

were beyond the reach of any bombing the Americans were prepared to carry out. The invasion of the South in 1972 moved the war on to a different level, and while they had a conventional invasion force in the south the North Vietnamese became much more vulnerable to a bombing campaign.

The war was, for the North Vietnamese, a total war involving the full commitment of their national assets. For the Americans the war was only ever a limited war. The strategic bombing theories grew out of the First World War and required the notion of total commitment to the destruction of an enemy's country. As they showed on many occasions, the North Vietnamese were prepared to escalate the war beyond anything the Americans wanted. American leaders, on the other hand, continually stated the limited nature of the war and the limited nature of the bombing. President Nixon might make statements in private like his famous 'The bastards have never been bombed like they are going to be bombed this time', but in public the emphasis was different and he attempted to play down the extent of the bombing. The Northern leadership always felt that they could outlast the Americans, who only had a limited commitment to a war that did not threaten any of their vital interests and would eventually tire of the conflict and simply leave.

For the Northern leadership to have abandoned its support for the war in the South it would have had to think that the situation could only get worse and that it had no choice but to give way. The Americans' statement of their limited position showed the North Vietnamese that they did have other choices. Carl von Clausewitz, the well-known German writer, stated,

> If the enemy is to be coerced you must put him in a situation that is even more unpleasant than the sacrifice you call on him to make. The hardship of that situation must not of course be merely transient, at least not in appearance. Otherwise the enemy would not give in but would wait for things to improve.[1]

The North Vietnamese did not give in, but did wait for things to improve and for the Americans to leave, as they had stated they would do.

It was an essential part of the strategic bombing theories that there were 'vital targets' that could be destroyed, bringing a country to its knees. This presupposed an advanced industrialised country with a complex infrastructure. It was thought that it would not be necessary to destroy the entire industry of a country, which would be an impossible task, but only vital parts of it,

---

[1] Clausewitz, Carl von, (ed. and trans. Howard, Michael, and Paret, Peter), *On War*, Princeton University Press (New Jersey, 1978), p. 77.

thereby disrupting the remainder. During the Second World War the German ball-bearings industry and the oil industry were at various times put forward as vital targets, with debatable results. But true vital targets were hard to find in North Vietnam. The lack of development in the country was part of its strength: there did not seem to be any targets that the North Vietnamese were not prepared to see bombed. As the bombing developed, industry was redeployed back to village level in order to avoid it. The lack of vital targets in North Vietnam meant that the strategic bombing of the North could not force the Northern leadership to abandon its commitment to the war in the South. Proponents of the idea that bombing alone could win wars had again failed to prove their case.

The real failure in American strategy was not in the bombing but in South Vietnam. Creating an independent South Vietnam was ostensibly the purpose of the war in Vietnam. This is a political problem and the main failing in the Americans' strategy was that they were seeking a military solution to a political problem. The governments in South Vietnam were corrupt dictatorships and were seen as such by most of the population. There was never enough backing for the governments in the South for the country to exist without American support, and it was a mistake to view the source of South Vietnam's troubles as being in the North rather than as the political situation in the South. A popular government in the South that had the support of the people would not have been seen as a target by the North. President Kennedy argued as early as 1961 that

> No amount of arms and armies can help stabilize those governments which are unable or unwilling to achieve social reform and economic development. Military pacts cannot help nations whose social injustices and economic chaos invite insurgency and penetration and subversion.[1]

It was this failure in South Vietnam that doomed all other aspects of US strategy. The people of South Vietnam were not prepared to back wholeheartedly any of the politicians who ruled in their country. A high proportion of the South Vietnamese Army deserted every year. Although the South Vietnamese Army performed considerably better than many thought it would when the North invaded in 1972, it would not have survived without the massive infusion of American air power. There was a long, slow decline in the morale of

---

[1] Kennedy, John, *New York Times*, 26 May 1961, p. 12.

the Southern population throughout this period. When the North invaded in 1975 the Army and the country quickly collapsed.

The 'Linebacker I' campaign was undoubtedly more effective on a tactical level than the 'Rolling Thunder' campaign of 1965–68. Controls on the bombing were relaxed and President Nixon gave his full support to it. The heaviest bombing during 'Rolling Thunder' occurred during 1967 when 106,996 sorties over North Vietnam dropped 247,410 tons of bombs; during 'Linebacker I' 41,653 sorties dropped 155,548 tons of bombs in five and a half months. The closing of Haiphong and other ports in North Vietnam during 'Linebacker I' was a major change from 'Rolling Thunder'. Closing the ports forced the movement of goods on to the rail lines and roads from China and these were heavily bombed. The lifting of the restrictions on bombing close to Hanoi and Haiphong together with the use of the laser-guided weapons increased the level of destruction, while the demolition of railway bridges forced the movement of supplies on to trucks for the journey south. Heavy bombing of the North Vietnamese oil storage system meant that the fuel available for transport became restricted towards the end of the campaign. The South Vietnamese Army kept up the pressure on the NVA in the South, keeping the level of supplies needed higher than could be maintained. This undoubtedly played a part in the defeat of the Northern army in the South.

The bombing, along with the practical defeat of their army in the South, did play a part in persuading the North Vietnamese to reach a settlement with the Americans in October 1972. Air power theorists would like to say that the bombing forced the North Vietnamese to reach an agreement. There seems little doubt that the bombing did indeed pressurise the North Vietnamese, but the actual terms of the agreement were very favourable to them. They were allowed to keep their army in South Vietnam, justifying their invasion and the destruction of large areas of the country. The ceasefire in place would allow them to re-group and rebuild their defeated army, ready for the the next attempt to take over the South—which is what in fact happened. The agreement allowed no effective way of stopping any violations of the ceasefire terms, which in reality allowed the North Vietnamese to do as they wished. The bombing had not forced the North Vietnamese to surrender, and the terms of the agreement gave them most of what they wanted—which is why President Thieu did not sign a ceasefire in October. When the Americans attempted to renegotiate the terms of the agreement to placate President Thieu the North Vietnamese refused to agree to less advantageous terms, although they must have real-

173

ised that a resumption of the bombing was possible, if not likely. The bombing, or the threat of more bombing, did not force the North Vietnamese to reach an agreement they did not want.

The North Vietnamese cannot have anticipated the extent of the bombing that took place during 'Linebacker II'. North Vietnamese claims that 'Linebacker II' was their victory can only be viewed as bravado. Since the end of the Vietnam War many of the advocates of strategic bombing have quoted the 'Linebacker II' campaign as an example of how air power should have been used, and see it as a vindication of the strategic bombing theories. Admiral Moorer has since said,

> I am convinced that Linebacker II served as a catalyst for the negotiations which resulted in the ceasefire. Air power, given its day in court after almost a decade of frustration, confirmed its effectiveness as an instrument of national power—in just 9½ flying days.[1]

Other commanders have also stated that 'Linebacker II' proved what bombing could accomplish. Here again, it is hard to justify these claims. 'Linebacker II' was an effective campaign in that it caused huge destruction. It has been said that the bombing forced the North Vietnamese back to the negotiating table. But the North Vietnamese refused to negotiate while the bombing continued: they made no concessions to stop the bombing, and when the talks re-started in January 1973 they had not changed their position since October 1972. The agreement was reached because the Americans forced President Thieu to sign a ceasefire that was only cosmetically different from the one he refused to sign the previous October. It can be said that 'Linebacker II' did help to bring a settlement, but it did not bring victory. Two years after Nixon's 'peace with honour' the North Vietnamese tanks rolled into Saigon.

---

[1] Moorer, T. H., 'The Decisiveness of Airpower in Vietnam', Air Force Policy Letter for Commanders, Supp. No 11 (November 1973), p. 9.

APPENDICES

APPENDIX 1: AIR-TO-AIR REFUELLING

During 1972 large numbers of tanker aircraft were stationed all round South-East Asia to support the 'Linebacker' campaigns. The bombing of the North could not have taken place without the use of these aircraft. The tactical bombers did not have the range to bomb the North while carrying a worthwhile bomb load without being refuelled in the air. The B-52s based in Thailand did not need the tankers but those based on Guam were dependent on tanker support. Although the aircraft carriers based at Yankee Station were closer to Hanoi than the Air Force bases in Thailand, Navy aircraft still made extensive use of air refuelling.

The Air Force and the Navy employed different systems of air refuelling. The Navy used the drogue and probe method. This involves the tanker aircraft trailing behind it a fuel line with a flexible cone attached to the end. The receiving aircraft is equipped with a probe that extends forward into the the pilot's field of view. It is the receiving pilot's responsibility to position his aircraft behind the tanker, and slot the probe into the drogue. Using this method, if the tanker is equipped with more than one drogue, several aircraft can be refuelled at the same time.

The Air Force originally used this system but had changed to the flying boom method by the mid-1960s. In this the tanker aircraft is fitted with a telescopic boom controlled by an operator. The receiving aircraft has only to position itself behind the tanker and the operator places the boom into a receptacle on the aircraft and pumps the fuel. Using this method fuel can be passed to the receiving aircraft more quickly than by the probe and drogue method, but only one aircraft at a time can be refuelled.

When the Air Force started its build-up in South-East Asia during the early 1960s it still had in service the Boeing KC-97, a propeller-driven aircraft used by Strategic Air Command, and the KB-50, a version of the Second World War Superfortress with two extra jet engines to give more speed, in use with Tactical Air Command. Both these tankers used the probe and drogue system. After 1964 the only Air Force tanker used in the war was the Boeing KC-135. This was developed from the Boeing 707 and was a large and fast aircraft capable of keeping up with the tactical jets and delivering over 50,000 gallons of fuel. The KC-135 used the flying boom system of refuelling but could be modified on the ground to use the probe and drogue. It had been decided that the tanker fleet would be concentrated under the control of Strategic Air Command, and throughout the war the tactical aircraft were dependent on SAC tankers.

With the bombing of North Vietnam during 'Rolling Thunder' between 1965 and 1968, and the B-52 'Arc Light' bombing raids from Guam, large numbers of KC-135 tankers were stationed throughout the area. In many cases the size of attacking forces was dependent on the availability of tanker aircraft rather than the availability of fighter-bombers. By late 1967 87 KC-135s were based in Thailand alone. During 1967 the KC-135s flew 22,891 sorties and carried out 103,415 transfers, and on average one tanker refuelled five tactical fighter-bombers on a mission over the North.

The Navy's large carriers normally carried a small number of tanker aircraft. At the start of the war the standard tanker was the Douglas KA-3. This was a large, twin-engine jet aircraft that had originally been designed as a long-range nuclear bomber; the Air Force used a version of this aircraft, the EB-66, as a radar-jammer. The KA-3 was one of the largest aircraft used by the carriers and thus the number available was always limited. Later in the war the standard tanker became the KA-6, a developed version of the A-6 Intruder.

During a major strike the tankers were always some of the first aircraft to take off. They were positioned close to the coast of North Vietnam to allow strike aircraft that were short of fuel to take on extra before heading out to the carriers. Many aircraft that would not have had enough fuel to reach safety were rescued in this way. To a limited extent the Navy also used what was known as the 'buddy-buddy' system. This involved ordinary strike aircraft (A-4s, A-6s or A-7s) carrying a special underwing package that included a drogue to allow other aircraft to take on fuel. Although this restricted the number of aircraft available to carry bombs, it did allow a temporary increase in tanking capability. However, the amount of fuel that could be carried by the strike aircraft meant that only a small quantity could be transferred to another aircraft.

With the halt in the bombing of the North in 1968 and the run-down of American forces, the numbers of tanking aircraft slowly declined to a low point in early 1972, but with the North Vietnamese invasion of the South, and the consequent massive increase in the numbers of aircraft in South-East Asia, the numbers of tankers were also increased. The redeployment of tactical fighters during the 'Constant Guard' series of reinforcements could not have taken place without tankers: tactical aircraft did not have the range to cross the Pacific without air refuelling. KC-135s were stationed at Takhli, Don Muang, Korat and U-Tapao in Thailand, Clark in the Philippines, Ching Chuan Kang in Taiwan, Kadena on Okinawa and Andersen on Guam, and by June there were 115 KC-135s at various air bases throughout the theatre.

The highest monthly totals for aerial refuellings during the entire war occurred in September 1972. During this month the tankers flew 3,902 sorties and carried out 12,509 refuellings. Of this total, 2,661 sorties were for refuelling tactical aircraft and 1,241 were for B-52s bombing South Vietnam. The number of tankers was increased again for the 'Linebacker II' raids in December 1972, when there were 195 KC-135s in the region. The total of tanker sorties flown between 17 and 28 December was 1,390, and 4,625 air refuellings were made. During the whole of of 1972 34,700 sorties were flown by the KC-135 tankers in support of the bombing operations, in the course of which 115,272 aerial refuellings were made and 106,913 to the tactical fighter forces. By the end of June 1973 the numbers of tankers in the region had been reduced to an average of 104. These were based at U-Tapao, Kadena and Andersen.

The enormous effort by the refuelling tankers had been central to the way that the bombing of the North had been carried out; indeed, the bombing could not have taken place without the commitment by SAC of large numbers of KC-135s. To refuel the tactical fighter-bombers the tankers flew in oval 'racetrack' patterns over Thailand, Laos and the Gulf of Tonkin. The tankers were in position before the strike aircraft arrived and passed between 10,000 and 12,000lb of fuel to them on the way into North Vietnam and some 5,000lb on the way out. While the 'Linebacker' bombing raids were taking place there were tanker aircraft at fifteen different positions around North Vietnam supporting the raids.

While they were bombing North Vietnam the B-52s from Guam were refuelled for their sixteen-hour flights by KC-135s from Kadena Air Base in Okinawa. The refuelling took place north of the Philippines over the sea. It took between 15 and 20 minutes to pass 100,000lb of fuel to each B-52. Large numbers of aircraft had to arrive in exactly the right place, at exactly the right moment and at exactly the right altitude for the 'Linebacker II' campaign to have taken place. Tankers refuelling the tactical aircraft were under the control of the ground radar network based in Thailand and South Vietnam. The KC-135s were not supposed to move from their allotted 'racetrack' positions but on occasions, when fighter aircraft had been damaged or were short of fuel, they would move north to meet them. On rare occasions they even flew into western North Vietnam to meet aircraft in desperate need.

Throughout the war the tankers flew 194,687 sorties and carried out 813,878 air refuellings. This involved the transfer of 1.4 billion gallons of fuel. Large numbers of aircraft that would not have reached their bases were saved and their pilots preserved from death or capture. Before the war it had been thought that air refuelling would only be used by tactical aircraft to allow overseas deployment to take place quickly, but the bombing of North Vietnam could not have taken place without the enormous effort put into air refuelling.

APPENDIX 2: RADAR COMMAND, CONTROL AND COMMUNICATIONS

On several occasions during the 1960s Tan Son Nhut airfield, close to Saigon, became the busiest airport in the world. The Americans had thousands of aircraft stationed in South-East Asia and by 1972 the South Vietnamese had the world's fourth largest air force. From being a quiet backwater in terms of aircraft Indo-China had become home to large numbers of aircraft. To provide control in the air for these aircraft the Americans developed an air traffic control system covering South Vietnam, Laos and Cambodia.

As early as 1964 ground radars had been set up at Pleiku, Da Nang and Saigon in South Vietnam. These were followed by other radars in Thailand and South Vietnam. The radar net was also used to provide early warning of any attack by aircraft from the North. Unidentified aircraft were detected flying over South Vietnam but none of these aircraft was ever intercepted. (They are more likely to have been flown by the CIA than by the North Vietnamese.) When the bombing of North Vietnam was started the radars in the northern part of Thailand and South Vietnam were used to provide some coverage for the strike aircraft entering North Vietnam.

By 1966 the SEAITACS (South East Asia Integrated Air Control System) had been introduced. This involved the use of four centres, two in Thailand and two in South Vietnam. The centre at Saigon controlled aircraft operating over South Vietnam and the centre at Da Nang (Monkey Mountain) provided radar control for aircraft over North Vietnam and the Gulf of Tonkin. Udorn centre in Thailand acted as a back up to Da Nang.

Range limitations on the ground-based radar restricted the coverage that could be given to the strike aircraft over North Vietnam. In order to give wider coverage over the North airborne command and control aircraft were introduced. The Air Force used the Lockeed EC-121D Warning Star for this purpose. This aircraft had originally been developed as an early warning aircraft, as part of the Continental US air defence network. Warning Stars were a development of the large, four-engine Super Constellation passenger airliner and were equipped with radar in a sail-like structure on the top of the fuselage. Operated by the 552nd AEWCW (Airborne Early Warning and Control Wing), the EC-121s were flown from various bases before moving to Korat.

EC-121Ds were equipped with the AN/APS-95 search radar and IFF (identification friend or foe) interrogation equipment, plus an extensive radio communications capability, to distribute the radar information they gathered. The EC-121D was developed into the EC-121D+ with improved equipment, and a later model, the EC-121T, was introduced before the end of the war. Because the radars used by the EC-121 had been developed to operate primarily over water they were limited in their effectiveness over land. However, the EC-121s were the only aircraft available to do the job. The types of radar then available had difficulty in tracking aircraft when looking down on to any type of ground as the reflected radar energy from the ground swamped the returns from an aircraft.

Between 10 December 1971 and March 1973 the EC-121s were credited with assisting in the destruction of twenty North Vietnamese MiGs. Included in that total was Steve Ritchie's fifth MiG kill. Ritchie's back-seat weapons systems operator, Chuck DeBellevue, who was credited with the destruction of six MiGs, was quoted as saying, 'Many times we would not have been able to intercept an enemy and effect an engagement without the information we received from them. It's invaluable support.'[1]

The detachment of EC-121s varied in size between five and eight aircraft. The Warning Stars originally used the code-name 'Big Eye' but this was later changed to 'College Eye'. The call-sign used by these aircraft in 1972 was 'Disco'. As large, relatively slow aircraft the Warning Stars had to be kept out of the way of the North Vietnamese defences. The radar aircraft were positioned over the Gulf, or over Laos, whenever aircraft were operating over North Vietnam. From these positions they could give radar coverage at high level over all of North Vietnam but low-level coverage was restricted and by flying at low level the North Vietnamese MiGs could avoid the EC-121's radar. However, by using two aircraft, one at high level to give long-range coverage at altitude and one at low level to give clearer, short-range coverage, the EC-121s were able to overcome some of the limitations of their equipment.

The EC-121s were responsible for directing American aircraft to intercept North Vietnamese fighters and for issuing MiG alerts. To ensure that there were no violations of the Chinese border warnings were given to aircraft coming close to the frontier, and warnings were also issued when SA-2 missiles were known to be active. During the early part of the war the airborne controllers were only advisory in nature, acting as a source of information to the strike aircraft. Decisions were taken by the strike commander who was flying in one of the strike aircraft. Later, during the 'Linebacker' campaigns, the EC-121s assumed more control of the fighter aircraft and would direct and position them to intercept the North Vietnamese MiGs.

The threat warning format used by the airborne controllers was originally a colour-coded system that gave general information to all aircraft over the North rather than to specific aircraft. This was broadcast on the guard channel of 243.0MHz and did not need to be acknowledged, which meant that it was not known whether the information had been received. By 1972 information was given to specific aircraft, who had to reply, and the position of MiGs was given in relation to 'Bull's Eye' (Hanoi) as a distance and direction. The pilots were given constant updates on the

---

[1] Cole, David K., 'The Connies of College Eye', *Airman*, XVI (March 1973), p. 6.

position of the MiGs in relation to the American fighters until the MiG was picked up on the fighter pilot's own radar. At this point the American pilots used the code word 'Judy' to tell the EC-121 that they would now be taking control of the intercept from the airborne controller. During one six-month period of the 'Linebacker' campaign six EC-121s flew 1,100 missions which involved 11,000 hours and supervised 27,000 flights of tactical fighters and strike aircraft.

During the later stages of the 'Linebacker' campaigns all Air Force aircraft entering North Vietnam came under the control of Tea Ball, the advanced headquarters based at Nakom Phanom in Thailand. Mission planning was still carried out in Saigon, but once the aircraft were in the air they were under the control of Tea Ball. By using the EC-121s and C-135 relay aircraft Tea Ball could be in constant radio communication with the strike aircraft, and by integrating all intelligence and radar information into one centre Tea Ball was able to give effective support to the attacking aircraft.

A version of the ubiquitous C-130 was used as an airborne combat command post. These aircraft did not have a radar set but were equipped with extensive communications equipment. They were used as airborne command centres to control strike aircraft operating in Laos and in RP 1 in North Vietnam. A crew of twelve was carried to operate the radio equipment. The C-130Es were under the command of the 7th ACCS (Airborne Command and Control Squadron) stationed at Udorn between 1965 and 1975. During the siege of Khe Sanh in 1968 the C-130 airborne command posts controlled up to 850 strike sorties a day.

The Navy equivalent of the EC-121 was the Grumman E-2 Hawkeye. This was a large, twin-engine aircraft with a circular radar mounted above the fuselage. All the aircraft carriers had a small number of Hawkeyes on board when operating from Yankee Station. The Navy established the PIRAZ (Positive Identification Radar Advisory Zone) area over the Gulf of Tonkin and the eastern part of North Vietnam. A radar network was established with the radars based on board the ships of Task Force 77, at Yankee Station, the airborne Hawkeyes and a forward screen of radar picket ships close to the coast of North Vietnam.

One cruiser equipped with high-quality radar and communications equipment was positioned off Haiphong to give some coverage of RP 6B. This ship operated under the code-name 'Red Crown'. The purpose of PIRAZ was both to provide early warning to the ships in Task Force 77 and to give some control of Navy aircraft operating over the North. Because of the distance between the Gulf and Hanoi, 'Red Crown' could only see aircraft above 10,000ft over Hanoi. 'Red Crown' also controlled Air Force aircraft operating in the eastern area of North Vietnam.When the full radar and communications network had been set up it was possible for the commanders on the ground at the Tea Ball command post in Thailand to follow and communicate with the aircraft operating over North Vietnam.

APPENDIX 3: THE 'WILD WEASEL' AND 'IRON HAND' MISSIONS

During the 'Rolling Thunder' campaign between 1965 and 1968 the North Vietnamese had time to develop their air defence system in response to the American bombing. To strengthen the defences the Soviets supplied the North Vietnamese with the SA-2 missile system. This was the missile that had shot down Gary Powers in his U-2 over the Soviet Union in 1961. The North Vietnamese started to build missile sites around the Hanoi area in 1965. The American forces did not attack these developments for perverted political reasons. The first Air Force aircraft to be shot down by an SA-2, an F-4C, fell on 24 July 1965 and the first Navy aircraft, an A-4, fell on 11 August. Both the Air Force and the Navy tried to attack the missile sites, but lost more aircraft through being forced to fly low to find the sites.

The majority of American aircraft shot down over the North were destroyed by anti-aircraft guns. Missiles never destroyed large numbers of aircraft, but did force strike aircraft to fly at a lower level than was thought ideal, and by flying at a lower altitude the American aircraft were much more vulnerable to anti-aircraft guns. The availability of jamming pods again allowed the strike aircraft fly at a higher altitude. By 1972 the majority of strikes into North Vietnam were flown at around 15,000ft. This was a compromise height, lower than ideal but low enough to restrict the SA-2 missile's effective envelope.

In response to the missile threat the US Air Force developed specialised aircraft and tactics to neutralise the SA-2s. When it became available the radar homing and warning system (RHAW) was carried by all US aircraft. This equipment detected when the aircraft had been picked up on North Vietnamese radar and indicated its direction. The SA-2 radar was known by the NATO code-name 'Fan Song' and operated in S-band, changing to L-band just before the missile was fired. The Air Force decided to develop a specialised type of aircraft, using the RHAW equipment, to counter the missile system. The programme code-name was 'Wild Weasel' and the anti-missile operations were known as 'Iron Hand'.

To assure the early availability of 'Wild Weasel' aircraft the first aircraft converted were F-100F two-seaters. The back-seat EWOs (electronic warfare officers) were transferred from SAC, the only branch of the Air Force with personnel experienced in operating electronic warfare equipment. The 'Iron Hand' missions were flown by two 'Wild Weasels' and two F-105Ds, operating as a 'hunter-killer team', the F-100s being the 'hunters' and the F-105s the 'killers'.

The 'Wild Weasel' teams escorted the strike aircraft into the target area and attacked any missile sites that could be detected. The RHAW equipment gave the direction of the active missile radar and the F-100F flew towards the missile site and marked it with rockets. Following behind, the F-105Ds attacked the site with cluster bombs and conventional bombs. As the first into the target area and the last out, the

'Iron Hand' missions suffered high casualty rates. To replace the F-100F the two-seat F-105F, which had a better range and load-carrying capacity, was developed into a 'Wild Weasel' aircraft. The F-105F was first deployed in May 1966 and operated over the North until the end of the 'Rolling Thunder' campaign in 1968.

One drawback with the RHAW equipment was that it did not give the range, from the aircraft, to the SA-2's radar. The 'Wild Weasels' had to fly in the general direction of the radar until it was possible to spot the site visually, and this made the aircraft vulnerable to flak batteries positioned around the site. The Shrike ARM (anti-radar missile) was introduced to the 'Wild Weasels' in 1966. This had a passive radar seeker head that could home on to and destroy the SA-2's 'Fan Song' radar, which was situated on top of a caravan-type vehicle. After launching the Shrike the 'Wild Weasel' aircraft could turn away, but the 'killer' F-105D had to follow the Shrike and bomb the missile site to assure its destruction. By the time of the 'Linebacker' campaigns in 1972 the 'killer' component of the 'Wild Weasel' team was made up of F-4 Phantoms.

The Shrike had a weight of only 400lb and a range of around six miles. A larger missile, the Standard ARM, was introduced in 1968. With a weight of 1,800lb and a range of 20 miles, this was a much more effective missile against the SA-2s. The drawback with both these weapons, however, was that if the SA-2 sites thought that they were under attack the 'Fan Song' radar would be turned off and the ARMs could no longer home in, although this would result in the missile sites becoming inactive—and the 'Wild Weasels' would achieve their primary objective of protecting the strike aircraft.

General William W. Momyer, who commanded the Seventh Air Force described the 'Wild Weasels':

> Of all the strike and support forces, the Iron Hand flights were truly the elite. These flights sought out the missile sites, and the battle of wits between the F-105 Wild Weasel pilots of the Iron Hand flights and the North Vietnamese controllers makes a most fascinating story. Of course, we knew where most of the active sites were, but there were always a number that were brought to bear against the strike forces that were not known until their radars came on the air.[1]

The 'Wild Weasels' suffered the highest casualties of the strike packages bombing North Vietnam.

A further development of the 'Wild Weasel' F-105F was the F-105G, which was introduced into South-East Asia in 1971. This version of the F-105 had better RHAW equipment, a built-in ECM capability and an improved missile-carrying fit. As well as giving the bearing of any radar detected the F-105G could now give a distance to

---

[1] Momyer, William W., 'The Evolution of Fighter Tactics in South-East Asia', *Air Force Magazine*, LVI (July 1973), p. 60.

it. The built-in ECM capability was achieved by splitting an AN/ALQ-105 pod in half and fixing these components on either side of the fuselage, underneath the wings, thereby releasing a weapons mount to carry another missile. In April 1972 sixteen F-105G 'Wild Weasels' were stationed at Korat Air Base as the 17th WWS. The 'Constant Guard I' deployment of aircraft included twelve F-105Gs of the 561st TFS, and these were moved to Korat on 11 April 1972 after the North Vietnamese invasion of the South.

A version of the F-4C was also converted to 'Wild Weasel' configuration. Only 36 of these aircraft were produced; half were stationed in Europe and the other half were used by the 67th TFS based at Kadena on Okinawa. The F-4C was not as well equipped as the F-105G, could not give the distance to a radar site and could not fire the Standard ARM missile. In October 1972 the 67th TFS was moved to Korat in Thailand. The F-4Cs carried out 460 sorties over the North, in support of the 'Linebacker I' and 'II' raids, without loss.

The Navy had approached the problem of the SA-2 missiles from a different direction. They had not developed specialised aircraft to attack the missile system, but had used the RHAW equipment fitted in their standard attack aircraft to allow all their aircraft to carry out the 'Iron Hand' mission. The larger carriers used the A-6B Intruder, which could carry two Shrike missiles and two Standard ARMs, for 'Iron Hand'; A-7E Corsairs could also carry Shrike missiles for defence-suppression missions. The smaller carriers, which could not carry the A-6B, used the A-4F Skyhawk equipped with the Bendix APS-107B RHAW and, for 'Iron Hand', with Shrike missiles. The Navy's approach meant that more aircraft were potentially available to carry out the 'Iron Hand' strikes, which allowed greater flexibility in mission planning, but the standard strike aircraft could never carry as much equipment as the specialised F-105G 'Wild Weasels'.

By 1972 the North Vietnamese had been using the SA-2 missiles for seven years and had become the most experienced air defence system operators in the world. They had reacted to every American development with changes in either equipment or tactics. They used electronic equipment that simulated the 'Fan Song' radar and surrounded this equipment with large numbers of anti-aircraft guns to draw American aircraft into flak traps. They became very adept at knowing when 'Iron Hand' aircraft were in the area and at switching their radar sets on and off to combat the threat.

Forty-eight 'Wild Weasel' aircraft were lost between 1965 and 1973, two F-100Fs and 46 F-105s; seven F-105Gs were lost during the 'Linebacker' campaigns, two from the 561st TFS and five from the 17th WWS. The whole concept of the 'Wild Weasels' was criticised and their effectiveness questioned by some sections of the Air Force. It was extremely difficult to confirm the destruction of missile sites by the 'Wild Weasel' aircraft, but the real criterion of success was not the destruction of the sites but the suppression of the missile system during the critical time that an attack was taking place. The real aim of the 'Iron Hand' missions was to enable strike aircraft being to operate without too much opposition from the missiles.The SA-2s were never very effective in the numbers of aircraft shot down. Indeed, compared to the numbers fired, they could be described as hopelessly ineffective: in 1967 one aircraft was lost for every 55 missiles fired, and by 1972 this total was one for every 87. However, the missiles did destroy more aircraft than were shot down by the North's MiGs. The Americans put considerable effort into combating the SA-2 missiles, but although the threat was contained it was never defeated.

APPENDIX 4: COMBAT SEARCH AND RESCUE

By 1972 the Americans had developed specialised search and rescue organisations that covered all of Indo-China and the Gulf of Tonkin. Over 5,000 aircraft had been lost in South Vietnam, Laos, Cambodia and North Vietnam, nearly 1,000 of which had been shot down over North Vietnam. The knowledge that everything possible would be done to recover downed aircrew was a boost to the morale of the forces involved. The Air Force had rescued over 2,600 personnel between 1964 and October 1972, while the Navy had rescued 458 of the 912 aircrew shot down between 1964 and November 1968.

The Air Force organisation controlling combat rescue was the 3rd Aerospace Rescue and Recovery Group based at Tan Son Nhut in South Vietnam. The 3rd ARRG had around 30 aircraft and 700 personnel under its direct control, but could draw on unlimited support from all American forces in the area. The Joint Rescue Coordination Center, code-named 'Joker', at Tan Son Nhut controlled rescue forces throughout the area, with the forces at Udorn in Thailand responsible for rescues over North Vietnam. The helicopters used included the Kaman HH-43 Huskie, which was a small helicopter intended for use close to airfields (a developed version the HH-43F had more powerful engine, extra armour and a machine-gun armament); the Sikorsky HH-3E (known as the 'Jolly Green Giant'), a twin-engine, armed and armoured helicopter with the range to operate over North Vietnam; and the Sikorsky HH-53 (known as the 'Super Jolly'), the ultimate rescue helicopter introduced during the war, which had extra range and lifting power for use over the North.

To coordinate and control the rescue missions a version of the Lockeed C-130 Hercules, the HC-130P, had been developed to act as an airborne command post and also as an airborne tanker for the HH-3s and HH-54s. When bombing missions were taking place over North Vietnam the helicopters were already in the air over Laos or positioned on landing strips there. These landing strips, called 'Lima sites', were often behind enemy lines in Laos and were controlled by the CIA; Lima Site 36 was only 170 miles west of Hanoi. The escort for the helicopters was provided by Douglas A-1s operating under the call-sign 'Sandy'. These propeller-driven aircraft had the range and endurance to stay with the helicopters and suppress any opposition on the ground.

The technique developed by the Air Force rescue services was that the helicopters worked in pairs, with one acting as back-up (the 'High Bird'), orbiting out of the immediate area of the rescue but close at hand. The other helicopter (the 'Low Bird') carried out the actual rescue. If the first helicopter were shot down, were severely damaged or went unserviceable the second helicopter moved in to replace it. A-1s working with the helicopters usually divided into the high flight, which escorted the helicopters, and the low flight, which searched for the downed pilot and made certain of the position and state of any ground defences. The flight leader of the low section of Skyraiders was nominated on-scene commander under the control of the airborne command post. The leader of the low flight could call in more air strikes against any defences or North Vietnamese troops as he saw fit, and the rescue helicopters would not enter the area until he considered it reasonably safe to do so.

One of the uncredited élite groups of the Vietnam conflict was the parajumpers. Their job was to go down on to the ground to help any survivors who needed medical attention or were too weak to get into the helicopter unaided. The 'PJs', as they were known, were trained in diving techniques by the Navy for over-water rescues and in first aid for injured aircrew. They were also fully qualified parachutists, trained in survival techniques and schooled in unarmed combat. On top of all this they were also expected to be fully conversant with all the armament carried by the helicopters. One parajumper was carried in the crew of the HH-43; the HH-53 carried two. Earl H. Tillford described the parajumpers:

> Pararescuemen were a special breed. The military produced several elites during the Vietnam conflict, mostly men dedicated to taking human lives in any number of ways. Air Force parajumpers were an elite committed to saving human lives.[1]

To lift people out of the thick jungle that covered large areas of Indo-China the rescue helicopters used a jungle penetrator. This device was a dart-shaped, 26lb weight that also incorporated three folding seats. If the downed pilot was wounded the helicopter's parajumper rode down on one of these seats. If the pilot was uninjured the penetrator was lowered through the foliage to him partially covered in canvas to protect it from snags. After releasing one of the seats the pilot strapped himself in and was lifted through the jungle canopy. The penetrator had been developed byKaman for the HH-43 but was used by all the rescue helicopters.

---

[1] Tilford, Earl H., *Search and Rescue in Southeast Asia 1961–1975*, Office of Air Force History (Washington, 1980), p. 87.

All the pilots flying over North Vietnam and Laos carried small rescue radios and spare batteries. It was intended that contact could be established between the shot-down aircrew and the rescue forces before rescue could take place. The North Vietnamese had obtained a supply of these radios from aircraft that had been brought down over the North, and it was considered essential that a positive identification be established before a rescue could take place as the North Vietnamese had attempted to draw rescue aircraft into traps using these radios. All aircrew operating over the North were supposed to register the responses to three personal questions that would have to be answered before a rescue could take place. The rescue forces had access to these answers and could satisfy themselves as to the identity of the airman before the helicopters would be committed. (However, one airman who could not remember his wife's maiden name was nevertheless picked up.)

The Navy rescue organisation was Helicopter Combat Support Squadron Seven (HC-7). To carry out the rescues the Navy used a version of the Kaman UH-2 Seasprite that had self-sealing fuel tanks, armour plate and a machine-gun armament. Also used was the Sikorsky SH-3 Sea King helicopter. When a major strike over North Vietnam was being carried out the Navy moved two destroyers to the Northern SAR station (approximately 20°N) and two destroyers to the Southern SAR station (about 19°N). The UH-2s were small enough to be stationed on the destroyers, but the SH-3s were based on board one of the carriers and were in the air during the raids over the North. The SH-3s could refuel from the destroyers by lowering a line and drawing up fuel into their tanks, without having to land on the ships. To provide combat support for the helicopters during a rescue mission over the North the Navy had four A-1 Skyraiders, A-4 Skyhawks or A-7 Corsairs already in the air.

Both the Air Force and Navy helicopter pilots were given survival training before they were sent to South-East Asia. The Navy school was at Warner Springs in California. Courses were divided into three sections—living off the land, evasion techniques and anti-interrogation techniques. An equivalent Air Force Jungle Survival School was situated in the Philippines close to Clark Field. Pilots on the way to Vietnam or Thailand had to spend three days at the school. They were given lectures on providing themselves with food in jungle conditions and what plants and animals to avoid. They were then transported into the jungle and expected to survive for three days before they were considered to have graduated.

The most famous mission carried out by the rescue forces was probably the raid on the prison at Son Tay that took place on 20 November 1970. By this time the North Vietnamese were holding several hundred American prisoners of war, mostly shot-down aircrew but also some Army personnel who had been captured in the South. There appeared to be no end in sight to the war and no chance that these prisoners would return home. In these circumstances it was decided to mount a rescue mission to bring out at least some of them. Son Tay, the prison camp chosen for

186

the raid, was on the Red River 28 miles north-west of Hanoi. The camp at Son Tay was close to an army camp and there were 12,000 troops within a four-mile radius, but it was thought possible to isolate the area long enough to carry out the raid.

The personnel involved, carefully selected to carry out the rescue attempt, spent several months training in secrecy close to Elgin Air Base in Florida. It was decided to mount the raid on 20 November 1970. The attacking force consisted of five HH-53 helicopters from Udorn in Thailand, to carry the special forces involved and to bring back the 55 prisoners thought to be at Son Tay. Also involved was one HH-3 helicopter that was small enough to crash-land inside the compound at the prison to place the troops directly where they were needed. To cover the raiding forces there were five A-1s and two C-130Es to provide command and control facilities and to drop flares. Fighter coverage was provided by ten F-4 Phantoms, while five F-105 'Wild Weasels' were intended to block the North Vietnamese radar and missile coverage.

This force crossed into North Vietnam at low altitude while Navy aircraft attacked targets in the Haiphong area to divert the attention of the defences. The attack on the prison went reasonably smoothly, although some of the American forces attacked the Vietnamese army camp instead of the prison 400yds away before they realised their mistake. A number of Vietnamese troops were killed during the capture of the prison, but no American prisoners were found—a local river had overflowed its banks and polluted the water supply for the prison and the inmates had been moved away several weeks beforehand.

Twenty-seven minutes after the start of the operation the last of the American troops were lifted out of the area. On the way out of North Vietnam one of the helicopters was attacked by a MiG fighter which fired a missile but missed. The F-105s had been suppressing the Vietnamese defences throughout the raid and two of these were damaged by SA-2s. One made it back to base but the other crashed in Laos. Two of the HH-53s refuelled in mid-air from a HC-130P and circled in the area of the crash site until morning, when they picked up the aircrew who had ejected.

Although the raid had been a tactical success the failure of intelligence meant that no prisoners had been rescued. After the raid the North Vietnamese reacted by moving all the prisoners into several large camps inside Hanoi. This was an improvement for many of the inmates who had been kept in solitary confinement for many years. The raid demonstrated the fact that the Americans could attack North Vietnam whenever they chose, even inside Hanoi's main air defence network.

With the ending of the bombing of North Vietnam in 1968, the policy of 'Vietnamisation' and the run-down in American forces there was also a decline in the numbers of rescue forces in South-East Asia. This changed after the North Vietnamese invasion of South Vietnam early in 1972, which forced the return of rescue assets to the theatre. On 20 April 1972 Lieutenant-Colonel Iceal E. Hambleton was shot down while on board an EB-66 close to the Demilitarised Zone. Hambleton landed close to large concentrations of North Vietnamese taking part in the invasion of the South, but A-1s found where he was hiding and attempted to isolate him from the surrounding troops. Four American Army helicopters attempted to move in to rescue him, without clearance from the rescue forces, and two of them were shot down, one crash resulting in the deaths of all the crew members on board. Over the next eleven days hundreds of air strikes were mounted in the area around Hambleton to prevent his capture. Two OV-10s were shot down while acting as forward air observers. Only one HH-53 attempted to reach Hambleton, but this was also shot down and its crew killed.

It was finally decided that it was impossible to place helicopters into the area around Hambleton and he was told to try to float down the Cam Lo river out of the area. Three days later he was picked up by a party of marines in a boat. (This incident was made into a feature film, *Bat 21*, starring Gene Hackman.) The attempts to rescue Hambleton by air showed the limitations of the rescue services when they tried to operate in areas of heavy defences and raised the question how long it was wise to continue trying to carry out a rescue when other lives were at stake. Five aircraft and eleven lives had been lost during the failed attempts to rescue Hambleton. A 17-mile control zone had been put around Hambleton's position on the ground and the use of artillery within this zone was strictly constrained. The zone was on the main axis of the North Vietnamese advance, and as a result the South Vietnamese 3rd Division was severely obstructed in its attempts to stop it. This situation gave rise to comments that the United States valued one American life more than a division of South Vietnamese.

On 10 May 1972 Roger Locher was shot down over North Vietnam. He parachuted down to land in a hilly area close to the airfield at Yen Bai. He hid from the North Vietnamese searching for him and moved over a period of days to the west, heading for a mountainous area on the other side of the Red River. It was 22 days before he managed to contact an American aircraft on his survival radio. The first rescue attempt was abandoned after the defences proved too strong. The next day, 2 June, all raids over the North were cancelled and 119 sorties were devoted to bringing back Captain Locher. Yen Bai airfield and anti-aircraft guns in the area were bombed. The entire rescue organisation went into operation and Locher was lifted out by an HH-53 and flown back to Thailand. This rescue had taken place further north in Vietnam than any previous rescue.

It was finally decided to replace the venerable A-1s in the rescue role by Vought A-7 Corsair IIs. It was intended to hand the Skyraiders over to the South Vietnamese Air Force as part of the process of 'Vietnamisation'. The A-7s were considerably faster than the Skyraiders and thus found it much more difficult to escort the helicopters, being forced to fly an oval pattern around them. Moreover, jet engines burn considerably more fuel when operated at very low level, which meant that the A-7s were obliged to spend more time in aerial refuelling. To provide a continuous escort for the helicopters the number of escort aircraft was increased from the four A-1s needed to six A-7s.

In South Vietnam the North American OV-10 Bronco was employed to work with the rescue forces. The OV-10 was primarily a FAC aircraft but was used to pinpoint any shot-down aircrew and to direct any attacks needed to protect them. The A-37 Dragonfly was also used in South Vietnam by the rescue forces as light attack aircraft, to supplement the A-1s and A-7s.

The Kaman HH-43 was still in use at the end of the American involvement in the Vietnam War, although it had been thought unsuitable from the very beginning. Even so, the HH-43 is credited with the fastest pick-up of the war. This occurred on 23 November 1972. Flown by Air Force Lieutenants William Latham and James Moulton, an HH-43 was already in the air when a distress call was heard from a OV-10. The helicopter was forced to take evasive action as the disabled aircraft passed within 300ft of it. Before it hit the ground the pilot of the OV-10 ejected at low level. Following the parachute down, the HH-43 landed in a paddyfield close to the survivor. As the helicopter started to come under fire, the pilot was helped aboard, and the HH-43 lifted away after spending several seconds stuck in the mud. It had taken 1min 32sec from ejection to pick up.

APPENDIX 5: THE ELECTRONIC COUNTERMEASURES WAR

The North Vietnamese had developed and expanded their air defence system and by 1972 it included hundreds of radars in an interlocking net covering most of their country. Long-range surveillance radars covered most of Laos and other radars based at Than Hoa and Vinh covered most of the Gulf of Tonkin. All these radars were Soviet sets, and the North Vietnamese air defence system was based on the Soviet model. Besides the long-range radars there were other short-range, height-finding radars, and the SA-2 missile guidance radars, plus the anti-aircraft gun aiming radars. The radar net was linked by land lines to several command centres that controlled the aircraft, missiles and guns that made up the air defence system. Other sources of information available to the North Vietnamese were the Soviet ships watching the aircraft carriers in the Gulf and spies stationed around the American air bases.

Faced with such an air defence system, it was nearly impossible for US aircraft to approach North Vietnam without being detected. The purpose of electronic countermeasures (ECM) is to cancel out or downgrade the electronic equipment used by an enemy—in this case the radar systems and radio links used by the North

Vietnamese. As most of the equipment used by the North Vietnamese was Soviet, the Americans had developed ECM equipment designed specifically to cancel out these radars and intended to be used by SAC bombers during an attack on the Soviet Union. However, the equipment tended to be bulky and little work had been done on ECM equipment for tactical aircraft.

The two main areas of development in the use of ECM were specialised ECM aircraft intended to jam the air defence radars, allowing the attacking aircraft to operate, and ECM pods, to be carried by all aircraft flying over the North. At the start of the war the only dedicated ECM aircraft in service with the Air Force was the Douglas EB-66. This was a version of the Navy's A-3 Skywarrior and was a large, twin-engine aircraft. The EB-66 carried a number of jammers and was used to create a path through the radar net by using 'noise' broadcast on the radar frequency to 'white out' the radar returns. These relatively slow, large and expensive aircraft or-bited outside the target area to cover the strike aircraft. As the North Vietnamese defences improved the EB-66s were forced to operate at greater ranges from the target area and hence became less effective. One EB-66 was shot down by an SA-2 in February 1966 and one by a MiG in January 1968. EB-66s were still in use in 1972, the 42nd Tactical Electronic Warfare Squadron operating them from Korat. As part of 'Constant Guard II' reinforcements the 39th TEWS, with eight EB-66s, was moved to Korat on 11 April 1972. One EB-66 was shot down by a missile on 20 April while operating over the Demilitarised Zone. The only other Air Force aircraft to operate as a jamming aircraft was a version of the F-105F fitted with a QRC-128 VHF jamming pod that blacked out the radio transmissions between the North Viet-namese MiGs and their ground control. These aircraft were only used to a limited extent and had left the region by 1969.

The Marine Corps had in service at the start of the Vietnam War an ECM version of the 1950s Douglas Skyknight, the EF-10B. This was used by a Marine squadron based at Da Nang until 1969 and accompanied both Navy and Air Force strikes over the North. By 1969 the EF-10B was completely obsolete and was replaced by the Grumman EA-6A, also based at Da Nang. The EA-6A was a version of the two-seat A-6 Intruder naval attack aircraft equipped with the necessary jammers.

At the start of the war the only Navy ECM aircraft was the EA-1, a version of the propeller-driven A-1 Skyraider. It was too slow to venture over North Vietnam and had to operate over the Gulf, close to the coast. The jamming equipment used by the EA-1 was based on valve technology and was of limited value. There was never enough space aboard the carriers and a version of the A-3, the EKA-3, was intro-duced in 1968 as a tanker and jamming aircraft, but the need for tankers meant that it was normally use as the former rather than the latter. The four-seat EA-6B Prowler version of the A-6 Intruder was introduced in June 1972 aboard the carrier USS *America*. This was an advanced aircraft that carried five jamming pods under the wings and fuselage. The Prowler was banned from flying over North Vietnam, but orbited off the coast. Electronic signals were detected by a large antenna on the top of the fin and a computer analysed the signal and used the jammers to send back signals to block the radar screens.

The development of ECM pods to be carried by individual strike aircraft provided a more flexible response to the North Vietnamese defences. The Air Force introduced ECM pods into service in Vietnam during 1966. At first they were unreliable, but by late 1966 they had become essential for operations over North Vietnam. Because of the North's SA-2 missiles, strike aircraft had been forced to operate at a much lower altitude, where the aircraft were more vulnerable to anti-aircraft fire, but by using the ECM equipment they were again able to operate at around 15,000ft. To achieve the most effective ECM coverage it was necessary for the four aircraft in a flight to maintain a specific formation, and after many trials the best arrangement was found to be line abreast, with 2,000ft horizontal spacings and a 500ft vertical separation between the aircraft. A flight of four aircraft in this formation carrying ECM pods created a large white 'blip' on the missile system's radar screen and individual aircraft could not be seen.

Although they did use pods the US Navy tried to install ECM gear inside all their attack aircraft so that all the weapons stations could be used for ordnance. However, this also meant that the basic weight of the aircraft was increased, and this weight had to be carried even in low-threat areas. The first piece of Navy ECM equipment was the crude 'Little Ear' which fitted inside the aircraft canopy with a rubber sucker and only gave an indication that the aircraft had been picked up on enemy radar. In 1966, in Project 'Shoe Horn', AN/ALQ-51 jamming sets were fitted in the diminutive A-4, for use against the 'Fan Song' radar used by the SA-2, giving the aircraft a hunch-back appearance.

The first of the ECM pods used by Air Force were the AN/ALQ-71 and the AN/ALQ-87 sets. These were noise jammers in that they broadcast on the same frequency as the radar to cover the real radar returns from the aircraft, the signals bouncing back from the aircraft being lost in 'noise' generated by the ECM set. US aircraft were also equipped with RHAW equipment to show when aircraft had been picked up on radar, the sets also giving an indication of the direction and type of any radar that had detected the aircraft. AN/ALQ-72 ECM pods were used to disrupt the radar carried by the MiG-21 known by the code-name 'Spin Can'; this operated at a higher frequency than the SA-2's 'Fan Song'.

More sophisticated types of deception ECM became available by 1969 and included the Westinghouse AN/ALQ-101. This set worked on the idea of detecting the pulse from the threat radar and sending back hundreds of identical signals, thereby producing hundreds of false targets on the radar set along the same bearing as the real aircraft. The radio command guidance for the SA-2 did not know which was the real target aircraft. It took nerve for the pilot of an aircraft to see an SA-2 missile heading towards his aircraft and to do nothing but rely on the ECM equipment to decoy it. (A later model of the Westinghouse AN/ALQ-101, the V-10, was used by RAF Jaguar fighters during the Gulf War.) Late in the war the Westinghouse AN/ALQ-131 pod was introduced, and this particular design combined both broad-band noise-jamming and deception-jamming in one installation, but it was a large and heavy piece of equipment. The use of chaff to disrupt the North Vietnamese radar defence system has been described elsewhere in this book.

North Vietnam's missile operators developed tactics to cancel out American superiority in the ECM war. Missiles were fired in a barrage with little chance of guiding in an attempt to break up the flight of attacking aircraft. Once a flight of aircraft had been separated they became more vulnerable, as a single ECM set gave inadequate coverage. The SA-2 operators also fired missiles to one side of a flight of aircraft, hoping to force them to turn into an area covered by further missiles. By 1972 it was reported that new types of missile were active in North Vietnam. A small number of SA-3s were thought to have been supplied to North Vietnam by the Soviets, and optically guided SA-2s were also reported to be active; it was thought to have been an optically guided SA-2 that shot down Randy Cunningham on 10 May 1972. The optically guided SA-2 gave no indication of launch or command guidance, making it harder to jam.

If everything else failed it was usually possible for the fighter aircraft to avoid a missile if the pilot could see it in time. It was fatal to turn away from the missile as it would follow: the escape manoeuvre was to turn into the missile and then at the right moment break to one side as sharply as possible. Having poor manoeuvrability, the SA-2 was unable to follow. If the missile launch was not seen then the missile could not be avoided, while when large numbers of missiles were fired avoiding one could place the aircraft in the path of another.

The Americans spent considerable amounts of money and expended great effort in the attempt to win the electronic war over North Vietnam, and to a large extent they did achieve success. However, right up to the end of the war the North Vietnamese did maintain a credible defence system that was capable destroying a percentage of the attacking American aircraft.

APPENDIX 6: RECONNAISSANCE

For the bombing that took place during the 'Linebacker' raids to have been effective it was essential that as much information as possible was available regarding potential targets. A clear understanding of the position and type of industrial development and of the transport system was necessary for the planning of a bombing campaign. When the campaign started it was also necessary to know how effective the bombing had been on individual targets, in order to attack them again if necessary.

There had been a steady build-up of reconnaissance forces in South-East Asia during the mid-1960s. The RB-57 had been use for sorties over South Vietnam and Laos by the 33rd TG, stationed at Tan Son Nhut, and this aircraft continued in use until 1971. For flights over North Vietnam during the early years of the war the RF-101 had been the standard Air Force aircraft. This was a unarmed, single-seat version of the F-101 Voodoo fighter carrying cameras in the nose. The RF-101 continued in use with the 460th TRW at Tan Son Nhut until 1971. Flying unarmed reconnaissance aircraft over North Vietnam remained a dangerous occupation throughout the war, and 39 RF-101s were shot down and twelve of their pilots killed.

Even before the war had started Lockeed U-2 aircraft were operating over North Vietnam. Aircraft from the 4028th Strategic Reconnaissance Squadron had been based at Bien Hoa between 1963 and 1966. The original plan for bombing North Vietnam, prepared by the Joint Chiefs of Staff in 1964, had been based on a list of 94 targets drawn up from information obtained by the U-2s. Between 1966 and 1976 the 349th SRS operated U-2s from U-Tapao on sigint (signals intelligence) and photographic missions. On a strategic level, SAC operated SR-71s as part of the 1st SRS. These aircraft were capable of over 2,000mph and were based at Kadena on Okinawa. At the time it was denied that the aircraft were stationed there, but the spectacular noise and sight of these aircraft taking off was witnessed by thousands of people and it became difficult to maintain the pretence. The CIA are reported to have had A-12 versions of the SR-71 also stationed at Kadena, and it can be assumed that these operated over North Vietnam. On the strategic level, satellite photographic coverage of North Vietnam was available throughout the Vietnam War, but the region was covered in cloud for long periods of time, blocking out satellite photography. The North Vietnamese also knew when American satellites were due over their country, and, when possible, anything that could be hidden was hidden.

The Navy tactical reconnaissance aircraft at the start of the war was the Vought RF-8A Crusader. In the same way that the Air Force had created the RF-101 from the Voodoo fighter, the Navy had used its standard fighter aircraft and replaced the armament with five cameras. During 1967 the RF-8A was replaced by the RF-8G, which had an uprated, 18,000lb thrust engine and improved navigational equipment. All the RF-8s were operated by one Navy Squadron, VFP-63, and detachments from this squadron were stationed on the smaller American aircraft carriers. During the war twenty RF-8s were shot down, two of them in 1972. The standard Navy heavy reconnaissance aircraft, operated from the larger carriers, was the North American RA-5C Vigilante. This was a version of the A-5A nuclear attack bomber, designed to replace the A-3 Skywarrior. After the A-5 had proved unsuccessful the design had been developed into the reconnaissance version. The Vigilante carried cameras but also used other sensors to provide reconnaissance coverage. Although it was a large aircraft, in clean condition the Vigilante was faster than the Phantom, which normally carried drop tanks and missiles when operating over the North. During the war eighteen RA-5s were shot down, including three in 1972.

By the time of the 'Linebacker' campaigns in 1972 the standard Air Force reconnaissance aircraft was the McDonnell RF-4C version of the Phantom. This had been introduced in 1965 and had replaced the RF-101 by 1971. The RF-4C had a full range of photographic cameras, plus other types of sensors, and was described by General William W. Momyer, Commander of the Seventh Air Force, thus:

> . . . the RF-4 was the most flexible tool for reconnaissance that I had. We could change missions while airborne and attain transitory target information more readily. Medium altitude reconnaissance proved both point and adjacent area coverage of immediate value in making decisions for restrike.[1]

The only RF-4C squadron operating during the 'Linebacker' campaign was the 14th Tactical Reconnaissance Squadron, flying from Udorn Air Base as part of the 432nd TRW. Although the 'Constant Guard' operations had brought in reinforcements for most of the categories of aircraft, no extra RF-4Cs were introduced into the region. During the course of the war 76 RF-4Cs were shot down, including six in 1972.

Large numbers of unmanned drones were also used over the North to provide various types of reconnaissance coverage. These were variants of the Ryan Q-2C target drone. These UAVs were known under the generic name of Ryan 147s but there was a range used for photographic, radar, sigint and elint (electronic intelligence) reconnaissance at low, medium and high level, and they were even used to drop leaflets over the North. The drones resembled small aircraft and were powered by a miniature jet engine. Operating from U-Tapao, the 350th Strategic Reconnaissance Squadron used the DC-130E, a version of the Hercules, to launch the drones. After being carried close to the border of the North under the wing of the DC-130, the drones were dropped and then flew a pre-programmed course or were controlled from another aircraft. To recover a drone a parachute was deployed and the machine was caught in mid-air by a CH-53 helicopter. Throughout the war 3,435 sorties were carried out by the Ryan drones and 578 were lost. The North Vietnamese claim to have shot down large numbers of them; indeed, the totals of aircraft quoted to have been shot down by their pilots and anti-aircraft gunners could include these drones.

To ensure that the results of a bombing strike would be known as soon as possible the commanders insisted that targets should be photographed directly after the strike had taken place. If reconnaissance aircraft had accompanied the strike force they

---

[1] Momyer, William W., *Air Power in Three Wars*, Department of the Air Force (Washington, 1978), p. 233.

would have had the protection of the strike package's fighters, chaff and jamming aircraft, but if the target were photographed during the raid then the smoke and dust caused by the bombing could obscure the amount of damage done. In practice the reconnaissance aircraft followed the strike aircraft and flew over the target some 5–7 minutes later. This placed the photographic aircraft in a vulnerable position. With experience, the Vietnamese knew that each bombing raid was closely followed by unarmed reconnaissance aircraft and the defences were alerted and waiting for their arrival. The reconnaissance aircraft of both the Navy and the Air Force suffered high casualties, and the predictability of the mission profiles flown by these aircraft played a part in these. Many examples exist during the Vietnam War of higher command ignoring the experience and opinions of the people carrying out the actual missions. If the reconnaissance pilots had been able to adjust their mission profiles and time on target then there is a good chance that fewer aircraft would have been lost.

Each individual strike aircraft was equipped with a strike camera by 1967. These cameras pointed backwards and photographed the impact of the bombs dropped by the aircraft carrying the camera. The quality of these photographs was not as good as that achieved by the specialist aircraft because the camera was only a small device, but a general view of the damage could be assessed. Instant information on the target could be achieved and the bombing accuracy of each pilot checked.

There had been a lot of discussion over the merits of one-aircraft as against two-aircraft reconnaissance missions. The RF-101s had operated singly over the North. Navy RF-8s and RA-5s usually operated throughout the war on their own, but with fighter escort in RP 6. Air Force RF-4s operated in elements of two since it was thought that the RF-4 acting as wingman could provide a look-out in high-threat areas for MiGs and any SA-2 launches; a second aircraft could also provide back-up if any of the lead aircraft's equipment failed to work. The argument for one aircraft was that as the reconnaissance aircraft were unarmed, two aircraft were not really better than one. A single aircraft had less chance of being detected and the faster an aircraft could be flown without worrying about another the more quickly a mission could be completed.

In addition to their photographic cameras the RF-4Cs also carried other sensors. These included the AN/AAS-18 infra-red line-scanner set, which functioned by recording the heat variations shown by the ground under the aircraft. Rather than a photograph of the reflected light from the target, the infra-red set produced an image of the target based on reflected heat. It was hence possible to produce images through some types of cloud and smoke, and at night. Trucks and other vehicles that used internal combustion engines gave clear pictures of the heat from their engines, and continued to do so for several hours after they had stopped, while different types of vegetation and terrain produced individual heat signatures clear enough for useful images to be produced.

A number of the RF-4Cs also carried the Goodyear AN/APQ-102A sideways-looking radar (SLR), mounted in the sides of the aircraft's nose. By looking out to the side of the aircraft the radar could produce a picture of the ground up to 30 miles away. This sensor gave the RF-4 a true all-weather capability as the radar could see through clouds, smoke or rain; moreover, the aircraft did not have to pass over the target but could operate from stand-off ranges of up to 30 miles when operating at 30,000ft. The limitation with the system was that only clearly defined objects would produce good radar returns: the radar would not, for example, produce good pictures of objects underneath trees or heavy camouflage.

No strategic bombing campaign could operate without effective reconnaissance coverage. Although the stereotyping of reconnaissance mission profiles did increase the casualty rate amongst the aircraft used, the reconnaissance effort was in general successful throughout the campaign. Whether the American commanders made the best use of the information obtained is another matter.

APPENDIX 7: THE AIR-TO-AIR WAR

In air-to-air combat during 'Rolling Thunder' the Americans lost 55 aircraft for the destruction of 116 North Vietnamese; they lost considerably more in total, but the overwhelming majority were downed by anti-aircraft guns and missiles rather than North Vietnamese fighters. This was a ratio of roughly 2:1 in favour of the Americans but fell far short of the 12:1 they reputedly achieved in the Korean War (if we accept these figures as accurate).

American defence strategy in the late 1950s and early 1960s had been one of 'massive retaliation'. This doctrine was first expounded by Eisenhower's Secretary of State, John Foster Dulles, in January 1954. The idea behind it was that any communist aggression anywhere in the world would be met by massive nuclear strikes against the Soviet Union and China (in reality it is doubtful whether this was ever a practical option). It was a policy based to some extent on Americas' long, frustrating experience of stalemate with conventional arms in Korea. Eisenhower, wishing to reduce defence spending, felt that nuclear weapons gave 'more bang for the buck'.

The result was the view, in the West, that the major task of air power was the delivery of nuclear bombs, or the destruction of enemy nuclear bombers by long-range missiles. (The British Defence White Paper of 1957 was of the opinion that manned aircraft were obsolete; the English Electric Lightning interceptor was seen as a temporary measure.) It was also thought by influential sections of the American military—although many of the pilots disagreed—that aircraft were now too fast to indulge in classic dogfighting, a view that had also been taken before the Second

World War and before the Korean War. It was this line of thinking that deleted a cannon armament from the original F-4 Phantoms (and took the cannon out of the Lightning F.3). Even the superlative F-86 Sabre air superiority fighter was converted into a one-way carrier for tactical nuclear weapons. General Chuck Yeager, the first man to break the sound barrier, who commanded a squadron of F-86s in Europe during the 1950s, said,

> Each Sabre carried one Mark XII tactical nuclear bomb which in those days was still heavy and cumbersome . . . Our Sabres could not be refuelled from airborne tankers, and we could keep flying only for a couple of hours before our tanks ran dry. All our targets were deep inside the Soviet sector . . . all of us would be forced to parachute down in enemy territory.[1]

Naval aviation had concentrated on nuclear weapons delivery in the same way as the US Air Force. Rear-Admiral Paul A. Peak, who commanded a wing during the Vietnam War, commented,

> . . . we came into the war totally unprepared for a conventional battle. For years the concentration, almost exclusively, was [on] the nuclear mission. I had to go back two or three tours to get anywhere near an alpha strike, and only on rare occasions did I see a multiple-carry bomb rack loaded with bombs.[2]

By concentrating on nuclear weapons delivery the Americans created a younger generation of fighter pilots whose main skills were not directed towards air-to-air combat.

During the 'Rolling Thunder' campaign of 1965–68 the successful air-to-air pilots tended to be the older men who had fought in the Second World War or Korea (or both) The highest-scoring American pilot during 'Rolling Thunder', with four MiGs to his name, was Colonel Robin Olds, who had been credited with destroying 24½ German aircraft during the Second World War (including aircraft destroyed on the ground). The younger pilots found themselves fighting in a different type of war from the one they had been trained for during the late 1950s and early 1960s. In a speech he gave on 4 October 1968 Olds said,

> . . . there was a time not ten years ago when the suggestion of a need for training in squadron-sized formations, for maintenance of qualifications in delivering conventional ordnance and for keeping current in aerial combat tactics was enough to get one laughed out of the conference room. One was a starry-eyed romanticist, a ghost from the past. The name of the game was nuclear deterrence. Everyone, even fighter pilots, worked at it.[3]

---

[1] Yeager, Chuck, *Yeager*, Arrow Books (London, 1986), p. 320–1.

[2] Levinson, Jeffrey, *Alpha Strike Vietnam*, Presidio Press (California, 1989), p. 225.

[3] Olds, Robin, 'Forty-Six Years a Fighter Pilot', *American Aviation Historical Society Journal*, XIII, Winter 1968, p. 237.

The American Navy's reaction to what they considered to be their poor showing during 'Rolling Thunder', when it was found that all the traditional lessons in air combat dating back to the First World War still applied and that air combat still did take place, was the review by Captain Frank Ault. This led to a list of recommendations to improve the Fleet's air-to-air capabilities.

To give training in realistic combat manoeuvring the Navy set up the now famous Top Gun fighter school at Miramar. The idea behind Top Gun was to create expertise in air combat manoeuvring and to distribute this expertise throughout the Fleet. The Air Force's reaction came later (too late to affect the Vietnam War) with the 'Red Flag' series of exercises and the setting up of the Aggressor squadrons. When the 'Linebacker' campaign started on 10 May 1972 many of the naval pilots who destroyed enemy aircraft during the campaign were graduates of Top Gun. They were a younger and better-trained generation of fighter pilots than had fought in 'Rolling Thunder'.

By the time the 'Linebacker' campaign got under way the North Vietnamese Air Force had only been in existence for around eight years. During the 'Rolling Thunder' campaign a large number of North Vietnamese aircraft had been shot down, most of the North Vietnamese pilots having had but a limited amount of experience, but by 1972 the North Vietnamese had a small number of very experienced, very effective pilots who had survived years of American attacks. Those who had survived in this Darwinian situation had learned their lessons well. However, although there was this small number of experienced pilots, most of the North's airmen were still relatively 'green'.

The organisation and training of the North Vietnamese Air Force were based firmly on the Soviet model and used Soviet aircraft. In May 1972 it was estimated that the North Vietnamese air defences were composed of up to 200 fighter aircraft, MiG-17s, -19s and -21s, with at least one-third being the newer MiG-21s. The northern part of the country was covered by an interlocking web of Soviet-designed radars and communications systems. The fighter aircraft flew under the tight control of Soviet-style GCI (ground controlled interception), which could often place the Vietnamese aircraft in an advantageous position. The North Vietnamese pilots were also flying over their own country, defending their homes and families. The defensive system included thousands of radar-controlled anti-aircraft guns and 300 surface-to-air missile sites (SA-2s) that had been placed to cover all the major targets in the North. Although not all these missile sites were in use at any one time, it was thought that the North Vietnamese had 35 active sites, with thirteen around Hanoi and ten around Haiphong.

All the North Vietnamese MiGs were lightweight, short-ranged aircraft. The MiG-17 was first introduced into Soviet service in the early 1950s but was still the most numerous type in North Vietnam's air arm. It had a maximum speed of around 700mph.

Its size was roughly that of a Second World War Mustang fighter, and it was only a quarter the weight of an F-4 Phantom. Although slower than the Phantom, the MiG-17 was considerably more manoeuverable. Its three cannon gave it a powerful close-in armament. While the American Phantoms carried no guns, provided the MiG could stay close to the F-4 it was safe, as the American missiles had a minimum range. The MiG-17s were clear-weather aircraft.

By 1972 the Soviets had supplied the North Vietnamese with the PF version of the MiG-21, which was a considerable improvement over the earlier F version. The MiG-21 was a small, short-ranged fighter aircraft, and in clean condition the PF version was faster than the F-4 at lower levels, but it only carried a modest armament and fire control system. The MiG-19 had been supplied to North Vietnam by China as the Chinese-built F-6. In 1972 North Vietnam had around 30 of these in service. Like all the Soviet-designed aircraft supplied to North Vietnam, it was a fast-climbing, manoeuverable aircraft, and it was capable of carrying a missile armament.

The MiG-21 carried the Russian 'Atoll' air-to-air missile. Like the Sidewinder, this was a short-ranged heat-seeker. It has been claimed that the 'Atoll' was based on the Sidewinder and that the Soviet Union had received several copies of the Sidewinder through espionage. In practice the 'Atoll' was faster but shorter-ranged than the Sidewinder and had to be launched well within 1½ miles of its target to be effective.

By 1972 the North Vietnamese had thirteen jet-capable airfields. The airfields in the southern part of North Vietnam did not have jet fighters permanently stationed, but were used as staging posts for aircraft from the air bases in the North. The main air bases were Phuc Yen, Hoa Lac and Kep.

The basic tactics used by the North Vietnamese MiGs remained the same during the 'Linebacker' campaign as they had earlier. If the North Vietnamese had attempted to meet the American fighters head-on they would undoubtedly have been heavily defeated, so their basic tactic was the hit-and-run attack against the formations of American strike aircraft. Even with the extensive jamming carried out by the American forces the North Vietnamese had enough radars available to know the exact position of the strike forces. The North Vietnamese MiGs were vectored into position to follow the American raids, and if the ground controllers thought they had the advantage the MiGs were ordered to carry out one fast attack; if this failed, they were to continue at high speed out of the area. By approaching the American formations at low level the North Vietnamese MiGs could obtain an element of surprise. Even if the MiGs were not successful they could compel the strike forces to drop their bombs in order to avoid the MiGs. General Momyer described the MiG tactics:

Instead of engaging in dogfights, the enemy chose to bring the in the MiG-21s at Mach 1.2 or thereabouts, in a stern attack with missiles. This was a very effective tactic since it capitalised on his excellent radar control system and employed surprise to the maximum extent. Furthermore our fighters were normally cruising at about 480 knots in order to conserve fuel, so a hit-and-run attack at the six o'clock position gave the MiGs the best probability of a kill, with the least exposure to fire from the F-4s.[1]

If the North Vietnamese felt themselves to be under threat they stood down for a period and even moved aircraft into China to re-group and develop new tactics. By using a modest approach and avoiding combat if they thought they were at a disadvantage, they remained a credible threat to the attacking Americans.

The F-4 Phantom was the standard American fighter aircraft by 1972 and was used by both the Air Force and the Navy, although deck space on the smaller aircraft carriers was restricted and here the F-8 Crusader was still the standard Navy fighter. The F-4 was a large, powerful aircraft and could carry a substantial external load, including bombs and air-to-air missiles. Early F-4s did not carry an internal gun although the later F-4E did. The standard missile armament was four Sparrows and four Sidewinders. The large numbers of aircraft that were on occasions in the air over North Vietnam forced the Americans to stipulate that, generally, fighter aircraft could not open fire without first obtaining visual identification. The theoretical range of the Sparrow missile was around ten miles, but by forcing the American fighter aircraft to close to visual range this long-range advantage was lost. Guidance of the Sparrow missile was by means of the radar on the launch aircraft focusing on the target aircraft and the seeker head in the missile homing on to the reflected radar energy. The Sparrow was an all-aspect missile and could therefore home on aircraft heading either towards or away from it. Most of the MiGs shot down by the US Air Force were accounted for using Sparrows.

Most of the MiGs shot down by US Navy aircraft, on the other hand, fell to Sidewinders. The Sidewinder was a smaller, shorter-ranged missile than the Sparrow, better suited for close-range combat. Most of the aircraft shot down by the Navy aircraft seem to have been MiG-17s. The guidance system was infra-red heat-seeking, and the early models used in Vietnam had to be launched from behind the aircraft under attack so that the missile could 'see' the heat from the jet exhaust.

All US strike aircraft carried a gun armament and MiGs were shot down by A-4s, F-105s and A-1s during the 'Rolling Thunder' campaign. However, during the 'Linebacker' campaigns all the North Vietnamese MiGs shot down were felled by various types of F-4, apart from two shot down by B-52 gunners. The only F-4 equipped with an internal gun was the the Air Force F-4E, although the F-4D could carry an external gun pod. During the campaign a significant number of MiGs were shot down using the F-4E's built-in 20mm cannon.

---

[1] Momyer, William W., 'The Evolution of Fighter Tactics in Southeast Asia, *Air Force Magazine*, LVI, July 1973, p. 61.

The numbers of missiles launched compared with the numbers of MiGs shot down show that the Sparrow and Sidewinder were never very effective. Between May 1972 and January 1973 100 Sidewinder missiles were launched by US Air Force aircraft at North Vietnamese MiGs, ten of which were shot down. In the same period 216 Sparrow missiles were launched and 23 aircraft shot down. The figures for the US Navy showed that the Navy found the Sidewinder more effective than the Air Force, with around one missile in five hitting its target. In the period 1972 to January 1973 34 North Vietnamese aircraft were shot down by Sidewinder missiles, 29 with Sparrow missiles, six with 20mm cannon fire, two with 0.5in calibre gunfire (from B-52s), one using combined Sidewinders and 20mm cannon fire and three using what are described as manoeuvring tactics. From this total of 75 North Vietnamese aircraft shot down the Air Force destroyed 51 and the Navy 24. From these totals it would seem that the Air Force had been roughly twice as successful as the Navy. However, the Air Force also lost considerably more aircraft to the North Vietnamese MiGs than did the Navy. Between 1970 and 1973 the Air Force lost 28 aircraft to the North's MiGs and the Navy four. General Vogt, commander of the Seventh Air Force in 1972, has commented,

> By July 1972, in the middle of the Linebacker operations, for the first time in the history of the USAF the loss-to-victory ratio swung in favour of the enemy. We were losing more aeroplanes than we were shooting down. This had never happened before anywhere in the world. Our losses were due . . . to our going blind into a heavily netted threat radar environment, confronting the best MiGs that the Soviets had available for export.[1]

The US Air Force's response to the low loss rate was to set up the Tea Ball control centre and to use more of the Sparrow missiles in the beyond-visual-range mode. The specialisation of certain fighter squadrons in the air-to-air role built up a reserve of the necessary expertise needed to combat the MiGs. There was also a recognition that more effort should be placed in air combat manoeuvring training, a decision that the Navy had already taken by instituting the Top Gun courses at Miramar. By August 1972 the Air Force was achieving a 4:1 loss ratio with the North Vietnamese.

During the full course of the air war from 1964 to 1973 the North Vietnamese lost 196 aircraft shot down by American aircraft (excluding two shot down by the CIA). The North Vietnamese MiGs shot down 92 American aircraft. These figures give an overall loss rate of 2.13:1 in favour of the Americans. Starting practically from scratch—some North Vietnamese pilots had never even driven a car—the North built up and maintained a credible Air Force in the face of a massive air attack by the most powerful nation on earth.

---

[1] Kohn, Richard H., and Harahan, Joseph P., *USAF Warrior Studies*, Office of Air Force History (Washington, 1986), p. 71.

APPENDIX 8: 'LINEBACKER II': TARGETS AND ACCURACY

The B-52 bombing in the course of 'Linebacker II' divides into a three-stage campaign. The first stage was the maximum effort, involving three waves each night attacking the Hanoi area between 18 and 20 December and ending with the loss of six B-52s on the 20th. The second stage was the reduced effort involving only the aircraft from Thailand in one wave to hit targets outside the Hanoi area. This lasted from the 21st to the 24th. Involved in the third stage were aircraft from Guam and Thailand in a maximum effort using new tactics to put the aircraft over the target in as short a time as possible. The third stage lasted from the 26th to the 29th and struck targets in Hanoi and Haiphong.

Although 'Linebacker II' was not intended to be an interdiction campaign, it was estimated that 60 per cent of the targets for both the B-52s and the tactical aircraft were associated with the North Vietnamese transport system. The other 40 per cent included power plants, radio sites, missile sites and communications. In fact there were seven main categories of target—railway yards, storage areas, radio communication facilities, power generation plants, airfields, missile sites and bridges. In the course of 'Linebacker II' 54 targets in these categories were struck by both the B-52s and the tactical bombers, and B-52s only bombed 34 of them. The Air Force alone directed 1,362 sorties against these 54 targets.

The North Vietnamese estimate of civilian casualties for the bombing was 1,300 in Hanoi and 300 in Haiphong. All civilian deaths are to be regretted, but, judged by the tonnage of bombs dropped, civilian casualties were minimal; the numbers of people killed during the North's invasion of the South were estimated at well over 100,000. The Germans killed 1,600 people in Guernica in one afternoon during the Spanish Civil War. On 4 May 1940 the Luftwaffe dropped 100 tons of bombs on Rotterdam and killed around 1,000 people. On the night of 14 November 1940 449 German bombers dropped 394 tons of high-explosive bombs and 54 tons of incendiaries on Coventry. These killed 400 people and badly injured 800. Bomber Command attacked the German town of Hamburg on the night of 24 July 1943 and estimates of the casualties vary between 30,000 and 100,000. The United States Army Air Forces bombed Berlin on 3 February 1945, causing up to 25,000 casualties. The attack by 800 RAF aircraft on Dresden during the night of 13 February 1945 caused enormous damage and casualties have been estimated at between 30,000 and 250,000. In one night attack on Tokyo on 9 March 1945 279 B-29 bombers killed 83,783 people—more than were killed in either of the atomic bomb attacks on Japan. On 13 June 1917 a flight of seventeen Gotha biplane bombers attacked London in daylight and dropped six tons of bombs which killed 162 people and wounded 432. The Americans have been accused of deliberately causing civilian casualties during 'Linebacker II', but, as can be seen from the examples quoted, the American military could have caused ten or even a hundred times as many casualties had they wished to.

Most of the bombing that took place as part of the 'Linebacker II' campaign was relatively accurate but some civilian targets were hit. A wing of the hospital at Bac Mai on the southern edge of Hanoi was struck, causing civilian casualties. When thousands of tons of bombs are dropped it is inevitable that a percentage will fall outside the target area. The hospital was just north of the airfield at Bac Mai and just east of a major oil storage facility. At first the American officials denied that the hospital had been hit, but after photographs showed the destruction the American investigation found that a B-52 attacking the airfield had released its bombs too early.

The B-52s were not, in any case, a precision bombing system. The measure of accuracy for a weapon system is the circular error of probability. This is the size of a circle within which, it is estimated, half the bombs will fall. The size of the circle for the B-52s was 1,250ft, and, on average, half the bombs dropped will fall within this circle. The CEP for the F-4 with laser-guided bombs was 20ft. Using visual bombing techniques, the CEP for the A-7 was 111ft and for the F-4 483ft; the F-111, using radar bombing, could achieve a CEP of 500ft whatever the weather. The LORAN bombing technique was supposed to have a CEP of 1,000ft but in practice achieved results considerably poorer than this.

Of the 20,000 tons of bombs dropped in the course of 'Linebacker II' 90 per cent were dropped using radar aiming, 7 per cent used LORAN, 2.6 per cent were aimed visually and 0.2 per cent were laser-guided. From photographic coverage of the targets after the campaign had finished, it was estimated that the effectiveness of a bomb dropped by visual aiming was eight times that of a bomb dropped by radar aiming, while a laser-aimed bomb was 124 times as effective in creating damage as one dropped by radar. The B-52s were most effectively employed against area-type targets like railyards and the laser bombs against pinpoint targets such as bridges and power stations. The LORAN bombing was found to have been inaccurate and many targets were missed altogether.

When bombing concentrated on targets with a single essential element such as a turbine house for an hydro-electric plant, a boiler house or an electrical transformer station it was found that only laser-guided bombs could give any guarantee of success. Targets like a bridge needed a direct hit on the structure for their destruction or even damage to the target to take place. Even very near misses were of little value if the structure of the bridge was not hit: one direct hit caused more damage than 100 near misses. The bad weather limited the use of the laser-guided bombs and the destruction of pinpoint targets. As stated earlier, the use of LORAN during bad weather was a failure. The F-111 had been used singly to attack individual targets, but one aircraft could not carry enough bombs to destroy an area target. Moreover, the radar bombing system on the F-111 was not accurate enough to allow pinpoint targets to be destroyed, although the use of F-111s to attack North Vietnamese airfields before major raids did disrupt their reaction to the bombing.

The concentration of the 'Linebacker II' bombing on area targets such as the railyards and storage facilities meant that the majority of the damage caused was to these types of targets. Since the war the lessons of the 'Linebacker' campaigns seem to have been taken to heart, and over the last twenty years the Americans have carried out enormous research into the production of improved precision weapon systems.

The choice of target lists had been in the hands of the Chiefs of Staff, with the local commanders given leeway in the choice of targets from the list, to suit local operational constraints. This list did include targets that the military had been asking to be able to bomb for years, and also included targets that had been excluded from the 'Rolling Thunder' campaign. Only a few major targets had been excluded, mainly for humanitarian reasons. However, the target list had been limited in scope, and an expanded list would have given local commanders more flexibility in the development of the campaign: with more options the reaction to the bad weather and the North Vietnamese defences could have been more varied. Many of the more lucrative targets had already been destroyed during 'Linebacker I', and the overall impact of 'Linebacker II' would have been greater if the targets had been attacked with the same intensity during 'Linebacker I', when the weather was better.

'Linebacker II':
Targets Attacked by B-52s and Tactical Aircraft

Rail Targets

Kinh Ho	Gia Lam	Giap Nhi	Haiphong	Yien Vien	Thai Nguyen
Kep	Trung Quan	Bac Giang	Duc Noi	Lang Dang	Hanoi
Viet Tri					

The number of Air Force sorties against these targets was 484, and 18,000 bombs were dropped. The overall damage to the rail targets was estimated as being 60 per cent.

Storage Facility Targets

Phuc Yen	Duc Noi	Bac Mai (storage on the airfield)		Gia Thu
Bac Mai	Van Dien	Quinh Loi	Hanoi	Viet Tri	Bac Giang
Trai Ca					

The total of sorties against storage targets was 339 and a 40 per cent destruction average was achieved.

Radar and Communication Targets

Hanoi (four separate targets in Hanoi were bombed, mostly by tactical aircraft)
Lang Truoc
Total sorties against radar and communications targets was 196. An average of only 32 per cent destruction was achieved, although one target was 90 per cent destroyed and one was untouched.

Power Generation Targets

Hanoi (two separate targets in Hanoi were attacked)   Haiphong   Bac Giang
Thai Nguyen Viet Tri
Total sorties against these targets 166. The average destruction was 29 per cent.

Airfield Targets

Hoa Lac   Kep   Phuc Yen   Quang Tri   Yien Bai
The number of sorties directed against airfields was 141, and 2,200 bombs were dropped. The average destruction to the five airfields was only 9 per cent.

SA-2 Missile Site Targets

Thirteen separate missile sites were bombed. The number of sorties directed against the missile sites was 29 and 1,300 bombs were dropped. The average destruction was 10 per cent but this included two sites where 50 per cent destruction was observed and eight sites where no destruction at all could be seen.

Bridge Targets

Hanoi (Canal des Rapides bridge)   Cao Nung   Lang Lau
The number of sorties was nine and 69 bombs were dropped. No B-52 sorties were involved. The average destruction was 33 per cent. However, the Canal des Rapides bridge was destroyed by laser-guided bombs and the other two bridges were untouched.

The overall damage inflicted on the 54 targets in the eleven days of bombing during 'Linebacker II' was estimated at 32 per cent.

APPENDIX 9:
THE 'LINEBACKER' RAIDS AND 'DESERT STORM' COMPARED

The 'Desert Storm' bombing campaign against Iraq was carried out from 16 January until 3 March 1991—a period of 42 days. As opposed to the bombing of North

Vietnam the bombing of Iraq was seen as a model of success and an example of what can be achieved by strategic attack. During the bombing the Allies carried out a total of 110,000 sorties and dropped a total of 88,500 tons of bombs, including 6,500 tons of precision-guided munitions or 'smart bombs'. The Allied aircraft were averaging something between 2,000 and 3,000 sorties a day. At the start of the war the Allied commanders had over 2,400 aircraft available within operational distance of Iraq. The vast majority of these aircraft were American but a significant number of British, French, Italian and Saudi Arabian aircraft also took part. The Allies lost 42 aircraft shot down by the Iraqi air defences.

During the 'Rolling Thunder' bombing campaign of 1965–68 against North Vietnam 605,000 tons of bombs were dropped in 297,000 sorties, an average of about 460 tons of bombs and 230 sorties a day over a period of three years and eight months. These are only average figures as there were several lengthy bombing pauses. The United States Air Force lost 928 aircraft, averaging one for every 650 sorties. The year of heaviest bombing was 1967, and the figures for that year alone were 299 sorties a day delivering on average 616 tons, and one aircraft lost for every 330 sorties.

The figures for 'Linebacker I' were, as stated earlier, 230 sorties a day delivering on average 864 tons of bombs; each sortie therefore delivered some 3.75 tons of bombs. One aircraft was lost for every 555 sorties. During 'Linebacker II' 20,000 tons of bombs were dropped in 1,945 sorties over eleven days. This gives an average of 1,818 tons a day from 177 sorties, each sortie delivering 10.27 tons. The total of aircraft lost during the eleven days was 25, giving an average of one aircraft for every 78 sorties.

'Desert Storm' averaged 2,600 sorties dropping 2,100 tons of bombs a day, and one aircraft was lost for every 2,600 sorties. The total of sorties includes large numbers of support missions, as well as actual bombing missions, made up of combat air patrols, air refuelling, defence suppression, etc. Even allowing for this, each 'Rolling Thunder' sortie delivered two tons of bombs compared with 0.8 tons during 'Desert Storm'.

The original planning for 'Desert Storm' was for a four-phase campaign. The start of the bombing was intended to damage Iraq's strategic capabilities and to achieve air superiority by attacking the airfields, any aircraft that managed to get airborne and the command and control network for the air defence system. The second phase was an attack on the air defence system in the Kuwaiti theatre of operations, including southern Iraq. The third and longest phase was the attack on the Iraqi Army and its support systems throughout the country. The last phase was the direct support of the Allied ground war during the re-taking of Kuwait. This air campaign was originally planned to last only 30 days, but 39 were needed to achieve the required results. The delay was caused by bad weather (some of the worst ever seen in the area), a lack of reconnaissance intelligence and the fact that the 'Scud' mobile targets were considerably more difficult to find and attack than had been imagined.

Over 300 strategic targets were bombed inside Iraq. These targets included the nuclear, chemical and biological industry. The military/industrial base was hit, including electrical production and oil production facilities. Also bombed were large numbers of direct military targets, including command and control facilities, communications networks and headquarters. The Allies attacked 66 airfields and 594 hardened aircraft shelters, and military bases and storage areas were targeted along with naval bases and ships. The transport infrastructure, including road and rail bridges, was heavily bombed. A major effort of the bombing was to destroy the government command and control network. The Iraqis had built up a modern system, with built-in redundancy. Bombing focused on the relay stations, the towers that held the microwave dishes, the nodes on the hardened land lines and the command centres. Later in the war many of the troops who surrendered in Kuwait stated that they had been out of communication with their headquarters since early in the war. Others stated that they had not been out of contact with their leaders but had been frightened to maintain contact in case they had been picked up by Allied listening equipment and targeted for bombing attacks.

In an attempt to cut off the Kuwaiti theatre of operations from the rest of Iraq, 54 major bridges on the route south from Baghdad were targeted for bombing. One of the few links left open between Iraq and the outside world was the road between Jordan and Baghdad, and this was also bombed. There were two main roads running from Basra in the south to Baghdad along the course of the Tigris and Euphrates rivers, and these, too, were heavily bombed. By the end of the war the amount of materials reaching the Iraqi front line had been reduced from 20,000 tons to 2,000 tons daily and 40 of the 54 bridges had been completely destroyed.

The bombing of the Iraqi capital city Baghdad involved less than 3,000 bombs weighing around 2,800 tons. This is a surprisingly low total given the overall volume of the bombing. The targets hit in the city included command and control facilities, bridges and power generation sites. It is estimated that around 2,000 civilians were killed in Baghdad. One of the reasons for the relatively low level of bombing was the fact that the Iraqi air defence system was focused on Baghdad, and to keep aircraft losses to a minimum only the most technically advanced attack aircraft were used to bomb the city at night.

Much has been made of the use of 'smart' weapons during 'Desert Storm' and the accuracy they achieved. The actual number of 'smart' bombs used was only a small percentage of the overall total of bombs dropped—just 6,500 tons out of a total of 88,000 tons, or 7.4 per cent. The most common type of 'smart' bomb was the laser-guided bomb, where a seeker head on the bomb homes on to the laser energy reflected from the target after the latter has been illuminated by a laser marker on board the attacking aircraft or an accompanying aircraft. Most of these were American Paveway types. Another common type of guided weapon was the glide bomb with a TV camera in the nose or imaging infra-red guidance. All the 'smart' weapons used seem to have been generally successful, but the vast majority of bombs dropped were of the conventional 'iron' type. Most of the weapons dropped were not dropped with 'surgical precision' and there have been some reports since the bombing that the percentage of guided weapons hitting their targets was not as high as first reported.

The Iraqi air defence system, although it was one of the most extensive and well-equipped, with both Soviet and Western radar and missiles, seems to have collapsed as a system very quickly. It is thought that the Iraqis had around 7,000 missiles and 9,000 anti-aircraft guns at the start of the war, including 3,000 guns and 60 missile batteries around Baghdad. The central control was destroyed in the first few days of bombing, reducing each of the individual systems and batteries to working under their own direction. Although the Iraqis managed to shoot down 42 Allied aircraft, their defences never managed seriously to affect the bombing campaign. The Iraqi Air Force played little part after the first few days and a large section of it fled to Iran or was dispersed off the air bases into the surrounding countryside.

The number of Iraqi deaths is estimated at around 110,000 during the 42-day war. The vast majority of these were Iraqi troops in the Kuwaiti theatre of operations. Before the start of the ground war it was estimated that the Iraqi Army had lost over 1,500 tanks, 1,500 artillery pieces and 1,200 armoured personnel carriers. This total was thought to be over 40 per cent of the equipment available in the Kuwaiti theatre. Most of the nuclear, bacteriological and chemical plants had been destroyed. The mobile 'Scud' launchers proved to be difficult targets to hit and many sorties were flown to this end, with some success.

The ground war that followed the bombing lasted only 100 hours and the speed of the victory has been use to support the view of a successful strategic bombing campaign. The American military and political leadership stated that they had learned the lessons of the bombing of North Vietnam. There was no attempt at gradualism and there was maximum effort from the first day, although there was a slight increase in the number of aircraft available during the course of the bombing. There was a clear military objective, which was the removal of Iraqi forces from Kuwait, and Allied efforts were not side-tracked into sortie totals or body counts. There was no attempt to halt the bombing for talks to take place or to divert resources from the central objective.

News reporters were not given free access to any of the Allied forces involved and in some cases even the pool reporters were refused access to anything the military did not want seen. The American public, seeing the horror of the Vietnam War on their television sets every evening, was in the long run responsible, to a certain extent, for the collapse of support for that conflict. By manipulating what was shown by the media, the military hoped to have a free hand long enough to carry out their plans unhindered. President Bush did not try to interfere with his commanders on a local level in the bombing and it was reported that he did not even know which targets were being bombed in Baghdad.

Perhaps the most important lesson learned and applied from the Vietnam War was the creation of a central commander of all the air power available. This was US Air Force General Charles Horner. At the start of the planning for the war General Schwarzkopf had stated, 'There will be one air commander and General Horner is it.' The targeting of 2,800 aircraft from one central point allowed the full flexibility of air power to be utilised.

'Desert Storm' was undoubtedly a success, but did it really fulfil the expectations of the strategic bombing theorists? Most of the bombing was in fact tactical rather than strategic. It is thought that between 20 and 30 per cent of the bombing missions took place against what could clearly be considered strategic targets in Iraq. However, during 'Rolling Thunder' only 5 per cent of the sorties flown against North Vietnam were directed against fixed strategic targets; the rest were armed reconnaissance missions against the transport system.

The bombing reduced the flow of supplies getting through to the troops in Kuwait and the level of conflict was raised above that which could be sustained by the Iraqis. The Allies held the initiative and controlled the level of the conflict to their best advantage. Iraq had no major source of aid from abroad as North Vietnam had possessed. The UN sanctions against Iraq were broken, but Jordan was the only country allowing large quantities of supplies to get through, and this was on a cash basis only.

The bombing did not cause the surrender of Iraq. Until the end the Iraqi leadership was still holding out and talking about the coming 'mother of battles' as deciding the issue. There had been no mass deaths of civilians and, as far as it is possible to judge in a dictatorship, the morale of the population generally had not collapsed. This cannot be said of the Iraqi Army, where there was clearly a complete breakdown in morale among the troops in the Kuwaiti theatre. The tactical bombing rather than the strategic bombing tore the heart out of the Iraqi Army—hardly surprising with over 100,000 deaths in 42 days, more than were suffered in eight years of war with Iran.

The Second World War only ended when Allied and Soviet troops met in the centre of Germany. The Gulf War ended when the Allied ground forces had captured a large portion of southern Iraq. No matter how successful the bombing, the ground campaign was still necessary. The 'hard slogging and professional skill on the ground'[1]

---

[1] Quoted in Armstrong, A., and Mason, R.A., *Air Power in the Nuclear Age*, University of Illinois Press (1983), p. 45.

was still needed. Air power still cannot succeed on its own in deciding the outcome of a major conflict.

The Iraqi capital Baghdad was extensively rebuilt after the war, and power and services were quickly back in operation. The bridges over the rivers in Baghdad have been repaired and within a year of the end of the war few signs remained of the bombing. All these are obviously prestige showpiece projects organised by a dictatorship anxious to eliminate memories of the war, but the bombing does not appear to have left any lasting effects. The civil wars in the north and south of the country after the Gulf War are alleged to have been more destructive than the bombing.

There is no doubt that air power is the decisive element in modern warfare, but the strategic doctrine that air power alone can win wars has still not been proved. The concept that there are 'vital targets' that a country cannot do without has again proved illusory. Although severely affected by the strategic bombing, Iraq was able to reorganise and absorb the effects of the bombing, at least to some extent. Iraqi society, government and culture survived untouched. The great German writer, Clausewitz, stated that, 'In war, the will is directed against an animate object that reacts.'[1] Countries have proved very adept at continuing to operate under even heavy bombing. They have suffered heavy damage without collapse. Ingenuity and effort have permitted states to continue to function at a reduced level of efficiency even after so-called vital targets have been bombed. Society has not been as fragile as was thought by the strategic bombing theorists but has proved to be infinitely adaptable. In 1917, during the First World War, Churchill's view of strategic bombing was that

> It is not reasonable to speak of an air offensive as if it were going to finish the war itself. It is improbable that any terrorization of the civil population which could be achieved by air attack could compel the Government of a great nation to surrender. Familiarity with bombardment, a good system of dug-outs and shelters, a strong control by police and military authorities, should be sufficient to preserve the national fighting power unimpaired.[2]

This seems to be a good description of the effects of the bombing of North Vietnam and 'Desert Storm'. The case for strategic bombing, with conventional munitions, as a war-winning policy is still unproven.

---

[1] Clausewitz, Carl von, (ed. and trans. Howard, Michael, and Paret, Peter), *On War*, Princeton University Press (New Jersey, 1978), p. 149.

[2] Quoted in Fuller, J. F. C., *The Conduct of War 1789–1965*, Eyre Methuen (London, 1972), p. 279.

BIBLIOGRAPHY

Allen, Michael, 'Sharing the Agony of Hanoi', *The Christian Century*, 24 January 1973

Anderton, David, *Republic F-105 Thunderchief*, Osprey Publishing (London, 1983)

————, *North American F-100 Super Sabre*, Osprey Publishing (London, 1987)

Anthis, Rollin, 'Air Power in Vietnam', *Air Force and Space Digest*, August 1967

Arbuckle, Tammy, 'Bombing was Pinpoint', *Washington Star*, 1 April 1973

Armitage, J., and Mason, R. A., *Air Power in the Nuclear Age*, University of Illinois (Chicago, 1983)

Ashmore, Harry S., and Baggs, William C., *Mission to Hanoi*, Putnam's Sons (New York, 1968)

Basil, G. I., *Pak Six*, Associated Creative Writers (La Mesa, 1982)

Bearden, Thomas E., 'What Really Happened in the Air Defense Battle of North Vietnam', *Air Defense Magazine*, April–June 1976

Bell, Ken, *100 Missions North*, Brassey's (McLean, 1993)

Berger, Carl, (ed.), *The United States Air Force in South East Asia*, Office of Air Force History (Washington, 1977)

Berrigan, Daniel, *Night Flight to Hanoi*, Macmillan (New York, 1968)

Berry, F. Clifton, *Strike Aircraft: The Illustrated History of the Vietnam War*, Bantam Books (New York, 1988)

Bonds, Ray, *The Vietnam War*, Salamander Books (London, 1979)

Boyne, Walter J., *Phantom in Combat*, Jane's (London, 1985)

Braybrook, Roy M., 'Under Combat Conditions', *Flying Review*, October 1966

Brodie, Bernard, *War and Politics*, Cassell (London, 1973)

————, 'Why We Were So (Strategically) Wrong', *Foreign Policy*, No 5, Winter 1971–72

Broughton, Jack, *Going Downtown: The War against Hanoi and Washington*, Orion Books (New York, 1985)

————, *Thud Ridge*, Bantam Books (New York, 1985)

Brownlow, Cecil, 'USAF Boosts North Vietnam ECM Jamming', *Aviation Week and Space Technology*, 6 February 1967

Burchett, Wilfred, *Grasshoppers and Elephants*, Urizen Books (New York, 1977)

Burns, Richard Dean, and Leitenburg, Milton, *The Wars in Vietnam, Cambodia and Laos 1945: A Bibliographic Guide*, ABC Information Services (Santa Barbara, 1984)

Cagel, Malcolm W., 'Task Force 77 in Action off Vietnam', *The Naval Review*, US Naval Institute (Annapolis, 1972)

Chanoff, David, and Toai, Doan Van, *Portrait of the Enemy*, I. B. Tauris & Co (London, 1986)

Chant, Christopher, *MiG 21*, Haynes Publishing Group (England, 1984)

Chinnery, Phil, *Air War in Vietnam*, Bison Books (London, 1987)

———, *Life on the Line: Stories of Vietnam Air Combat*, Blandford Press (London, 1988)

———, 'The Air War over Vietnam', *Aeroplane*, January–October 1986 (10 vols)

Chodes, John J., *The Myth of America's Military Power*, Branden Press, (Boston)

Clark, Wesley K., 'Gradualism and American Military Strategy', *Military Review*, 55, September 1975

Clodfelter, Mark, *Red River Rats*, Turner Publishing Co (Kentucky, 1989)

———, *The Limits of Air Power*, The Free Press (New York, 1989)

Cole, David K., 'The Connies of College Eye', *Airman*, XVI, March 1973

Collins, John M., 'Vietnam: A Senseless Strategy', *Parameters*, 8, March 1978

Colvin, J., 'Hanoi in My Time', *The Washington Quarterly*, 4, Spring 1981

———, *Volcano under Snow*, Quartet Books (London, 1996)

Coonts, Stephen, *Flight of the Intruder*, Pan Books (London, 1986)

Cooper, Chester, *The Lost Crusade: America in Vietnam*, Dodd Mead (New York, 1970)

Cunningham, R., and Ethell, J., *Fox Two*, Champlin Fighter Museum (Mesa, 1984)

Clausewitz, Carl von, (trans. Howard, Michael, and Paret, Peter), *On War*, Princeton University Press (Princeton, 1976)

Davis, Larry, *Wild Weasel: The Sam Suppression Story*, Squadron/Signal Publications (Carrollton, 1986)

Decornoy, Jacques, 'Eye Witness Reports of the Bombing: How the North Survives', *The Observer*, 1 January 1967

DeWeerd H. A., 'Strategic Decision Making in Vietnam 65–68, *Yale Review*, 67, 1976

Donovan, James A., *Militarism USA*, Scribner's (New York, 1970)

Dorr, Robert F., *A-6 Intruder*, Arms & Armour Press (London, 1991)

———, *Air War Hanoi*, Blandford Press (London, 1988)

———, *Air War South Vietnam*, Arms & Armour Press (London, 1990)

———, *F-105 Thunderchief*, Arms & Armour Press (London, 1988)

———, *McDonnell Douglas F-4 Phantom II*, Osprey Publishing (London, 1984)

———, *McDonnell F-101 Voodoo*, Osprey Publishing (London, 1987)

———, 'Navy Phantoms in Vietnam', *Wings of Fame*, Vol. 1, Aerospace Publishing (London, 1995)

———, 'Southeast Asian Spad: The Skyraider's War', *Air Enthusiast*, 36, May–August 1988

———, *Vietnam: Combat from the Cockpit*, Airlife Publishing (England, 1989)

———, *Vietnam MiG Killers*, Motor Books International (Osceola, 1988)

Douhet, Giulio, *The Command of the Air*, Rivista Aeronautica (Rome, 1958)

Doyle, Edward; Lipsman, Samuel; and Maitland, Terrence, *The North*, Boston Publishing

Co. (Boston, 1986)

Drendel, Lou, *Air War over Southeast Asia*, 2 vols, Squadron/Signal Publications (Texas, 1982)

———, *. . . and Kills MiGs*, Squadron/Signal Publications (Texas, 1984)

———, *The Air War in Vietnam*, Arco (New York, 1968)

———, *Thud*, Squadron/Signal Publications (Texas, 1986)

———, *USAF Phantoms in Combat*, Squadron/Signal Publications (Texas, 1987)

———, *USN Phantoms in Combat*, Squadron/Signal Publications (Texas, 1988)

Duncan, Scott, 'Rolling Thunder', *Airman*, Vol. 18, October 1974

Duncanston, Dennis J., 'The Ceasefire in Vietnam', *The World Today*, March 1973

Enthoven, Alain C., and Smith, K. Wayn, *How Much is Enough?*, Harper & Row (New York, 1971)

Ethell, Jeffrey, and Price, Alfred, *One Day in a Long War*, Random House (New York, 1989)

Fall, Bernard, *Vietnam Witness 1953–66*, Prager (New York, 1966)

Flight of the Intruder, Spectrum Holobyte, Mirrorsoft (London) (computer game)

Flintham, Victor, *Air Wars and Aircraft*, Arms & Armour Press (London, 1989)

Francillon, Rene J., *Tonkin Gulf Yacht Club*, Conway Maritime Press (London, 1988)

———, *Vietnam Air Wars*, Temple Press Aerospace (London, 1987)

Freeman, Roger, *The US Strategic Bomber*, Macdonald & Janes (London, 1975)

Fricker, John, 'Air Armaments', *Flying Review*, March 1968

Futrell, Frank, et al., *Aces and Aerial Victories: The United States Air Force in Southeast Asia 1965–73*, Office of Air Force History, Washington, 1976).

Gallucci, Robert, *Neither Peace nor Honour*, Johns Hopkins University Press (Baltimore, 1975)

Gelb, Leslie H., and Betts, Richard K., *The Irony of Vietnam: The System Worked*, The Brookings Institute (Washington 1979)

Gerassi, John, *North Vietnam: A Documentary*, George Allen & Unwin (London, 1968)

Giap, General Vo Nguyen, *People's War against US Aero-Naval War*, Foreign Languages Publishing House (Hanoi, 1975)

Gillcrist, Paul T., *Feet Wet*, Pocket Books (New York, 1990)

Gilster, Herman L., *The Air War in Southeast Asia*, Air University Press (Maxwell AFB, 1993)

Ginsberg, Robert N., 'Strategy and Air Power: The Lessons of Southeast Asia', *Strategic Review*, I, Summer 1973

———, 'The Tides of War', *Air Force and Space Digest*, February 1968

Goodman, Alan, *The Lost Peace: America's Search for a Negotiated Settlement of the Vietnam War*, Hoover Institute (Stanford, 1978)

Gorn, Michael, and Gross, Charles, 'Published Airforce History Still on the Runway', *Aerospace Historian*, 31 No I, March 1984

Goulding, Phil G., *Confirm or Deny: Informing the People on National Security*, Harper & Row (New York, 1970)

Graff, Henry F., *The Tuesday Cabinet*, Prentice-Hall (New Jersey, 1970)

Grant, Zalin, *Over The Beach: Air War in Vietnam*, Norton (New York, 1986)

Greer, Thomas H., *The Development of Air Force Doctrine in the Army Air Arm 1917–1941*, Office of Air Force History, United States Air Force (Washington, 1985)

Grindler, Lawrence E., 'How They Lost: Doctrines, Strategies and Outcomes of the Vietnam War', *Asian Survey*, 15, December 1975

Gunston, Bill, *Mikoyan MiG-21*, Osprey Publishing (London, 1986)

Gurney, Gene, *Vietnam: The War in the Air*, Crown Publishers (New York, 1985)

Halberstam, David, *The Best and the Brightest*, Random House (New York, 1973)

————, 'The Programming of Robert McNamara', *Harpers Magazine*, February 1971

Hanoi, International Travel Maps (Vancouver) (map)

Harvey, Frank, *Air War Vietnam*, Bantam Books (New York, 1967)

Herman, Edwards S., *Atrocities in Vietnam: Myths and Realities*, Pilgrim Press (Boston, 1970)

Herring, George C., *America's Longest War*, John Wiley & Sons (New York, 1979)

Higham, Robin, *Air Power: A Concise History*, Macdonald (London, 1972)

Hoeffding, Oleg, *Bombing North Vietnam: An Appraisal of Economic and Political Effects*, Rand Corporation (Santa Monica, 1968)

Hoopes, Townsend, *The Limits of Intervention*, David McKay Co (New York, 1969)

Hopkins, Charles K., 'Linebacker II: A First Hand View', *Aerospace Historian*, September 1976

————, *SAC Tanker Operations in the Southeast Asia War*, Office of the Historian, Headquarters Strategic Air Command (1979)

Janis, Irving L., *Victims of Groupthink*, Haughton Miffin (Boston, 1972)

Johnson, Lyndon B., *The Vantage Point: Perspectives on the Presidency*, Holt (New York, 1971)

Jones, Neville, *The Origins of Strategic Bombing*, William Kimber (London, 1973)

Kasler, J. H., 'The Hanoi POL Strike', *Air University Review*, 16, November–December 1974

Kennan, George F., *American Diplomacy*, University of Chicago Press (1951)

Kennett, Lee, *A History of Strategic Bombing*, Charles Scribner's Sons (New York, 1982)

Kilduff, Peter, *A-4 Skyhawk*, Osprey Publishing (London, 1983)

Kirk, William L., *Gradualism in the Air War over North Vietnam*, Air University (Maxwell AFB, 1970)

Kohn, Richard H., and Harahan, Joseph P., *Air Interdiction in WWII, Korea and Vietnam*, Office of Air Force History, US Air Force (Washington, 1986)

Lane, John J., *Command and Control and Communications Structures in Southeast Asia*, Air War College (Maxwell AFB, 1981)

Lavalle, A. J. C., *Air Power and the 1972 Spring Invasion*, USAF Southeast Asia Monograph Series, Vol. II No 3 (Washington, 1977)

————, *The Vietnamese Air Force 1951–1975*, Office of Air Force History (Washington, 1977)

Levinson, Jeffrey L., *Alpha Strike Vietnam*, Presidio Press (USA, 1989)

Lewy, Gunther, *America in Vietnam*, Oxford University Press (New York, 1978)

Littaur, R., and Uphoff, N., *The Air War in Indochina*, Beacon Press (Boston, 1972)

Lonie, Frank R., 'Interdiction in a Southeast Asian Limited War', *Royal Air Force Quarterly*, 9, Winter 1969

Lowe, James Trapier, *A Philosophy of Air Power*, University Press of America (Lanham, 1984)

MacIsaac, David, 'Voices From the Central Blue: The Air Power Theorists', *Makers of Modern Strategy* (ed. Paret, Peter), Clarenden Press (Oxford, 1986)

Mack, Jerold R., and Williams, Richard M., 'The 552nd Airborne Early Warning and Control Wing in Southeast Asia: A Case Study in Airborne Control', *Air University Review*, XXV, November–December 1973

Maclear, Michael, *Vietnam: The Ten Thousand Day War*, Thames Methuen (London 1981)

Marolda, Edward J., *A Short History of the United States Navy and the Southeast Asian Conflict 1950-75*, Naval Historical Center, Department of the Navy (Washington, 1984)

———, *Carrier Operations: The Illustrated History of the Vietnam War*, Bantam Books (New York, 1987)

Marolda, E. J., et al., *A Select Bibliography of the United States Navy and the Southeast Asia Conflict 1950–75*, Naval Historical Center (Washington, 1983)

Mason, R. A., *War in the Third Dimension*, Brassey's (London, 1986)

McCarthy, James R., *Linebacker II: A View from the Rock*, Air War College (Maxwell AFB, 1979)

McLellan, D. S., 'The Myth of Air Power', *World View*, 15, November 1972

Menault, S. W. B., 'The Use of Air Power in Vietnam', *Royal United Services Institute for Defence Studies Journal*, June 1971

Mersky, Peter B., and Polmar, Norman, *The Naval Air War in Vietnam*, The Nautical & Aviation Publishing Company of America (Annapolis, 1981)

Middleton, Drew, *Air War Vietnam*, Arms & Armour Press (London, 1978)

Momyer, William W., *Air Power in Three Wars*, Department of the Air Force (Washington, 1978)

———, 'The Evolution of Fighter Tactics in Southeast Asia', *Air Force Magazine*, LVI, July 1973

Morrocco, John, *Rain of Fire: Air War 1969–1973*, Boston Publishing Co (Boston, 1985)

———, *Thunder from Above*, Boston Publishing Co (Boston, 1984)

Mrozek, Donald J., *Air Power and the Ground War in Vietnam*, Pergamon Brassey's (London, 1989)

Myers, Charles E., 'Deep Strike Interdiction', *US Naval Institute Proceedings*, Vol. 106, November 1980

Nichols, John B., and Tillman, Barret, *On Yankee Station*, Airlife (England, 1987)

Nordeen, Lon O., *Air Warfare in the Missile Age*, Arms & Armour Press (London, 1985)

Olds, Robin, 'Forty-Six Years a Fighter Pilot', *American Aviation Historical Society Journal*, XIII, Winter 1968

————, 'How I Got My First MiG', *Air Force and Space Digest*, July 1967

————, 'The Lessons of Clobber College', *Flight International*, 26 June 1969

Palmer, David, *Summons of the Trumpet*, Presidio Press (California, 1977)

Palmer, Gregory, *The McNamara Strategy and the Vietnam War*, Greenwood Press (Connecticut, 1978)

Parks, W. Hayes, 'Rolling Thunder and the Law of War', *Air University Review*, January–February 1982

Parrish, Noel F., *The Influence of Air Power upon Historians*, US Air Force Academy (Colorado, 1979)

Peacock, Lindsay, 'Connies in Combat', *Air World*, June 1995

————, *RA-5C*, Osprey Publishing (London, 1987)

Pickerill, James H., *Vietnam in the Mud*, Bobbs Merrill (Indianapolis, 1967)

Pike, Douglas, *PAVN: People's Army of Vietnam*, Brassey's Defence Publishers (London, 1986)

Pisor, Robert, *The End of the Line*, W. W. Norton & Co (1982)

Price, Alfred, *Instruments of Darkness*, Macdonald & Janes (London, 1977)

Pro-Communist Eye Witness Reports of US Bombings of Civilians in North Vietnam, Washington Joint Publications Research (Washington, 1967)

Roberts, John, *The Fighter Pilot's Handbook*, Arms & Armour Press (London, 1992)

Robinson, Daniel, and Cummings, Joe, *Vietnam, Laos and Cambodia*, Lonely Planet Publications (Australia, 1991) (Vietnam guidebook)

Russet, Bruce M., 'Vietnam and Restraints on Aerial Warfare', *Ventures*, Vol. 9, spring 1969

Salisbury, Harrison E., *Behind the Lines: Hanoi, December 23 1966–January 7 1967*, Harper & Row (New York, 1967)

Salmon, Malcolm, 'North Vietnam: A First Hand Account of the Blitz', *Sydney Tribune* (Sydney, 1969?)

Santoli, Al, *To Bear Any Burden*, Abacus (London, 1986)

Saunby, Robert, 'The Ethics of Bombing', *Air Force And Space Digest*, No 50, June 1967

Schandler, Herbert Y., *The Unmaking of a President: Lyndon Johnson and Vietnam*, Princeton University Press (Princeton, 1977)

Schmaltz, Robert E., 'The Uncertainty of Predicting Results of an Interdiction Campaign', *Aerospace Historian*, 17 December 1970

Schneider, Donald K., *Air Force Heroes in Vietnam*, Air War College (Maxwell AFB, 1979)

Scutts, Jerry, *Wolf Pack*, Airlife (England, 1987)

Shaplen, Robert, *The Road from War: Vietnam 1965–70*, Harper & Row (New York, 1970)

Sharp, U. S. Grant, 'Airpower Could Have Won in Vietnam', *Air Force*, Vol. 54, September 1971

————, *Report on the War in Vietnam*, Washington DC GPO (1968)

————, *Strategy for Defeat: Vietnam in Retrospect*, Presidio Press (San Rafael, 1978)

Sheehan, Neil, *The Pentagon Papers*, Bantam Books (New York, 1971)

Showalter, Dennis E., and Albert, John, *An American Dilemma*, Imprint Publications (Chicago, 1993)

Smith Jr, Melden E., 'The Strategic Bombing Debate', *Journal of Contemporary History*, Vol. 12, January 1977

Smith, John T., *Rolling Thunder*, Air Research Publications (London, 1995)

Sochurek, H., 'Air Rescue behind Enemy Lines', *National Geographic Magazine*, 134, 1968

Staudenmaier, William O., 'Vietnam, Mao and Clausewitz', *Parameters*, 7, March 1967

Stockdale, Jim, *In Love and War*, Harper & Row (New York, 1984)

Sullivan, Cornelius D., 'Air War against the North', *The Vietnam War: Its Conduct and Higher Direction*, Georgetown University Center for Strategic Studies (Washington, 1968)

Sullivan, Jim, *F-8 Crusader in Action*, Squadron/Signal Publications (Texas, 1985)

Summers, Harry G., *On Strategy: The Vietnam War in Context*, Strategic Studies Institute, US Army War College (Carlisle Barracks, 1981)

Szulc, Tad, *The Illusion of Peace*, Viking Press (New York, 1978)

Taylor, Telford, 'Report and Comments—North Vietnam', *Atlantic Monthly*, May 1973.

The Pentagon Papers, The Senator Gravel Edition, Beacon Press, Boston

Thies, Wallace J., *When Governments Collide: Coercion and Diplomacy in the Vietnam Conflict 1964–68*, University of California (1980)

Thompson, James C., *Rolling Thunder: Understanding Policy and Program Failure*, University of North Carolina Press (Chapel Hill, 1980)

Thompson, W.; Scott, Donaldson; and Frizzel, D., *The Lessons of Vietnam*, Crane, Russak & Co (New York)

Thornborough, Anthony M., *The Phantom Story*, Arms & Armour Press (London, 1994)

———, *Wild Weasels*, Osprey Publishing (London, 1992)

Tilford, Earl H., *Search and Rescue in Southeast Asia 1961–1975*, Office of Air Force History (Washington, 1980)

Tillman, Barrett, *MiG Master: The Story of the F-8 Crusader*, Patrick Stephens (England, 1980)

Trotti, John, *Phantom over Vietnam*, Airlife (England, 1984)

Thu, Hai, *North Vietnam against US Air Force*, Foreign Languages Publishing House (Hanoi, 1967)

Ulsamer, Edgar, 'Air Rescue in Southeast Asia: Right from Hanoi's Own Backyard', *Air Force Magazine*, 55, October 1972

US Congress, Senate Committee on Foreign Relations, *Bombing as a Tool in Vietnam: Effectiveness*, Study No 5, 92nd Congress, 2nd Session (Washington GPO, 1972)

US Senate, Hearings before the Preparedness Investigations Subcommittee, 9 and 10 August 1967

Van Dyke, Jon M., *North Vietnam's Strategy for Survival*, Pacific Books Publishers (Palo Alto, 1972)

Verrier, Anthony, 'Strategic Bombing: The Lessons of World War II and the American Experience in Vietnam', *Journal of the Royal United Services Institute*, CXII, May 1968

217

Vietnam Destruction War Damage, Foreign Languages Publishing House (Hanoi, 1977)

Watts, Barry D., *The Foundations of US Air Doctrine: The Problem of Friction in War*, Air University Press (Maxwell AFB, 1984)

Weigley, Russell F., *The American Way of War*, Macmillan (New York, 1973)

Weiss, Steve, *Rolling Thunder*, Group Three Games (New York, 1985) (war game)

Welsh, Douglas, *The History of the Vietnam War*, Hamlyn (London, 1981)

Witze, Claude, 'How Not to Win', *Air Force Magazine*, 53, 1970

Wolf, Charles, 'The Logic of Failure: A Vietnam Lesson', *Journal of Conflict Resolution*, September 1972

Wolfe, Tom, 'The Truest Sport: Jousting with Sam and Charley', *Mauve Gloves and Madmen, Clutter and Vine*, Farrar, Straus & Giroux (New York, 1976)

Yenne, Bill, *The History of the US Air Force*, Hamlyn

Yudkin, Richard A., 'Vietnam: Policy, Strategy and Air Power', *Air Force Magazine*, 56, February 1973.

INDEX

Vought F-8/RF-8 Crusader, 26,
31, 93–4, 193, 195, 200

Walleye bombs, 84, 94
Warner Springs, 186
Watson, George D., 111
Webb, Lt Omri, 110
Wells, H. G., 8
Westmoreland, Gen William, 32
Westphalia, Lt-Col Curtis D.,
113
Weyand, Gen Frederick C., 85
'White Bandits', 96
White, Capt Sam, 101
'Wild Weasel', 29, 34, 55, 94,
125, 127, 135, 181–4
Wilkinson, Capt D., 67
Williams, Capt Jim, 78
Wise, Lt James A., 141
Wolf FAC, 110
Wolf, Capt Robert E., 125
Wright brothers, 9

Xom Bong, 28
Xuan Mai, 100

Yahmed, Bechir Ben, 152
Yankee Station, 29, 61, 77,
175, 180
Yeager, Gen Chuck, 197
Yen Bai, 65, 67, 77–8, 107,
110, 133, 188
Yen Vien, 63 67, 124, 126,

129–30, 204
Yien Bai, 205
Youth Shock Brigades, 151

Zeppelin, 8, 10

1st Division, 53, 80
1st SRS, 193
2nd Air Division, 23, 32, 57
3rd ARRG, 184
3rd Division, 52, 188
3rd TFW, 54-5
4th TFS, 90, 101, 140
7th ACCS, 180
7th Air Force, 20, 32, 46, 57,
96, 120, 182, 194
7th Fleet, 29
8th Air Force, 132
8th TBS, 26
8th TFW, 33, 63, 65, 74-5, 83,
86, 100, 105
13th Air Force, 23
13th TBS, 26, 79
13th TFW, 92
14th TRS, 194
15th TRS, 31
17th WWS, 183
20mm Vulcan cannon, 79, 83,
85, 111, 200–1, 105, 107
20th TRS, 31
21st Division, 86
25th TFS, 91
34th TFS, 110

35th TFS, 106
36th TAS, 55
36th TFS, 26
39th TEWS, 190
42nd TEWS, 56, 190
45th TFS, 28
49th TFW, 55, 108
58th TFS, 55, 99, 112
61st TALS, 55
95th Regiment, 147
307th SW, 58, 119
308th TFS, 55, 112
325th Division, 147
349th SRS, 193
350th SRS, 194
354th TFW, 112
366th TFS, 92,99
374th TALW, 55
388th TFW, 61, 63, 65, 107,
111
432nd TRW, 61, 67, 109, 194
433rd TFS, 75
460th TRW, 193
469th TFS, 85
497th TFS, 100
509th FIS, 25
552nd AEWCW, 178
555th TFS, 61, 65, 77, 79, 91,
105, 107, 109, 112, 137
615th TFS, 26
4028th SRS, 193
4400th CTS, 23